Praise for Nathan J. W
and Redemption

Praise for the Book

"*Redemption* is a passionate advocacy for ending the killing of homeless dogs and cats in shelters. Telling the story of how the movement of animal sheltering in the United States was born of compassion and lost its way... *Redemption* offers hope that America can yet change its ways. Highly recommended."
—*Midwest Book Review*

"An important work."   —*The Bark magazine*

"Within its pages, readers and animal lovers can find the blueprint not so much for our failure to save the animals in our communities, but for our ability to start doing so today."   —*San Francisco Chronicle (SFGate.com)*

"One of the most important books you'll read this year."
—*Pajiba.com*

"I cannot remember any work that has so dramatically altered my point of view on any subject—nor another book that has me so excited to think of what real reform can do to save the lives of shelter pets." —*Petconnection.com*

"For anyone who has ever loved an animal, this book, like no other non-fiction, takes you through the full spectrum of emotions: from sadness to anger, from fear to hope. But redemption? That is ultimately left up to each and every one of us..."
—*Air America Radio*

"[A] unique and important book."   —*Library Journal*

"Love animals? Then don't miss Nathan Winograd's *Redemption*."
—*Dogpolitics.com*

"[An] excellent, empowering new book." —*Fetchdog.com*

"[T]he most provocative and best-informed overview of animal sheltering ever written."   —*Animal People*

REDEMPTION

*The Myth of Pet Overpopulation and the
No Kill Revolution in America*

NATHAN J. WINOGRAD

ALMADEN

Second Edition

Cover and Interior Design:
Judith Arisman, arismandesign.com

Cover Photos:
Dog, istockphoto.com/susaro
Cat, istockphoto.com/silberkorn

Library of Congress Control Number: 2006936683
ISBN 13: 978-0-9790743-1-8
ISBN 10: 0-9790743-1-2
Printed in the United States of America

To my wife, Jennifer. Who believed,
long before I did.

Table of Contents

A Revolution in Sheltering

SINCE ITS RELEASE in September 2007, *Redemption* has become the most critically acclaimed book ever written on its topic. Not only has the book helped shift the national debate about killing, it is also playing a direct role in helping to transform communities. A shelter manager in Washington says the book completely changed her views and she is committing herself to saving all animals in her shelter. Another in Ohio reported that the book gave her the "conviction to move forward" with her No Kill ambitions. Yet another in Louisiana reported to her staff, "We've been doing it wrong, and we are going to start doing it right."

After reading *Redemption*, county commissioners in an Indiana community succeeded in taking to No Kill a shelter that previously killed the vast majority of dogs and cats, often cruelly. As *Redemption* celebrates its continuing success, Tompkins County, New York, finished its seventh No Kill year, Charlottesville, Virginia, entered its third, and new communities like those in Reno, Nevada, entered the No Kill club. Other communities in other states have also embraced No Kill or are aggressively moving in that direction. No Kill is on the agenda of local governments nationwide as advocates in communities as diverse as Seattle, Washington, and Indianapolis, Indiana, are using *Redemption* and the model it advocates to force changes in the practices of local shelters.

There have been other notable changes as well. The Humane Society of the United States' (HSUS) favorite misnomer "euthanasia" has lost its cache. Rescue groups and animal advocates have stopped using it and other

HSUS euphemisms such as "putting them to sleep" to describe the abhorrent practice of systematic shelter killing. People are more aware of widespread mistreatment of animals in shelters. And they are less tolerant of the poor care and the killing, the excuses built up over the decades to justify it, and the legitimacy that groups like HSUS give to it. This has put the large national humane groups on the defensive, trying to take credit for the decline in killing nationally even as they opposed and in some cases continue to oppose the programs responsible for it, and by softening their anti-No Kill positions.

Redemption debunks the myth of pet overpopulation and puts the blame for the killing where it belongs: on the shoulders of the very shelter directors who find killing easier than doing what is necessary to stop it, on the local governments who continue to underfund their shelters or place them under the regressive oversight of health and police departments (and even under sanitation!), and on shelter managers who protect uncaring and even cruel staff members at the expense of the animals.

More than all of that, average people are now aware that shelters kill. And they are aware that there are some shelters and communities that do not kill. After reading the book, one animal lover in Los Angeles, California, told me: "At least now we know what—or more accurately, who—the problem is." We also know how to make them stop. And in more communities nationwide, we have.

THE MYTH OF PET OVERPOPULATION

Unfortunately, many shelter directors remain steadfast in their refusal to embrace the No Kill paradigm. To them, the culprit for the killing remains "pet overpopulation," a dogma they cling to with the fervor of religious faith and which they deem to be simply beyond question—outside the realm of factual confirmation, data, and analysis.

When I argue in this book that pet overpopulation is a myth, I am not saying that people aren't irresponsible with animals. It doesn't mean there aren't a lot of animals entering shelters. It doesn't mean it wouldn't be better if there were fewer of them being impounded. Nor am I saying shelters don't have institutional obstacles to success. But it does mean that these problems are not insurmountable. And it does mean we can do something other than killing for all savable animals right now, today: if all shelter directors cultivate the desire and will to do so, and then earnestly follow through. That is good news. It is news we should celebrate. And it should be the focal point with which we target our advocacy efforts to achieve the greatest declines in killing possible in the shortest amount of time.

Current estimates from a wide range of groups indicate that between four million and five million dogs and cats are killed in shelters every year. Of these, given data on the incidence of aggression in dogs (based on dog bite extrapolation) and save rates at the best performing shelters in the country from diverse regions and demographics, about 90 percent of all shelter animals are "savable." The remainder consists of hopelessly ill or injured animals and vicious dogs whose prognosis for rehabilitation is poor or grave. That would put the number of savable dogs and cats at roughly 3.6 million on the low end and 4.5 million on the high end of the spectrum.

But even at the high end, it means that we only need to increase the market for shelter pets by three percent in order to eliminate killing. Today, there are about 165 million dogs and cats in homes. Of those, about 20 percent come from shelters. Three percent of 165 million equates to 4.9 million, more than all the savable animals being killed in shelters. This is a combination of what statisticians call "stock" and "flow." In layman's terms, some of the market will be replacement life (someone has a dog or cat die or run away and they want another one), some of that will be expanding markets (someone doesn't have a dog or cat but wants one, or they have dogs or cats but want another one). But it all comes down to increasing where people get their dogs or cats from.

These same demographics also tell us that every year about twice as many people are looking to bring a new dog into their home than the total number of dogs entering shelters, and every year more people are looking to bring a new cat into their home than the total number of cats entering shelters. On top of that, not all animals entering shelters need adoption: Some will be lost strays who will be reclaimed by their family (shelters which are comprehensive in their lost pet reclaim efforts, for example, have demonstrated that as many as two-thirds of stray dogs can be reunited with their families). Others are unsocialized feral cats who need neuter and release. Some will be vicious dogs or are irremediably suffering and will be killed. In the end, a shelter only needs to find new homes for less than half of all incoming animals.

And since this book was released, even one of the chief architects of the current paradigm of killing—the Humane Society of the United States—

has stopped ignoring these facts and in late 2008 conceded that "increasing the percentage of people who obtain their pets through adoption—by just a few percentage points—we can solve the problem of euthanasia of healthy and treatable dogs and cats."*

All the data point to the same conclusion, and even HSUS can no longer deny it: it is not pet overpopulation if kittens are being killed in shelters because the shelter refuses to put in place a foster care program which would eliminate the "need" to kill kittens, as too many shelters in this country do. It is the shelter's decision to kill kittens instead of implementing a foster care program that is killing kittens. It is not pet overpopulation if Pit Bull-type dogs are being killed because the shelter kills dogs based on arbitrary criteria and unfair stereotypes, even if the individual dogs are healthy and friendly. It is the shelter's decision to adhere to an arbitrary policy that dictates that Pit Bull-type dogs should be killed that is killing those dogs. The same is true of sick dogs, shy cats or any of the other categories of shelter animals who could be saved with a targeted program that shelter directors simply refuse to implement.

The reality, for example, is that short of leaving them alone or outlawing their trapping, a shelter cannot save feral cats in its facility without a Trap-Neuter-Release (TNR) program, just as it cannot save kittens or puppies without a program such as foster care. Any shelter director who says they oppose No Kill is making the thoroughly unethical argument that they want to continue killing. How do you save animals without embracing alternatives to killing? You cannot. But while any level of lifesaving is not possible without these programs, No Kill is precluded unless they are comprehensively implemented to the point that they replace killing entirely. (See Appendix II for further discussion.)

From the perspective of achievability, therefore, the prognosis for widespread No Kill success is very good. And we have seen this in action in various

*Unfortunately, while HSUS may have a new language, they still continue to act in old ways. In April of 2008, Randolph, Iowa officials announced a bounty on stray cats, offering residents $5.00 for every cat they rounded up and brought to the shelter to be killed. While cat lovers protested, HSUS officials said they "didn't have a problem with humanely killing a stray cat." In 2007, HSUS asked the King County Council in Washington not to vote on a measure to mandate an 85 percent rate of lifesaving at its animal control shelter, setting itself up against animal activists working to reform their local shelter. And in August 2008, HSUS defended the decision by the Hammond, Louisiana animal control shelter to kill every single animal in its facility.

communities throughout the country. Some are urban, some rural, some in the North, some in the South, some in what we call "liberal" or "blue" states, and some are in very conservative parts of the country. Demographically, these communities share little in common. What they do share, however, is shelter leadership committed to saving all the lives at risk. And they are proving the validity of the data, which shows that it can be done.

Statistics aside, the fundamental lesson from the experiences of these communities is that the choices made by shelter managers are the most significant variables in whether animals live or die. Several communities are more than doubling adoptions and cutting killing by as much as 75 percent—and it isn't taking them five years or more to do it. They are doing it virtually overnight. In Reno, Nevada, for example, the Nevada Humane Society has led an incredible renaissance in lifesaving that saw adoptions increase as much as 80 percent and deaths decline by 51 percent, despite taking in a combined 16,000 dogs and cats a year with Washoe County Animal Services. Reno's success occurred immediately after the hiring of a new shelter director committed to No Kill and passionate about saving lives. Her appointment followed the 20-plus year reign of a darling of HSUS—a member of their national sheltering committee—who for two decades found killing easier than doing what was necessary to stop it.

In addition to the speed with which it was attained, what also makes Reno's success so impressive is that the community takes in over two times the number of animals per capita than the national average, over three times the rate of Los Angeles, and over four times the rate of San Francisco. So if "pet overpopulation" were really a problem, it would be a problem in Reno. But in 2007, 92 percent of all dogs and 78 percent of all cats were saved countywide, and in 2008 Washoe County become the safest community for homeless cats in the U.S.—despite an economic and foreclosure crisis that hit the community hard. With an overall rate of lifesaving of roughly 90 percent, they are proving that shelters can quickly save the vast majority of animals once they commit to do so, even in the face of public irresponsibility or economic crisis.

WHAT IF PET OVERPOPULATION IS REAL?

But let's put all this aside. Let's assume "pet overpopulation" is real and insurmountable. To do that, we have to ignore the data. We also have to ignore the experiences of successful communities. We have to pretend the knowledge and the results do not exist.

To make that leap, critics of the No Kill philosophy like to point out that the Philadelphia Animal Care & Control Association (PACCA), which plays prominently at the end of *Redemption*, failed to achieve No Kill. After decreasing the death rate from a staggering 88 percent to less than 40 percent, PACCA leadership got sidetracked, which resulted in infighting and open hostility with local government. The agency effectively ceased to exist on January 1, 2009, when the Philadelphia Department of Public Health essentially disbanded it and gave the contract for animal control back to the Pennsylvania SPCA.

Does this reflect the inefficacy of the No Kill paradigm? It does not. While PACCA leadership failed to implement all the recommended programs to replace killing, effectively abandoning the goal, new communities have emerged that not only were as cruel and hostile to animals as PACCA once was, but have already achieved better than 90 percent rates of lifesaving—communities which take in more animals per capita than Philadelphia. The criticism also ignores that I specifically warned in *Redemption* that,

> There is still a long way to go, some of the programs are not being comprehensively put into place, and there are still far too many Philadelphia animals facing death... It will also take continued leadership and commitment to make No Kill a reality in Philadelphia and to overcome the real but not insurmountable roadblocks PACCA faces. The prognosis for that success remains guarded at best due to a poor infrastructure, hostility to reform from the health department that oversees PACCA, lack of support for the No Kill initiative by the two other community shelters, and its unfavorable location relative to retail and residential sectors of the city.

With continued hostility from the health department, with shelter managers responsible for the staggering decline in killing having left the organization, and with my faith in the shelter's director having been misplaced, sadly those fears came to pass. So while we have had some important victories since *Redemption* was first published, we have also had some losses. But the conclusion is not that No Kill isn't possible. It is that No Kill depends too much on the actions of individual leaders. Failure in Philadelphia or San Francisco or anywhere else is nothing more than a failure of leadership. If there is a lesson in Philadelphia, it is that we need to move past a system where the lives of animals are subject to the discretion and commitment level of shelter leaders or health department bureaucrats. In *Redemption*, I wrote that,

> *No Kill is only succeeding in some communities because of the commitment by individual shelter leaders, who are few and far between. Traditional sheltering, by contrast, is institutionalized. In a shelter reliant on killing, directors can come and go and the shelter keeps killing, local government keeps ignoring that failure, and the public keeps believing "there is no other way." By contrast, the success of an organization's No Kill policies depends on the commitment and vision of its leader. When that leader leaves the organization, the vision can quickly be doomed. It is why an SPCA can be progressive one day, and moving in the opposite direction the next.*

That is why we have to focus on institutionalizing No Kill by giving shelter animals the rights and protections afforded by law. The answer lies in passing and enforcing shelter reform legislation (See Appendix III). By adopting this approach, we will force shelter leadership to embrace No Kill and operate their shelters in a progressive, life-affirming way, removing the discretion which has for too long allowed shelter leaders to ignore what is in the best interests of the animals and kill them needlessly, even in spite of tremendous public opposition and hunger for change.

Another argument used against No Kill since this book was published is that the Tompkins County SPCA, which spearheaded the nation's first No Kill community and has been No Kill for seven years, is in the process of moving away from administering animal control based on the costs of doing so. Even though the legal mandate to provide animal control services rests with government, the Tompkins County SPCA has been performing the service under contract as many private humane societies do. For far too many years, local government was underpaying for the service. Critics of No Kill ignore the fact that the Tompkins County SPCA was No Kill for seven years while receiving animal control funding that was less than one-fourth of what HSUS recommended for municipalities and far less than the national average. If anything, this fact substantiates the viability of No Kill. When the Tompkins County SPCA asked for a modest fee increase to make the arrangement more equitable, some town administrators refused and contracted for services elsewhere.

If this was any other shelter, groups like HSUS would have rallied around the shelter, because its request for an increase from $1.65 to $3.00

per capita would still have given them less than half of the high end of the $5.00 to $7.00 HSUS recommends for shelters nationally, and far less than surrounding counties were paying. But because it is a symbol for No Kill, they attack it as financially unsustainable, an unfair and deceitful double standard.

But let's ignore this, and continue to assume that "pet overpopulation" is again very real and very insurmountable. How does this change our support for the No Kill philosophy and the programs and services that make it possible (as discussed throughout this book and in Appendix II)? Once again, it doesn't. Shelters nationally are killing roughly half or more of all incoming animals. If I can borrow from an overused sports analogy: that puts us at the 50-yard line. And although the evidence is overwhelming to the contrary, let's say that we can never cross the goal line because of "pet overpopulation." What is wrong with moving the ball forward? If all shelters put in place the programs and services of the No Kill Equation, the model which brought rates of shelter killing to all-time lows in communities from San Francisco, California, to Ithaca, New York; from Reno, Nevada, to Charlottesville, Virginia, and points in between, we can save millions of lives nationally, regardless of whether we ever achieve an entirely No Kill nation. Even if people do not believe, as I do, that a No Kill nation is inevitable, that is worth doing and worth doing without delay. Because every year we delay, indeed every day we delay, the body count increases. It is indefensible for shelter directors to refuse to implement programs that would dramatically lower death rates at their shelter because they lack the belief that those programs can eliminate killing entirely.

THE RIGHT TO LIVE

Even if we were simply to surrender reality and accept as fact that there is no practical way to end the killing, that doesn't make killing animals ethical, merciful, or defensible. Animal lovers would still be morally bound to reject it. Any "practical" or utilitarian consideration about killing cannot hold sway over an animal's right to his or her very life. Just as other social movements reject what is claimed to be practical when it violates the rights of individuals for which they advocate, we, too, should reject the idea that killing animals is acceptable because of the claim that there are "too many" for the "too few homes which are available." Simply put, killing healthy or treatable animals is immoral.

Indeed, it does not necessarily follow that killing of any hopelessly ill, injured or vicious animal is actually ethical. Most animal advocates are not calling for hopelessly ill or injured sheltered animals to be put up for adoption while irremediably suffering, because that is cruel. And few, if any, are calling for truly vicious dogs to be adopted into homes in the community, because that is dangerous. While over 90 percent of dogs and cats entering shelters would fall outside this limited range of exceptions, it does not follow philosophically that the remainder should be killed. The reality is that while fewer than 10 percent of shelter animals may not be healthy or treatable, the vast majority of those are not suffering. This might include a dog with cancer whose prognosis is grave, but who still has a good quality of life for a limited time. It might include a cat with renal disease in its early stages. In fact, not only are some "unadoptable" animals living without pain, they enjoy a good quality of life and can continue to do so, at least for a time, until they succumb to their illness.

Today, the great challenge in sheltering is between No Kill advocates working to ensure that healthy animals, animals with treatable medical conditions, and feral animals, are no longer killed in shelters and the defenders of tradition who claim that killing healthy and treatable animals under the guise of "euthanasia" is both necessary and proper. As the No Kill paradigm's hegemony becomes more established, however, the humane movement will have to confront other ethical quandaries within our philosophy.

The ethical quandaries surrounding killing dogs who are aggressive but can lead happy lives in sanctuaries where they cannot harm the public and carrying out what are considered "mercy" killings or true "euthanasia" for hopelessly ill animals in shelters rather than giving them hospice care will become paramount. In fact, even today, the idea of killing at all is being challenged by a small but growing movement of sanctuaries and hospice care groups. They argue for a "third door" between adoption and killing. That these issues have not yet been rigorously debated within the movement does not mean they shouldn't be. They should. Compassion must be embraced whenever it presents itself, especially when it furthers an animal's right to live.

Dismantling the Killing Paradigm

Realistically, however, if I can come back to my sports metaphor, we will cross the goal line and achieve a No Kill nation. To paraphrase abolitionist

Theodore Parker and Martin Luther King, Jr., the arc of history may be wide, but it bends toward greater justice and compassion. And compassion dictates we will get there. But to do that, we must dismantle the current paradigm that says it is acceptable to adopt out only a precious few and systematically put the remainder to death, a paradigm long championed by the very institutions that should have been working to create a No Kill nation. Beginning over 40 years ago with their first Vice President of Companion Animals, Phyllis Wright, the Humane Society of the United States abandoned what should have been its primary mission of ending the killing of companion animals in shelters and instead chose to champion a philosophy which excused killing, often promoted it, and cemented its hegemony, all of it at the expense of the animals.

In her seminal and cataclysmic essay "Why We Must Euthanize," Wright wrote that she "put 70,000 dogs and cats to sleep.... But I tell you one thing: I don't worry about one of those animals that was put to sleep." The essay not only coined one of the biggest misnomers of them all ("putting them to sleep") and created an emotionally acceptable pretext for killing, it helped cement the paradigm which allows groups like HSUS to claim that killing is morally acceptable, indeed an imperative. Wright's world-view informs HSUS' historical and present positions, including the myths that no one wants to kill, that killing is the public's fault, that killing is kindness, and that shelters have no choice in the matter—all of which have been proven false. These have been the backbone of the paradigm that is responsible for the mass extermination of dogs and cats in shelters. Every animal who enters a U.S. shelter today faces the very real potential for being killed as a direct result of the broken animal shelter system HSUS helped to create.

That paradigm not only shuts the door to No Kill in many communities, but it also undermines all the other goals that groups like HSUS should, by virtue of their mission to protect animals, support. To defend the killing of healthy and treatable animals and refer to it as "euthanasia," or "putting them to sleep," or "moral," or "ethical," or "necessary," or "kind," or "proper", obscures the truth and the ends they should be seeking, while hindering progress that would benefit all animals.

The right to life is universally acknowledged as a basic or fundamental right. It is basic or fundamental because the enjoyment of the right to life is a necessary condition of the enjoyment of all other rights. No "right" is guaranteed when it can be taken away by killing. A movement cannot be "rights" oriented as many of these groups claim to be, yet ignore the fundamental

right to life. By asserting that humans should have the right to deny animals their lives—they make the attainment of any rights for animals
inherently impossible to achieve.

In both a philosophical and absolute sense, all animals really have is
their life. If that is taken, there isn't anything left. Once they are killed,
these animals can no longer think and feel and run and play and eat and
sleep and purr and bark and love and be loved. It is over. Forever. Because
they never wake up.

In failing to champion the right of dogs and cats to live, these
organizations are also missing the opportunity to harness the public's
progressive attitudes and great love for these animals. It is that love and
compassion which could yield laws banning killing in animal shelters altogether. This achievement—the attainment of a legally guaranteed right to
life for a species of non-human animal—will be a seminal event for animals
and the animal protection movement, a crossing of the Rubicon from which
our society will never return. As history and the human rights movement
predicts, that door—once opened—will be forced open even wider to accommodate other species of animals currently exploited or killed in other
contexts.

Right now, however, the nation's largest self-proclaimed "animal
rights" groups, including People for the Ethical Treatment of Animals
(PETA), are fighting to keep that door closed—by actively and proactively arguing that dogs and cats do not have the right to life and by telling
us, in some variation or another, that "killing is kindness," "killing is not
killing," and even that "killing is a gift." It is beyond ironic. It is beyond
hypocritical. It is beyond a betrayal. It is beyond self-defeating. It is insane.

Groups like PETA may claim to be leaders of the animal rights movement, and the larger public may equate animal rights with PETA, but their
positions and actions show that they do not truly believe in the concept.
By claiming to be "animal rights" advocates while advocating for the right
of humans to kill animals and killing animals themselves in staggering
numbers,* they advance hypocritical and irreconcilable propositions which

---

*In 2006, PETA took in 3,043 animals and killed 2,981 of them. Despite nearly $30 million
in revenues, and millions of animal loving supporters, they killed 97 percent of the animals.
In 2007, despite record rates of lifesaving in shelters which take in thousands more animals
at a fraction of PETA's budget and despite that new figures report that rates of shelter killing
dropped to their lowest levels ever as more shelters embraced the lifesaving programs of the
No Kill Equation, PETA's killing showed little sign of subsiding. PETA killed roughly 91
percent of the animals they impounded, taking in 1,997 and putting 1,815 to death.

result in a deadly double standard that is—at its very core—antithetical to their proclaimed mission. Because the treatment they condone, encourage, and even practice for animals is treatment they would never accept for themselves, given that no one—and I mean not one solitary person on the planet—would be an advocate for killing if they were the one unnecessarily facing the needle.

RECLAIMING OUR MOVEMENT

Thankfully, the public is increasingly aware of just how broken our shelter system is and supports the No Kill alternative. Not only do approximately 165 million dogs and cats share our homes and not only are we spending over $40 billion per year on their care and comfort, but study after study confirms that people will cut back on their own needs during periods of economic downturn, rather than curtail the care they provide their animal companions. Indeed, the average American is far more progressive about dogs and cats than every animal welfare and animal rights organization in the United States, with rare exception. The success of No Kill does not depend on winning the hearts and minds of the American public. We don't need to gain their support because we already have it. While the voices of tradition chant "kill, kill, kill," most dog and cat lovers, armed with the facts, find it abhorrent.

We must therefore recognize that the battle to save companion animals is not against the public: The battle is within. Our battle is against the cowards of our movement who refuse to stand up to their colleagues and friends running shelters that are mired in the failed and defunct philosophies that allow (indeed, cause) killing. Our battle is against those who claim to be part of our movement but fail to recognize the killing of millions of animals every year as an unnecessary and cruel slaughter and to call it what it is. It is against those who will not do for the animals that thing which is their solemn duty to do: to change themselves and to demand that their colleagues change, when that is what the situation calls for.

The only thing standing between the system of mass killing we are living under today and the No Kill nation we can immediately achieve is that the leaders of the large national organizations refuse to seize the opportunity to act. Instead they are determined to fail—to ensure that the paradigm they have championed for so long is not upended—by blocking reform efforts which challenge their hegemony; by protecting and defending draconian shelter practices, uncaring shelter directors; and by squandering the potential represented by the great love people have for companion animals.

What would it look like if the large national groups instead embraced No Kill? In practice, it means reporting to the public and shelter administrators that No Kill has been achieved, requiring full implementation of the No Kill Equation, and demanding the removal of shelter leaders who refuse to do so. It means promoting the communities, which have achieved levels of No Kill success that others have not. It means arguing in all publications, advocacy efforts, educational materials, media interactions and conferences that No Kill is the only legitimate standard for animal sheltering–and must be embraced by all shelters with sincere commitment and with all deliberate speed. It means stating unequivocally that shelters must modernize and innovate by replacing century old ways of doing business with the life-affirming programs and services of the No Kill Equation as outlined in the U.S. No Kill Declaration. (See Appendix I.) It means assisting activists who are trying to reform their shelters rather than fighting them–even when doing so means confronting a fractious shelter director who refuses to change. It means no longer rewarding failing shelter directors with speaking engagements at their conferences, with features in their magazines, with national awards, or with hundreds of thousands of dollars to be squandered. That, of course, would be quickly followed by investing their huge resources in lobbying for and funding change in communities, including a widespread effort to reform shelters, remove entrenched kill-oriented directors, and provide the infrastructure needed to achieve success.

With a group like HSUS leading the charge, our nation could very easily outlaw the shelter killing of savable companion animals. If one of these organizations were to champion such a law in any given community, who would dare oppose such an effort? What animal control director could stand up against HSUS political muscle and the will of their community? Who would be left to legitimize their refusal to change or to parrot their diversionary platitudes about public irresponsibility, pet overpopulation, or the need to kill?

Only time will tell how long they will allow allegiance to their kill-oriented colleagues, to their antiquated philosophies, and to their failed models, to hold them back from the success they and this movement can achieve the moment they decide to embrace it.

Nathan J. Winograd
January 2009

re·demp·tion

1: to get back; 2: to free from what distresses or harms; 3: to change for the better; 4: to make good; 5: to atone for.

To the Reader

WE ARE A NATION of animal lovers. Collectively, we share our homes with ninety million cats and seventy-five million dogs. We talk to them, keep their pictures in our wallets, celebrate their birthdays, travel with them, and greet them upon coming home even before saying hello to the spouse and kids. We include them in holiday celebrations and take time off from work to care for them when they get sick. And when it is time to say good-bye, we grieve.

Every year, we spend more than thirty-eight billion dollars on our animal companions. And we donate billions of dollars more to charities that promise to help animals in need, with the largest of these having annual budgets in excess of one hundred million dollars.

Most Americans today hold the humane treatment of animals as a personal value, reflected in our laws, the proliferation of organizations founded for animal protection, increased per capita spending on animal care, and great advancements in veterinary medicine. However, the agencies that the public expects to protect animals are instead killing more than five million annually.

How did this happen? How did the very charities founded on the highest ideals of compassion become the nation's leading killers of dogs and cats? How did a nationwide system of tax-funded animal shelters that the public expects to provide a second chance for homeless animals become a network of agencies that does little more than kill them? And why does the animal-loving American public, the very same people who talk to their own pets and celebrate their birthdays, not only accept this situation but continue to foot the bill for the daily killing of animals through taxes and voluntary donations?

Shelter killing is the leading cause of death for healthy dogs and cats in the United States: some five million are killed in our nation's shelters every year. The numbers are staggering. For far too long, we have been led to believe there is no other way. More than that, we have been told that this killing is the right thing to do.

In 1994, however, one shelter embarked on a bold and revolutionary approach to animal sheltering. Although every national animal welfare agency said it was impossible and every other community in the country continued to kill animals at an astonishing rate, San Francisco became the first city in the United States to end the killing of healthy homeless dogs and cats in shelters. The "No Kill" movement it inspired has the potential to end, once and for all, the century-old notion that the best we can do for homeless dogs and cats is to adopt out a few, and kill the rest.

This is the story of animal sheltering in the United States, a movement that was born of compassion and then lost its way. It is the story of the No Kill movement, which says we can and must stop the killing. It is about heroes and villains, betrayal and redemption. And it is about a social movement as noble and just as those that have come before. But most of all, it is a story about believing in the community and trusting in the power of compassion.

Part I

THE CONTROVERSY OVER
SAVING LIVES

Betrayal

"Ownerless animals must be destroyed. It is as simple as that."
—Dr. John B. DeHoff, Health Commissioner, Baltimore, MD,
Proceedings of the National Conference on Dog and Cat Control (1976)

AS DIRECTOR FOR the little known Peninsula Humane Society in San Mateo, California, Kim Sturla oversaw an animal shelter that took in thousands of dogs and cats every year, the majority of whom were put to death. Her record was hardly impressive. But on October 27, 1990, reporters from across the nation converged upon a small room in her shelter, and she had their full and rapt attention.

While cameras clicked and onlookers gasped, Sturla took a tan-and-gray calico cat and her four tiger-striped kittens—all healthy, adoptable animals—and injected them in the stomach with poison from a bottle marked "Fatal Plus." One by one, their tiny bodies went limp and they slumped to the table. By the time she had finished, Sturla had killed eight animals, five cats and three dogs on television. Dubbed a "public execution," the first-of-its-kind public relations ploy was an instant sensation.

People for the Ethical Treatment of Animals (PETA), an organization whose hard-line advocacy on behalf of animals is legendary, should have decried the killings. At least, that is the reaction one would expect—and hope for—when animals are killed as a public relations gimmick. But it didn't happen. PETA, in fact, labeled the acts "courageous."

5

In a series of speeches to groups across the country, Ingrid Newkirk, PETA's founder, rallied behind Kim Sturla. As the centerpiece of the speech, Newkirk hailed Sturla as a visionary and a tireless fighter and dubbed her and her colleagues "dark angels," doing the necessary dirty work for society with compassion and dedication. To SPCAs (Societies for the Prevention of Cruelty to Animals) and humane societies across the country, Sturla had become a hero.*

In Greensboro, North Carolina, in Nevada City at the foothills of the Sierras, and elsewhere, shelter directors turned to killing healthy animals on television in the hope that shocking the public would lower shelter intakes. Mitchell Fox, a shelter administrator in Seattle, Washington, put it bluntly:

> *We are killing animals every night at 6 o'clock behind closed doors and we want very much to change that, to go public with it. We want to do this killing on the steps of city hall and in the parking lots of populated malls and in parks. We want people to see it because there is nothing like that experience.*

Again, PETA applauded the move: "We're hoping that this sort of approach is going to catch on," a spokesperson said.

How had it come to this? How was it that humane societies, which were founded to save animals, were instead killing them on television, while the nation's most strident animal rights group was applauding? Perhaps most disturbing of all, why didn't any of these organizations put to the test the question: do we really have to kill these animals in the first place? The answer to this would have put an end to these sensationalist and immoral ploys.

Instead, content to regurgitate clichés about "pet overpopulation" and pass the blame to others, Fox gleefully proclaimed to the national press corps that the killing would be brought to where people work, live and play. In Seattle, as in San Mateo, New York, Atlanta, St. Louis, Los Angeles, and Boston, in cities great and small, shelter directors earning high salaries, with multi-million dollar budgets and endowments, would continue to kill

---

* In fact, the Peninsula Humane Society under Kim Sturla would put to death an astonishing 9,038 dogs and cats in 1990 alone, over 75 percent of all cats the shelter took in. (The number is actually higher because the agency failed to report the dogs and cats it killed ostensibly at the *request* of the people who were relinquishing them to the shelter).

most of the animals entrusted to them while that simple question went unanswered before real reflection began: *Do we have to kill these animals in the first place?* To see why, we have to understand how a movement that was founded to save animals became a collection of agencies whose primary purpose is to kill animals, regardless of whether the animals are suffering. In other words, we have to answer the question: what went wrong?

THE GREAT MEDDLER

The modern humane movement began in earnest in the United States with the 1866 founding of the first Society for the Prevention of Cruelty to Animals (SPCA) in New York City by Henry Bergh, the son of a wealthy ship builder. At the time, New York City had the distinction of having more animal residents than people. Twenty thousand hogs and countless sheep roamed the streets, eating garbage on behalf of the cleaning department. Cows lumbering through the streets on the way to the slaughterhouse were as commonplace as the dogs and cats drowned in the East River or shot on sight by the police, acting to rid the city streets of "unwanted" strays. Even wild pigeons were peddled from wagons and carts at a few cents a dozen.

But no animal was such an integral part of the New York City landscape, so responsible for the city's meteoric rise in size, and perhaps so consistently abused, as the working draft horse. At the time, all inland travel was done by horse—on horseback, in wagons, or in carriages. Horses straining under heavy loads with bleeding noses, who could be seen starving and dying in the streets or being beaten by caretakers, were a fact of New York City life, and scarcely resulted in a passing glance.

By the time of the Civil War, the aristocratic Bergh had moved to St. Petersburg, Russia, where he had been granted a diplomatic post by President Abraham Lincoln in the court of Czar Alexander II. Finding the duties tiring and mundane, Bergh spent less time on official duties and more time taking aimless carriage rides throughout the city. When he witnessed a peasant beating his donkey on one such ride, Bergh ordered the man to stop, which the man did in deference to Bergh, who looked like a well-dressed gentleman of official position. According to legend, the experience completely transformed Henry Bergh and left him with an abiding sense of accomplishment. Bergh spent his remaining time in Russia traveling daily by carriage in search of such transgressions, which he could prevent by reason of his social class, official position and immense physical stature.

On his return to the United States, he stopped in London for an extended visit with the president of the Royal Society for the Prevention of Cruelty to Animals. The conversion was complete. Bergh had found his calling. "At last," Bergh wrote, "I've found a way to utilize my gold lace—and about the best use that can be made of it."

In early 1866, Bergh returned to his native New York City, a city now filled with a million residents, and discovered—on every street, in every corner, as part of virtually every industry—an overcrowded city built upon the suffering of animals and crying out for reform. On February 8, 1866, to a well-filled room of attendees including the mayor, Bergh delivered the first lecture on animal protection in the United States. He called upon the gathering to undertake a moral fight to better the plight of animals: "This is a matter purely of conscience. It has no perplexing side issues. Politics have no more to do with it than astronomy. No, it is a moral question in all its aspects."

One hundred signatories came forward and signed Bergh's *Declaration of the Rights of Animals*, pledging themselves to suppressing cruelty and showing mercy to animals. Armed with the *Declaration*, Bergh secured a charter from the State of New York, creating the country's first humane society, the American Society for the Prevention of Cruelty to Animals (ASPCA). Nine days later, on April 19, 1866, the state passed a new law prohibiting cruelty to animals, and the fledgling ASPCA was given the power to enforce that law. Henry Bergh went to war.

Bergh would spend the better part of the next two decades in a daily struggle for the animals in and around New York City. Turning to the event in the streets of St. Petersburg that inspired him, his first order of business was to better the plight of New York City's much abused working draft horses. In 1832, New York had established the first horse railway in the world. By 1863, sixteen lines of horse railways criss-crossed the city and 500 horse-drawn cars made their way through traffic daily. Sickly and uncared for horses struggled to pull over-laden cars through the streets, often weighted down beyond their capacity, while impatient drivers lashed at them to proceed. Henry Bergh's answer was simple—the practice would be stopped immediately. The annals of the ASPCA describe the first such encounter:

The driver of a cart laden with coal is whipping his horse. Passersby on the New York City street stop to gawk not so much at the weak, emaciated equine, but at the tall man, elegant in top hat and spats, who is explaining to the driver that it is now against the law to beat one's animal. Thus, America first encounters "The Great Meddler."

With top hat and cane, gentleman-turned-humane officer Henry Bergh began enforcing the law on the spot, ordering passengers to unload and drivers to return to their stables under threat of arrest and prosecution. One evening in February of 1871 during the evening commute, working people rushed for the cars, and the horses began to strain with heavy loads through snow and slush. As one overloaded car reached the corner near where Bergh stood, the driver was ready to give the horses another lash when the call came to "Stop!" and "Unload!" It was Bergh. "Who the hell are you?" came the reply from the driver. "Unload!" called the order again. When the driver refused, Bergh reportedly pitched him into a snow bank and unhitched the horses. Often, Bergh would completely stop traffic on the lines, causing traffic jams that would leave thousands of people stranded and cursing to no avail—because one man had stopped all the traffic to protect a single horse.

For over two decades, Bergh spent each and every night tending to sick animals and hauling drivers who overworked them off to the local justice for prosecution on charges of cruelty. Although the owners of the lines complained, Bergh would carry the day. Within two years of the ASPCA's incorporation, limits on passengers were common, horses were better cared for, and water troughs and buckets for thirsty horses could be seen throughout the city. One chronicler of Bergh's life noted that it was horses that Bergh championed above any other animals. In reality, Bergh's ASPCA labored equally hard to protect the city's stray dogs, particularly against abuses at the hands of city dogcatchers.

Every year for a ninety-day period beginning in June, the New York City pound opened its doors to round up stray dogs with the help of local boys and men. The payment of fifty cents for each dog brought to the pound led to a profitable trade in dogs.*

---

* Stray or not, dogs were rounded up off the street, from yards, and from people's arms, and turned into the pound. At the time, it was not possible to punish the thieves, because many courts held that dogs were not property under the statutes for larceny.

The pound was nothing more than a rough shed where as many as 300 dogs were kept with little or no shelter and no food or water. The dogs were left lying in their own waste, tied up in close proximity, and sometimes fighting each other until they were killed. Every afternoon, unclaimed dogs were drowned in a watertight cistern with a slatted cover. As many as eighty dogs at a time were drowned, with the largest dogs beaten on the head with a club until they stayed underwater. Alternatively, they were killed in what the *New York Telegram*, one of the city's preeminent newspapers, called "the terrible iron crate," where struggling dogs were dropped several times in the East River in front of a crowd of neighborhood children until all the dogs had drowned. Every day, the *Daily News* reported the toll in dog lives: "Monday, 320; Tuesday, 218; Wednesday, 140; Thursday 118; Friday, 93."

Bergh privately championed leaving the dogs alone, noting later in life that once the sweeping generalizations, scare tactics, and hyperbole were put aside, stray dogs posed very little threat to the public health and welfare: "Let us abolish the pound!" he would write. Publicly, however, Bergh was more of a pragmatist, making incremental changes to better the situation. He succeeded in reducing the reward paid per dog from fifty cents to twenty-five cents, and in making it unlawful for the poundmaster to accept dogs from boys under the age of eighteen, thereby discouraging "thieving gangs of young dog catchers." As a result, the number of dogs killed declined significantly (in a two-month period, the number of dogs executed dropped from 5,825 to 938 for the same period the following year).

In the spring of 1869, however, New York City was in the grip of a rabies scare. Although cases of rabies were rare, in the era before vaccinations it did not take much to alarm the public. Bergh's biographer wrote:

> *This convulsive disease, transmitted by the bite of a mad dog, was in those days widely dreaded and completely uncontrolled. Cases of [rabies] were relatively few, but the agony of the disease was so terrible, and death… inevitable, that the danger of mad dogs whipped the public into a hysteria of apprehension.*

Once again, stray dogs were threatened with mass slaughter. However, Bergh's painstaking precinct-by-precinct search yielded only one possible case of human rabies, which was not attributable to a bite from a "mad dog." While the authorities could not argue with the facts, they nonetheless claimed that killing these dogs before they had a chance to bite was preventing rabies, noting that many dogs were "destroyed when in paroxysms of madness." Bergh was undeterred. The reality, he noted, was that most of these dogs, shot by police or clubbed by crowds of angry men and boys, were more scared than mad. In the end, the debate was academic— the pound simply failed to open that summer, but not because of Bergh.

Bureaucratic infighting between the mayor and health board president kept the doors of the pound closed for the duration of the summer. Although he could not take credit, Bergh was relieved. "The present season," he wrote, "has been happily free from the demoralizing massacres of preceding ones." Even the *New York Telegram* noted that despite the lack of a pound, "the poor animals have not disturbed anyone."

That year, tired of fighting the ASPCA and hoping for a break in the stalemate, New York City offered Bergh's ASPCA money to run the dog pound. New York's alderman were ready not only to pay the ASPCA its costs to run the pound, but offered to allow the ASPCA to keep any fines the ASPCA should levy for whatever purpose it saw fit. Henry Bergh refused.

He believed the ASPCA was a tool to champion and protect life, not to end it. He believed that its role to protect *animals* from *people* was fundamentally at odds with that of a pound. Bergh understood implicitly that animal welfare and animal control were two separate and distinct movements, each opposing the other on fundamental issues of life and death. To this day, this tension can be bridged somewhat, but never eliminated. Bergh's answer was clear. "This Society," he wrote, "could not stultify its principles so far as to encourage the tortures which the proposed give rise to…" Henry Bergh would not allow his ASPCA to do the city's bidding in killing unwanted dogs.

Rebuffed by Bergh, New York City officials attempted to crack down on dogs with more zeal than before. First, they proposed a law requiring all dogs to be muzzled in public. They also proposed outlawing a breed of dog called the Spitz which at the time was irrationally feared to be highly susceptible to rabies. Finally, they gave the mayor the power to appoint dogcatchers to round up strays. Undeterred, Bergh fought them every step of the way.

Because of intense ASPCA opposition, the proposed muzzling law failed to pass. While the Spitz was outlawed in many states, and ordered killed on sight in others, the breed ran free in New York City. And in one year alone, the ASPCA prosecuted twelve cases of cruelty by city dog-catchers. The tenacity of Bergh led to the christening of a more modern dog pound in New York City. The dogs were to be housed in individual runs supplied with fresh running water until they met their fate.

Whether fighting for the rights of horses, opposing hunting, trying to clean up slaughterhouses, or protecting stray dogs, Bergh's ASPCA grew in both scope and influence. In a very short period of time, Canada and twenty-five states and territories across North America had used the ASPCA as a model for their own, independent humane societies and SPCAs, and the numbers continued to grow. By the end of the first decade of the twentieth century, virtually every major city in the United States had an SPCA or humane society.

Each SPCA and humane society was a unique entity with its own funding, leadership, staff, set of rules, policies, and governing structure. In other words, no SPCA was (nor to this day is) affiliated with or gets fund-ing from any other SPCA or humane society. Nonetheless, they have al-ways had similar histories. Early humane efforts throughout the United States focused on prosecuting cruelty and providing water troughs for overworked horses. Following the ASPCA's lead, many also turned their attention to the cruelties inflicted by local dogcatchers, including the theft of dogs to sell at the pound, withholding food in order to realize greater profits, and cruel methods of killing—clubbing, drowning, or shooting. And all of them owed their existence and their platform to a single man, The Great Meddler, whose life was irrefutably changed by one act of com-passion on the streets of St. Petersburg. But then, something happened. Somewhere along the path, the humane movement lost its way.

UNINTENDED CONSEQUENCES

On March 12, 1888, as a storm whipped the city and gales tore the roofs off of houses, New York's overworked horses struggled to pull carloads of people through the snow. But for once, after two decades of policing the streets on their behalf, Bergh was not there to protect them. In the early hours of the morning, Henry Bergh had died. Of Bergh, the poet Henry Wadsworth Longfellow once wrote:

Among the noblest of the land;
Though he may count himself the least;
That man I honor and revere;
Who, without favor, without fear;
In the great city dares to stand;
The friend of every friendless beast.

And the *New York Post*, in a prophetic statement, noted that:

His society was distinctly a one man power. The Society for the Prevention of Cruelty to Animals was Henry Bergh and Henry Bergh was the Society for the Prevention of Cruelty to Animals.

Indeed, Bergh himself had often lamented, "I hate to think what will become of this society when I am gone." It did not take long for the fears Bergh harbored about the future of his ASPCA to come to pass. Following his death—and contrary to Bergh's wishes—the ASPCA capitulated and accepted a contract from New York City to run the dog pound. It was a tragic mistake. In little more than a decade, animal sheltering became the ASPCA's primary role. By 1910, the ASPCA was doing little more than impounding dogs and cats on behalf of the city, with all but a small percentage put to death. Other SPCAs around the nation fell in line. The guaranteed source of income provided by contracts helped sway many SPCAs and humane societies to abandon their traditional platforms of advocacy and cruelty prosecutions in favor of administering dog control for cities and counties. In virtually every American city or county, the pound work was placed in the hands of the SPCA. Within a decade or two, most mainstream humane societies and SPCAs did little more than kill dogs and cats.

While by far the largest, the ASPCA was not the first SPCA to make the transition from prosecuting animal cruelty to running the dog pound. In 1872, in an effort to reduce the public exhibition of cruelty favored at the time by Philadelphians in ridding the city of stray dogs, the Women's

Pennsylvania SPCA accepted the first pound contract in the United States by a private humane society and established a three-pronged approach to stray animals. First, it began a humane education program promoting lifetime commitments and the importance of keeping animals in the home. Second, it offered homeless animals for adoption. Third, it introduced the use of a gas chamber to replace old, slow, and more painful practices of killing stray animals, primarily in the form of drowning, beating, and shooting.

These three approaches—education, adoption and killing—were endorsed on a national scale in 1879 with the founding of the first *national* companion animal organization, the American Humane Association (AHA), and have become the mainstay of sheltering ever since. In 1910, for example, the Animal Rescue League of Boston adopted the following policy, more or less identical in practice to most shelters:

> *We keep all dogs we receive, unless very sick or vicious, five days; then those unclaimed are humanely put to death except a limited number of desirable ones for which we can find good homes. We keep from twenty to thirty of the best of the cats and kittens to place in homes and the rest are put to death… We do not keep a large number of animals alive.*

From the ASPCA in New York City to humane societies throughout California, the twentieth century saw killing become the centerpiece of shelter strategy. It is the paradigm we live with to this very day. And while many of these organizations became very large and influential, they also became bureaucratic, with none of the zeal for reform that characterized the movement's early founders.

The disparity behind the motives for founding the Mobile, Alabama humane movement and the reality of high contemporary rates of shelter killing in Mobile County is illustrative of the national shift away from a tenacious focus on saving lives to pound work that results in high rates of killing. In *The Quality of Mercy*, author William Allen Swallow recounts how Mobile, Alabama

> *received nationwide attention in 1892 arising from the arrest and conviction of a groom for using a cruel over check rein [a strap which connects the bit of the bridle to the harness back band; the check rein keeps the horse's head up]. At the time it was said to be the first such conviction in the world.*

Over a century later, however, Mobile County's notoriety stemmed from a deplorable record of killing dogs and cats, at the time arguably one of the worst in the nation. In 1999, 27,930 dogs and cats were killed in county shelters, roughly seventy animals for every 1,000 people, or thirty-two times higher than the San Francisco rate of killing for the same time frame.*

While industry-absent, indigent Mobile might seek to blame its historical rate of killing on a lack of money, economic arguments of this kind are misleading as even wealthy communities and wealthy humane societies kill at alarming rates. With assets at one time reaching nearly one hundred million dollars, the Massachusetts SPCA (MSPCA) is perhaps the richest animal shelter in the world, but roughly 60 percent of all dogs and cats who entered the MSPCA shelter system throughout the 1990s were killed. Indeed, from coast to coast, from community to community, the picture is virtually identical. A critic of this shift, Ed Duvin, summarized it accurately:

> Historically, SPCAs made the tragic mistake of moving from compassionate oversight of animal control agencies to operating the majority of kill shelters. The consequences in terms of resource allocation and sacrificing a coherent moral foundation have been devastating.

Put more bluntly, when the ASPCA took over the pound contract in New York City following Henry Bergh's death, it began a century of squandering not only his life work, but more significantly the ASPCA's vast potential. Bergh's ideal of a humane agency founded to save the lives of animals was replaced with shelters across the country whose primary purpose was—and still is—killing animals, whether or not they are suffering. And for the majority of the animals "rescued" by these agencies, death would remain a virtual certainty even though in many cases, it was not "necessary."

In the end, if Mitchell Fox and Kim Sturla are to be blamed, it is pri-

---

* The community of Mobile, Alabama, can also show the opposite: how refocusing on saving lives can start to turn things around. The Mobile SPCA has led a resurgent focus on lifesaving, helping to significantly lower the county shelter's death rate. While still killing over 12,000 dogs and cats per year as of 2005, the county shelter has begun moving in a more positive direction.

marily for their blind adherence to a century-old tradition of killing, and to the rationalizations that have been built up over decades to justify it—with one notable exception. While the Women's Pennsylvania SPCA took over the pound contract to reduce the public displays of killing, shelter administrators like Sturla and Fox tried to place the killing back into the public squares.

Blaming the Victim

"I am sick over the fact that we can call an agency to come and 'rescue' a pet—only for the pet to be taken to a 'shelter' and [killed]. What the heck kind of rescue is that?"

—Maryann Gandolfo, Letter to Editor,
Best Friends Magazine (2002)

FOR MUCH OF HISTORY, animals were considered commodities who pulled our wagons, provided the products for our farms, herded our sheep, and kept our barns free of mice. After the second World War, however, social and demographic changes in American society at large led to progress in the status of animals as well. Many animals—dogs and cats in particular—were now overwhelmingly seen as "companions" instead of servants.

Six out of ten American families have animal companions, spending tens of billions of dollars every year on their care and comfort. Pet cemeteries are growing in popularity, and in a 1987 study by the U.S. National Institutes of Health, 99 percent of people with pets admitted they talk to their animals; about four out of ten keep pictures of their animal companions in their wallets or celebrate their pet's birthday. A subsequent study in 1999 found that nearly nine out of ten of people include their pets in holiday celebrations, over half will take time off from work to care for a sick pet, and 52 percent prepare special meals for them. An earlier study in 1983 found that nearly three out of four "think of their pets as family members." More recently, the etiquette columnist for the *New York Times* agreed that having a dog carry the flowers or the ring in a wedding is appropriate, if the dog "is a member of the family." In the United States, pet dogs and cats moved from the *barn* to the *backyard* and now into our *bedrooms.*

Three other key changes in our relationship with cats and dogs since World War II have become evident. The first is technical—veterinarians have gained the ability to perform widespread and high volume sterilization of animals easily, safely, and at relatively low cost. By partnering with veterinarians, shelters are able to dramatically reduce unwanted births and thus the number of animals surrendered, and subsequently killed in shelters.

The second change is economic. The growth of the middle class after World War II meant a spread of America's wealth across a wider range of people. This wealth, combined with our unfolding humane ethic, meant donations and bequests to animal welfare organizations increased on a scale previously unimaginable. The wealth made available to these agencies, combined with a prospering economy, resulted in shelters with annual budgets exceeding one million dollars, and shelter directors earning high salaries. By the 1980s, top organizations such as the Humane Society of the United States (HSUS) and the Massachusetts SPCA each had assets ranging from forty million to one hundred million dollars.* Today, donations to animal causes is the fastest growing segment of American philanthropy.

The third and perhaps most important change is suburbanization. People moved from farms into cities, and eventually out of cities into suburbs. These households had yards, nearby parks, and open space. Since there was no longer a "need" for animals as "workers," suburban households became homes for pets, and often homes for multiple animals. Americans opened their hearts and homes like never before, vastly increasing the number of homes available for animal companions. With 165 million dogs and cats in homes today, it is the pet-less household of suburbia that has become the anomaly.

These moral, technical, economic, and demographic changes could—and should—have ended the era of mass killing in American shelters. A caring public who spends billions on their animals, talks to their pets, celebrates their birthdays, and grieves their deaths, combined with wealthy

---

* The Humane Society of the United States is the largest and wealthiest humane agency in the world. In 2006 alone, its operating budget was 103 million dollars.

SPCAs and humane societies, and the ability to halt pet reproduction, offered a recipe for success. All the shelter in a community had to do was to tap into that compassion and channel it towards lifesaving. But they did not. Instead, an institutionalized mentality of killing came to prevail. And the leaders of the new millionaire national organizations ensured, in many cases, that progress would be limited.

INSTITUTIONALIZING DEFEATISM

In 1969, a little known "shelter crusader" named Phyllis Wright joined the Humane Society of the United States. Founded in 1954, HSUS had quickly grown into the world's largest animal-protection organization. By the end of the 20th century, it claimed the support of seven million members.

Although the HSUS was not a shelter and did not provide sheltering services to dogs and cats, Wright succeeded in establishing the organization as the standard bearer for shelter practices nationally. In a review of its own history, HSUS describes Wright, its late vice president, as

> *a fierce advocate for animal shelters, [who] became a mentor and surrogate mother to many shelter employees, while teaching animal-sheltering skills and fostering humane policies. The "Phyllis Wright Road Show," as her many workshops across the nation were known, was a mecca where kindred souls gathered to learn, feel, and embrace the new professionalism.*

HSUS also tried to create "national standards" and "best practices" through workshops, conferences, position papers, and its industry magazine, *Shelter Sense*, which was provided by subscription to local shelters.* Some of the changes that resulted were for the better. HSUS took important stands on many abhorrent shelter practices, including advocating for the abolition of the high-pressure decompression chamber, shooting, and other cruel shelter methods of killing animals. It advocated for better training of shelter personnel, and called on municipalities to provide adequate funding. But Wright's primary legacy was not benign. In an essay entitled "Why We Must Euthanize," Wright wrote that she "personally put 70,000 dogs and

---

* In 1995, *Shelter Sense* became *Animal Sheltering* magazine.

cats to sleep" and that "I don't worry about one of those animals who was put to sleep." According to *Animal People* magazine, the essay created an emotionally acceptable pretext for killing animals: shelter workers "were now 'putting animals to sleep,' albeit permanently." The charade that "killing is kindness" became a national fixture.

Unfortunately, the Humane Society of the United States also worked to limit local initiatives that were at odds with its policies, a course of action that has also not benefited animals. For example, at a time when many organizations were seeking to reduce the number of cats being killed in shelters through an innovative program to neuter and release feral (wild) cats, HSUS condemned the move, calling mass killing the only "practical and humane solution." (A detailed discussion of feral cats is provided in a subsequent chapter.)

And despite the proliferation of breed-specific rescue groups, such as German Shepherd Clubs, Himalayan Rescue, and others that focused on a particular breed and whose members were willing to take animals out of shelters and place them into homes, HSUS claimed that shelters should not allow rescue groups to take animals because the shelter could not guarantee adoption standards or, in a ludicrous argument, because transport to a new shelter might "stress" the animal, despite the fact that the alternative often meant death. Barbara Cassidy, Director of Animal Sheltering and Control for HSUS in 1990, wrote that it "would not recommend the transfer of animals to another facility for adoption... Transport and changes in environment are stressful for animals that are already experiencing stress from the loss of their home."

In 2003, for example, volunteers from "A Forever Home"—a high-volume adoption rescue group—offered to save dogs from the county shelter in Page County, Virginia. In a series of meetings with the county administrator and then-shelter leadership, they demonstrated not only how the group could save the lives of dogs in the shelter (by transporting them to private foster homes and then placing them up for adoption in more populated areas of Virginia), but save the county money as well: they offered to pay for the veterinary exam, vaccination, sterilization, transport, and adoption of these dogs. They had just one request: a telephone call to let them know which dogs faced death so that they could come and save them. With their efforts meeting resistance at the local level, A Forever Home turned to HSUS, assuming that the nation's largest animal welfare group would help. Instead, HSUS sided with the shelter.

In a meeting between the rescue community and local officials, HSUS' representative argued that the rescue groups were trying to hold the shelter "hostage," that their requests for pre-killing notification were unreasonable and that they should not be implemented.* While some of these policies have since been modified, others (as will be discussed later) have not. For many agencies, the HSUS standard became the gold standard. To this day, it is not uncommon to see job descriptions for shelters state they are "run in line with HSUS policies." Shelters are often publicly judged by whether they follow HSUS principles. And when local shelters come under scrutiny by community groups for various perceived failures, HSUS personnel are often requested to do an "external audit" of procedures.

Unfortunately, HSUS has not been alone in supporting or promoting shelter practices that unnecessarily lead to higher death rates for animals. For example, cats and kittens in shelters are highly susceptible to respiratory infections or colds. This is a somewhat inevitable outcome of placing a large number of mammals in one room in a stressful environment. To prevent the spread of colds, some groups have promoted the holding of fewer pets and creating distance between the animals by keeping every other shelter cage empty, a practice that continues in some shelters today. While the problem can be controlled to a significant degree by simply modifying cleaning and/or vaccination protocols, creating an infirmary for sick cats to be treated while isolated from the remainder of the shelter population, or sending sick animals into temporary foster homes, this preferred "solution" of empty cage space leads to more killing since the shelter's capacity is unnecessarily cut in half.

Some shelters also began to operate under the oversimplified theory that shelters must act like department stores and display "quality" merchandise in order to maintain public support. Consequently, they promoted the view that only young and attractive animals should be made available for adoption. Otherwise, it was claimed, local shelters would gain an unfavorable reputation from potential adopters that shelters were filled with "inferior" animals and adopters would increasingly turn to pet stores and breeders for their pets. Unfortunately, the end result was that many shelter animals deemed "less desirable" were relegated to certain death, without ever being

---

* HSUS took this position five years after California made it illegal for a shelter to kill a dog or cat if a rescue group was willing to save that animal's life, a law HSUS did not support as discussed in a subsequent chapter.

offered for adoption. Not only did these shelters have no real evidence to support the claim, they ignored the common shelter experience that many families want an older animal to avoid the training and other issues inherent with very young animals, particularly dogs.

The zeal with which these maxims were offered as truth encouraged shelters to go a step further. Under the theory that too many black cats or Shepherd-type dogs would also turn the public off, but with no proven definition of what constitutes "too many" or proof that it would actually reduce adoptions, many shelters killed animals on the basis of arbitrary criteria such as age, color, or breed in order to keep the "merchandise" diversified.*

These practices inescapably resulted in increased killing and stifled innovation that could have decreased it; a tragedy that could have been avoided. However, the deadly end result of these policies was seen as inevitable only because the national groups perpetuated the idea that the public, and not the shelters themselves, are to blame for high rates of shelter killing. Since national giants like the Humane Society of the United States legitimized, and even encouraged, this perspective, local shelters blamed the public and turned against the very community whose help they needed in the form of adoptions, funding, and volunteers to save animal lives—an idea that had its genesis in 1974, at the first modern-era meeting of national animal protection groups in the United States.

THE BLAME GAME

From May 21-23, 1974, self-proclaimed "leaders" of the animal welfare movement, including the Humane Society of the United States and the American Humane Association, met in Chicago to look for causes and to find solutions to what they termed "the surplus dog and cat problem." It had little hope of success.

With stated goals of finding "consensus" and adopting a "unified" approach, the involvement of private practice veterinarians, the American Veterinary Medical Association (AVMA), and the American Kennel Club

---

* At the same meeting in Page County where HSUS argued that the local shelter should not be required to notify rescue groups before killing animals, HSUS also argued that these rescue groups should not try to save older dogs, dogs with medical issues or pregnant dogs. As these rescue groups provided the only viable safety net, the alternative was a near certain death.

ensured the rejection of any program perceived to interfere with the business interests of these entities. As a result, the meeting turned into the search for a scapegoat to blame for shelter killing, rather than an attempt to see how shelters could operate differently and more efficiently and more effectively at saving lives.

From the beginning of the conference, the AVMA opposed the endorsement of municipal- or SPCA- administered spay/neuter clinics that provided the poor an alternative to the prohibitively high prices charged by some private practice veterinarians. Despite the fact that low-cost spay/neuter services aimed at lower income people with pets had a well documented rate of success in getting more animals altered and reducing the numbers of animals surrendered to shelters in a community, the AVMA would not agree to any program that threatened the profits of veterinarians, even though poor people were not, and were unlikely to ever be their customers.*

But it was the shelter leaders themselves who doomed the effort from the start. In an astonishing keynote address, Roger Caras of the Humane Society of the United States who would later go on to lead the ASPCA, likened free roaming dogs and cats to "inhabitants of an interstellar craft… brought here with the purpose of disrupting our ecosystem." He described them as a threat of the highest magnitude, damaging property and decimating wildlife, and the notion of creating successful programs to save them as so impossible that it was "not worthy of a passing daydream."

When Rutherford T. Phillips, the executive director of the American Humane Association took his turn at the podium, he dismissed claims that veterinarians had any moral culpability for the killing due to the high price of spay/neuter surgeries, yet he ignored their opposition to low-cost alternatives for the poor. Despite the large numbers of animals dying from lack of adoptions in shelters, he failed to directly fault the American Kennel Club for their "increasing number of breeder promotions" to encourage the sale of unsterilized dogs, which results in higher birth rates. Finally, he thoroughly rejected any blame for animal shelters despite a candid admission that "they are destroying 90 percent of the animals received and only placing 10 percent." Instead, Phillips, the head of the then-largest

---

* Regional veterinary associations and private practice veterinarians, at different times and in different places, sued humane societies or sought legislative action to prevent the establishment of low-cost clinics. In 1986, for example, Congress was asked to impose taxes on not-for-profits for providing spay/neuter surgeries and vaccination of animals at humane society operated clinics.

animal welfare agency in the country, blamed the public *and the animals* for their own demise.

Phillips claimed that it was the animals' "unadoptability" which required their killing. If they aren't young enough, do not like to be confined, or have bonded to the family that surrendered them, they—as he put it— "must be put down." Indeed, aside from puppies and kittens, few animals could pass his litmus test of "adoptability."* Any notion of increasing adoptions was further rebutted with an unusual claim, reeking with racial overtones, that only certain kinds of people were worthy of having pets. To prove his point, he claimed that past adoptions in "ghetto areas" were a failure, and that these dogs were now doing little more than "attacking children in schoolyards."

To Phillips and his allies, most of the 90 percent of animals killed in shelters were not worthy of our best efforts to save them. By this logic, these animals would be killed even in the best case scenario since few were considered adoptable: "the ratio of animals received by animal shelters to those which are placeable and usually adopted or returned to their owners runs closer to 40 percent." In one large sweep, Phillips surmised that shelters had an obligation to kill 60 percent of all the animals they took in.

But the public, opined Phillips, was responsible for the bulk of the blame. He blasted "pet owners" for not doing more to confine their animals. He urged the participants to "try to educate the public to the fact that irresponsible companion animal owners are at fault rather than the agencies which serve them." He even provided a solution: "The only answer will be for the public to become responsible pet animal owners. We must have adequate animal control laws and they must be enforced." The view that the public's irresponsibility was the cause of high rates of shelter killing was adopted by the participants with fervor. And to the question of how to make the public more responsible, the national groups erroneously believed they had the answer.

THE NEW ORDER

In order to force the public to become "responsible pet owners," the participants of the Chicago conference came up with a plan that was aptly nick

---

* However, the attendees also agreed that all kittens and puppies under six weeks old should be killed as a matter of policy.

named "LES" (pronounced *less*). LES was an acronym for Legislation, Education, and Sterilization. The first prong promoted legislation aimed at requiring people to keep better track of their pets, usually through licensing and confinement laws. The second prong was aimed at educating children about "responsible pet ownership," in hopes they would grow up with humane attitudes. The third involved punitive measures to force people to spay and neuter their pets.

LES was widely popular among local shelters. Like the conference that nationalized the viewpoint, however, it was doomed to fail in reducing shelter death rates. First, LES did not put any responsibility onto the shelters that were actually doing the killing, nor did it question if a shelter's own actions were leading to increases in shelter death rates (as indeed many did). Second, it took the onus off of poorly performing shelters by blaming the public for shelter failures. Third, it did not question the perceived need to kill. Finally, the plan did not focus on services like affordable spay/neuter programs, which had demonstrated success at reducing death rates at shelters that were utilizing them.

Legislation

A flurry of legislation aimed at making people responsible was promoted and passed in localities nationwide. Among the many laws favored, the most common were those that,

1. Required dogs and cats to be confined in homes;
2. Required dogs and cats to be licensed with local authorities;
3. Limited the number of animals a family could care for;
4. Prohibited the feeding of stray cats; and
5. Provided authority for animal control officers to seize and destroy pets they deemed a "nuisance."

The theory behind these laws was to severely curtail not only the public's "bad" behavior, but also the "bad" behavior of the animals. In practice, however, the laws ended up being ignored or targeting the wrong people.

In a convoluted reading of these laws, for example, anyone who fed a stray animal—or left food out for a hungry cat—was considered that animal's "owner." As the animal's "owner," these individuals were required to do a host of things, including licensing and confining the animal indoors. Failure to comply would often result in fines, or worse, the confiscation and killing of the animal. In towns and communities throughout the United

States, well-meaning people, many of them elderly, found themselves threatened by animal control authorities for feeding the stray cats who wandered into their backyards in search of food. As "owners" under these new ordinances, they were violating the law for "allowing" the cats outside, a curious twist of facts since these people were merely allowing stray animals to have occasional food. Not only were humane societies and SPCAs punishing people for their compassion toward stray animals, they were alienating the people most likely to be sympathetic to their mission, and mostly likely to support them through adoptions, volunteerism, and donations.

Dogs faired little better under these new laws. Dogs picked up by the "dogcatcher" were held on threat of execution if their "owners" did not pay licensing fees, impoundment penalties, and other fines for the return of their pet. Many localities passed laws prohibiting dogs from being in any street or public place unless collared and leashed, thus preventing people with dogs from exercising and socializing their dogs in parks and other places.

Since the legislation prong of LES was premised on the notion that the public was "bad" and had to be "punished" and "coerced" into doing the right thing, it ignored the obvious. Even if HSUS and the others were right, the law would nevertheless miss its intended target since responsible people acted responsibly whether there was a law or not, while truly irresponsible people would merely ignore it. In the end, however, since failure to comply with these laws often resulted in the pet's impoundment and death, the net effect of the legislation was to exacerbate shelter killing.

This point is worth underscoring: at a time when shelters were killing the vast majority of animals they were taking in, they were successfully seeking legislation which gave them authority to impound even more animals. Since they claimed they had little choice but to kill most animals, the animals now in violation of a new law or ordinance had little hope of getting out alive. It is hardly surprising that many jurisdictions actually saw impound and kill rates increase after passage of these laws.*

Moreover, to encourage health and local government officials to pass

---

* At the same time, shelters succeeded in passing laws that limited the number of animals a family could have in their home in order to control the community pet population. As a result, people who already had pets were barred from further adopting from the shelter, which ultimately prevented lives from being saved.

these type of laws, HSUS ultimately would encourage local shelters to blame cats for everything from plagues to car accidents, arguing that they are a human health threat and that they erode the foundations of neighborhoods. The very groups which were founded to protect animals, elevate their status in society, and promote the viewpoint that their lives are precious and they are entitled to care, compassion, and the right to be free of suffering, were instead denigrating and condemning animals.

In contrast, when dogs were being blamed for rabies in the late nineteenth century, Henry Bergh had proven that dogs were not a public health risk. The end result of the backtracking in organizational philosophy underscores Ed Duvin's earlier point: by taking over the killing of animals, humane societies and SPCAs sacrificed "a coherent moral foundation." HSUS, however, took the issue one step further: *it asked shelters to essentially vilify the animals they were founded to protect.*

Education

While localities were being encouraged to pass such laws, the national groups were also encouraging shelters to educate schoolchildren in the hope they would grow up with more humane views than their parents—a program called "humane education." In communities nationwide, shelter employees with dogs and cats in tow entered classroom after classroom to meet with wide-eyed school children. Meanwhile, generations of shelter directors boasted to their constituents about the number of children they were reaching with their humane message and promised that the light at the end of the tunnel, the mythical place where all animals were loved and had lifelong homes, would come when the children became responsible adults. It was, and remains, a lovely thought.

But this effort has never been challenged to see if it can achieve results. In fact, no shelter director—*not a single one*—can point to any results even today. Were more animals being sterilized because of these efforts? Were people keeping their pets longer? Was the death rate at the shelter declining because of it? Would these children grow up to be more responsible with pets? No one has any answers.

Despite tight budgets and cuts in the areas of animal care, shelters continue to send staff members into classrooms without any proof that it can ever hope to decrease the death rate in shelters. Over thirty years of humane education has yet to produce a single study showing it has made any impact, while millions of dollars are diverted to the effort nationwide.

Sterilization

The third aspect of their national approach was sterilization. It was here that the participants had the potential to make a positive and decisive impact. Sterilization of animals to curb their reproductive capacity thus leading to the birth of fewer dogs and cats and consequently fewer surrenders to shelters, is one of the keys to substantially reducing shelter killing. In fact, had the national "leaders" focused on promoting affordable spay/neuter, had they demanded it and helped to fund it, the end result could have been a drastically reduced death rate today. But they did not.

In order to increase the number of animals sterilized—the one thing that would have had dramatic results—they encouraged the passing of even more laws, this time to force people to spay/neuter their companion animals. Many localities took up the banner, passing laws that required people to spay or neuter their dogs and cats on threats of fines, increased licensing costs, and ultimately impoundment and killing of their pets.

Despite studies showing that simply providing a low-cost option doubled the number of poor people who spayed or neutered their pets, and that the wealthiest communities voluntarily spayed/neutered their pets at four times the rate of their poor counterparts, local shelters failed to provide meaningful solutions to obstacles that prevented people from acting the way shelters wanted them to act. While laws were passed to force people to spay or neuter their pets, little was done about the high cost of sterilization that kept poor people from complying. Even in more impoverished communities, where the federal government was subsidizing the cost of home heating oil to prevent families from freezing during the winter, these groups made no effort to provide affordable spay/neuter surgeries in order to appease veterinarians, who continued to oppose perceived threats to their profits.

Not surprisingly, LES has not achieved its intended results. In fact, since LES was not reducing the perceived need to kill animals to any significant degree, the end result was a culture of defeatism ("there is nothing we can do") that perpetuates a distrust—almost hatred—of the public, whom shelter workers blame for the killing. Virtually every major shelter endorsed this view. Shelters nationwide had a new enemy: *the American public.* And, in turn, the public had even more reason to avoid their local shelter: *these agencies did little more than kill animals.*

Never Mind the Laws

The genesis of the failed model can be found in the 1974 meeting at which self-proclaimed animal welfare "leaders" failed to demand the one thing that could have achieved results: low-cost and free spay/neuter, particularly for the pets of the poor. With the AVMA opposed to such programs and private practice veterinarians balking at any real or imagined threat to business profits, neither AHA nor HSUS was willing to take a decisive stand.

While AHA demanded enforcement of animal control laws and increasing penalties for those who did not comply, they backed down from making the same sort of demands for affordable spay/neuter for fear of betraying unity with the industry groups present. Instead, AHA President Rutherford Phillips merely supported "research to come up with a more economical sterilization program." But the research was unnecessary since the solution was already at hand, as Phillips and his allies were well aware.

Study after study had already confirmed that unaltered pets tend to belong to the people with the lowest incomes. If there was a solution in front of them, it was not hard to see: make spay/neuter affordable. A full three years before the Chicago conference, an organization called Mercy Crusade of Los Angeles did just that. On February 17, 1971, it opened the first low-cost spay/neuter clinic in the country, with the City of Los Angeles paying for the veterinary staff. By 1973, two more clinics opened and the first was expanded. In 1979, a fourth clinic became operational. The effort was so successful, that within the first decade of the program Los Angeles shelters were killing half the number of animals they had been prior to the clinics. Every dollar invested in the program was saving taxpayers ten dollars in animal control costs, due to the reduced numbers of animals these shelters were handling. And despite outcry from private veterinarians and their associations when the program first began, there was no discernible loss of business over time. With four clinics operating, private veterinarians were still performing 87 percent of all neutering within Los Angeles, because the clinics were being used by poor people who would not otherwise have had their pets altered. While national "leaders" were trying to appease private veterinarians, Los Angeles had begun the march to save the animals.*

---

* In 1976, the large national groups met for a second time in Denver, Colorado. Once again, they reaffirmed the findings from the Chicago conference, ignoring the success of publicly funded low-cost spay/neuter programs which was presented by a Los Angeles official.

Unfortunately, after two decades, the clinics were closed in a round of budget cuts, and Los Angeles began following a different path: the thoroughly discredited road to LES. On March 22, 2000, at the urging of then animal control director Dan C. Knapp, the Los Angeles City Council passed the nation's strongest law based on the LES-model. During the legislative process, the shelter director proposed penalties of up to six months in jail, which made the punishment for failing to license a dog on par with weapons possession and domestic violence. The final ordinance that was passed, while less draconian, nonetheless punished people with fines of up to five hundred dollars and empowered animal control officers to go door-to-door with the ability to fine owners and confiscate and subsequently kill animals. Low-cost spay/neuter was not written into the law and no effort was made to reopen the spay/neuter clinics that had brought Los Angeles to the lowest third of pet killing per capita in the United States. Not surprisingly, the law has thus far failed to achieve the desired results, the city remains a battleground between shelter bureaucrats and animal advocates over unnecessarily high killing rates, and tens of thousands of dogs and cats continue to lose their lives every year.

In the end, if the national leaders of the second half of the twentieth century left a legacy, it is one of stifled innovation, institutionalized defeatism, and promotion of the notion that shelters are required—indeed, morally obligated—to kill the bulk of their occupants. In a very short period of time, this view hardened to the point that any efforts to break the status quo—to save feral cats, promote more adoptions, or stop animal killing altogether—was met with virulent opposition and a backlash of national proportions.

BETRAYAL

It was upon Henry Bergh's death that this great betrayal first began to take place. The irony, of course, is that the very vehicle Bergh created to save animals from abuse has so altered its scope and mission that it hardly resembles the SPCA of his day. Bergh's dream of creating a truly humane society was pushed aside by the day-to-day ordeal of intake and disposition of dogs and cats in shelters across the country. Hope was replaced with despair. And despair turned to anger. Shelters began to blame the very people they needed to embrace in order to save the lives of animals in their care. Shelters across the country enacted laws that put a stranglehold on the community—pet limits, registries, even laws making it a crime to feed stray cats. As a result, compassion became control. And animals—the healthy and treatable side-by-side with the hopelessly ill—died in shelters by the millions.

To cope with the deaths, SPCAs and humane societies assured themselves there was no other way. They generated innovative workshops to help shelter employees "cope" with "euthanasia." But innovation that would change the status quo got lost in the now all-too-familiar cliché that there are just "too many animals, and not enough homes." Until one SPCA decided to recapture its roots.

Miracle on 16th Street

"What is unconscionable, abominable and outrageous is that animals, healthy and well-behaved, are being killed because someone says there are too many. That is something we do not accept. That is something we find intolerable."

—Richard Avanzino, President,
San Francisco Society for the Prevention
of Cruelty to Animals (1997)

THE TRANSAMERICA BUILDING rises above San Francisco's skyline like the city's once-official bird, the mythical phoenix. At the base is a small park, shaded by redwood trees, populated by local businesspeople who spend their lunchtime eating, reading, or taking in the sights. Nestled near the center of the park, in a stone planter, sits a thirty-by-twenty-inch brass plaque.

Like plaques in many parks around the country, it is a dedication—but one uniquely different in the object of its affections. It is not, like so many others, an expression of gratitude to the founders of the park, nor to war heroes of yore. It is not placed in memory of those who have suffered in the name of progress or intolerance, nor does it honor those who are remembered for significant accomplishments. Nothing about the plaque signifies that the dedication is a thank you for contributions to the public good. In fact, the plaque does nothing more than recall the misadventures of

32

Bummer and Lazarus, two stray dogs who captured the heart of the city during the Civil War.

In 1861, two dogs took to the streets of San Francisco in a vicious fight. As people gathered to see what was happening, the larger dog bit the smaller one's leg, nearly severing it. Another street dog heard the barking and dashed into the fray to rescue the injured animal. Bummer, as the locals knew him, escorted the injured Lazarus to the safety of a doorway where the two of them slept every night until the injured leg recovered. Though the newspapers seem to have played up the fact that the dogs were ugly, their fascinating and inseparable bond of friendship delighted a generation of San Franciscans.

Despite the fame of these two particular dogs, stray dogs in general were not welcome in nineteenth century San Francisco. A newly enacted ordinance specifically prohibited dogs from being without a collar and leash on city streets and without a muzzle in certain sections. On weekday mornings, a horse-drawn van made its daily pilgrimage through the city. Two men would sit on the van, with a third on horseback behind them ready for the chase. A policeman also rode ready to arrest anybody who interfered with the enforcement of the dog law. "As the van jolts along over the rough cobblestone pavement," wrote one historian, "the imprisoned canines give vent to mournful howls, on hearing which every… dog on the street takes to his heels and flees."

In only the first month after enactment, city dogcatchers impounded 255 dogs and all but twenty were killed. According to the local newspaper:

> The pound keeper makes the arrests, and keeps the records, while the executioner takes the unredeemed to some dark and lonely spot, and dispatches his victims. They are then buried without ceremony or pomp—the dainty poodle and the mangy cur, the bristling terrier and the sleek spaniel, all lie in one common grave, and are soon forgotten.

Not only was the poundmaster authorized to seize any dog found in violation and kill the dog if not redeemed within a forty-eight hour period on payment of a penalty, but police officers were authorized to shoot such dogs on sight. This was San Francisco's answer to the existence of stray dogs and it was popularly known as the "Canine Murder Law."

But when the poundkeeper picked up Lazarus along with other strays, the story made headlines. "It was hoped," pleaded the *Daily Alta*, "that the dogslayer would spare the life of the poor vagrant dog known as 'Lazarus,' the inseparable companion of another canine brute, 'Bummer.'"

In response, Lazarus made bail, thanks to the payment of five dollars from an anonymous source, and thereafter a petition containing several hundred signatures was presented to the Board of Supervisors "praying that the dogs 'Bummer' and 'Lazarus' be exempted from the canine murder order." The petition was approved, and Bummer and Lazarus gained their freedom and more fame. They even appeared onstage at the Metropolitan Theatre in a play entitled "Life in San Francisco." Upon their death, the reporter Samuel Clemens, later known as Mark Twain, reverently wrote that they died "full of years, and honor, and disease, and fleas."

Within a few short decades of the poundkeeper's impoundment of Lazarus which had led to the petition signed by hundreds of citizens, his zealousness in rounding up and killing stray dogs had alienated many more. Calls for reform would ultimately number in the thousands and would come to include some of the most influential members of San Francisco high society, until they finally found a voice in a successful San Francisco banker—and friend of Henry Bergh—named James Sloan Hutchinson.

In the late 1860s, San Francisco's cobblestone streets bustled with horse-drawn carriages, streetcars, and wagons. In this rough-and-tumble pioneer city, "progress" often came at a price. Too often, that price was intolerance or cruelty toward overworked draft horses, animals on overcrowded feedlots and farms, and stray dogs who were rounded up and killed by the overzealous poundmaster.

On a spring morning in April 1868, Hutchinson found himself face-to-face with such cruelty when he witnessed two men dragging a squealing boar off to market along the street's rough cobblestones. Hutchinson described the incident:

> *Two vaqueros mounted on spirited horses [were] attempting to lasso a boar which had been separated from its drove and was running up Washington Street. Both vaqueros caught the animal about the same time, one about the fore and the other about the hind legs, and started dragging him over the cobblestones toward the city front.*

Hutchinson sprang into the street and stopped them, with many passers-by coming to his aid. And like Henry Bergh's epiphany in St. Petersburg under similar circumstances, the incident affected Hutchinson very deeply and moved him to call together a group of fellow humanitarians to found the San Francisco SPCA.

On April 18, 1868, the San Francisco SPCA received its charter from the State of California, becoming the fourth SPCA in the nation and the first west of the Rocky Mountains. Like virtually all the SPCAs of the day, for the next few years it focused on bettering the lives of the city's animals, especially San Francisco's overworked and underfed horses. The San Francisco SPCA built and maintained public drinking fountains for the horses, and following the lead of the ASPCA in New York, constructed a horse ambulance, the first of its kind in the West. The SPCA continued to grow both in support and esteem throughout Northern California. Over time, however, another concern caught the society's attention, the same concern that had once gripped Henry Bergh: abuse of city strays at the hands of unscrupulous dogcatchers. The San Francisco SPCA wrote:

> *The public pound as then conducted was a disgrace to the city. The pound-men grabbed pet dogs from the arms of women and children in broad daylight and broke down fences in order to take [pets] to the public pound. They made a practice of stealing animals, and greatly mistreated them after being impounded.*

A Changing of the Guard

The San Francisco SPCA gathered signatures demanding change. John Partridge, the SPCA's president described it as "one of the greatest petitions ever filed with the board of supervisors. The document contained over 13,000 names of our best citizens, demanding the public pound to be placed under the control of the society." According to the SPCA:

> *The board of supervisors informed the society that if [we] would purchase a lot, erect suitable buildings, and furnish horses, wagons, harness, etc., for carrying on the public pound without cost to the city, they would then appoint the society's nominee pound keeper.*

Under the agreement, the San Francisco SPCA owned the property, the equipment, and paid all expenses for running the pound. All the money received as fines and fees, however, were paid to the treasurer of the city, except for fees specified by statute. The society's members and supporters would now be paying for the SPCA to kill animals at the behest of the city. "The result," wrote one commentator, "has been a loss to the society and considerable profit to the city."

A few critics of the financial aspects aside, virtually all supporters viewed the arrangement as a cause to celebrate. San Francisco, wrote the SPCA's Board of Directors:

> *comes nearer today to realizing the hopes, ambitions and dreams of its founders than at any time in its history. For the real object of humane work is far more than the remedying of individual cases of cruelty. It is the application of the principles of justice, of humanity and mercy to our daily life, and in laboring to better effect to attain a general recognition of these objects…*

Ultimately, however, the celebration turned out to be premature—the justification little more than rhetoric. What was supposed to be an application of the principles of justice, humanity, and mercy, quickly deteriorated into a more efficient system of killing. The San Francisco SPCA constructed what it deemed an ambulance department, but two of the vehicles were instead used to round up animals and take them to the pound, *where the vast majority were put to death.*

Although the city had begun the process of collecting and killing stray dogs under the notorious "Canine Murder Law," the SPCA ambulances added efficiency to the dog eradication effort. Of the 4,139 dogs impounded by the SPCA in one year, 3,004 were killed—almost three out of every four dogs. Cats were also impounded for the first time in San Francisco despite the fact the city did not ask for nor pay for it—it was an initiative the SPCA adopted of its own accord. In one year, the San Francisco SPCA rounded up 5,936 stray cats *and killed each and every one,* even though no one asked them to do so. And for nearly a century, like many humane societies throughout the country, the San Francisco SPCA's primary role became killing animals, ostensibly on behalf of the city.

Although the SPCA received increasing contractual payments throughout the coming years, the fundamental logic of the arrangement did not change over the next eight decades. By the late 1970s, the San Francisco SPCA was still subsidizing the killing of dogs and cats to the point that it had driven itself to near bankruptcy. The shelter was housed in a crumbling, old building on 16th Street, between a cement factory and a trucking operation, in the city's decaying mission district. Efforts to negotiate with the city for more funding to adequately care for the animals fell on deaf ears in a political bureaucracy that saw the SPCA as an agency which would retain the contract no matter what it was paid.

In an effort to get out of this quagmire, the San Francisco SPCA Board of Directors conducted a search for a new president, hoping to infuse the society with both business acumen and political skill. They wanted a leader who could negotiate with the city in order to restore society finances. The candidate they hired was Richard Avanzino.

Avanzino was no stranger to either business or politics. Prior to taking the helm at the San Francisco SPCA, he had had a relatively lucrative career as a lobbyist for the pharmaceutical industry, had been mayor of his hometown in a wealthy enclave of San Francisco's East Bay, and was both a lawyer and pharmacist by trade. Ultimately, however, Avanzino would do no better than his predecessors at convincing the city to pay fully for the services the SPCA was providing. In the end, however, it didn't matter; Avanzino's real passion turned out to be saving lives—a passion which not only saved thousands of dogs and cats every year, but also turned the SPCA in San Francisco into one of the richest and most progressive humane societies in the world.

THE OUTSIDER

When Richard Avanzino took over the San Francisco SPCA in April 1976, humane societies and SPCAs throughout the country had not only been serving as poundmasters for their communities for close to a century, they were slavishly following the tenets being promoted by national organizations like the Humane Society of the United States.

Chief among these precepts was that SPCAs were required to kill the bulk of animals in their care because there were simply too many animals and not enough homes. This view, a gospel upon which the bedrock of animal sheltering depended, was a mantra so ingrained as truth it was simply beyond questioning. A corollary of that principle blamed the public for the level of killing because of its failure to spay/neuter pets or make life-time commitments to them. As a result, it was believed that shelter work-ers—through no fault of their own—were mercifully performing the public's dirty work.

If the pet-loving public was slow to back the San Francisco SPCA fi-nancially, and was even slower to visit in order to adopt animals, it should have come as no surprise. Many potential adopters refused to go into a shelter that had poor customer service, limited hours, a remote location and, more importantly, did little more than kill the bulk of its occupants. Instead, people went other places to get animals—friends, neighbors, newspaper advertisements, breeders, pet stores and rescue groups.

While pet lovers understood the reluctance to visit the shelter, many within the shelter industry did not, and in fact still don't today. As many shelters did then and continue to do now, the San Francisco SPCA simply tallied up the number of people who came to the shelter to adopt animals and the number of people who came to surrender animals, and came to the conclusion that since more animals were being surrendered every day than people who came to adopt, the number of animals exceeded the communi-ty's ability to care for them. As the cages became full and adopters failed to come, the remainder of the animals was simply executed.

Although shelter leadership argued that there were "not enough homes," in fact—as will be shown in greater detail in later chapters—there were plenty. Shelters, however, did not proactively reach out to those homes, nor did they provide an environment that encouraged adopters to visit. With pet stores, breeders, friends, rescue groups, and "free to good home" opportunities legion, people who wanted dogs and cats had other avenues to get them, while shelters did precious little to compete with these sources. And with agencies like the Humane Society of the United States vindicating their point of view of "not enough homes," the San Francisco SPCA and thousands of shelters nationwide continued to kill healthy dogs and cats under the belief that there were no alternatives—un-less the "bad" public could finally be made responsible at some mythical time in the future.

Avanzino had two facts working in his favor that allowed him to see beyond this false assumption. First, as an outsider to the animal shelter in-dustry, he was not schooled in conventional sheltering wisdom and could see the possibilities for more lives saved through innovative, lifesaving pro-grams in total contravention of LES. Second, with Mercy Crusade's spay/neuter effort in full swing, and Los Angeles experiencing a dramatic decline in deaths as a result, the seeds of an alternative model were being planted nearby. Avanzino would adopt the Mercy Crusade approach, and radicalize it.

The challenge, he believed, was getting pet lovers to adopt from the shelter instead of from pet stores or backyard breeders. To do that, Avanzino began to implement changes to make the shelter better serve the public, in his belief that this would help the animals. The strategy for saving lives—a strategy that became the cornerstone of his revolutionary new approach to animal sheltering—was to make it easy for people to do the right thing.

At a time when every shelter in the country was telling people to spay and neuter their pets, many of these shelters were not altering the animals in their own care prior to adoption. Avanzino realized he could not expect his SPCA to get people to understand the importance of spaying their animals when the SPCA itself was adopting them out without neutering them. And he saw the hypocrisy of impounding and killing the offspring of the animals he himself had adopted out when he had the power to change the situation by spaying them, thus ensuring that the SPCA's animals were not contributing to shelter killing in San Francisco.

To prevent accidental or needless breeding because people failed to spay or neuter their animals, Avanzino began sterilizing animals before adoption.* But that was not enough. Understanding that the high cost charged by private veterinarians was the primary barrier to spay/neuter, he also began a low-cost spay/neuter clinic so people could sterilize their pets regardless of their economic status.

As Avanzino worked to prevent future generations of unwanted animals from entering his shelter, he also worked to prevent killing those animals already born. Avanzino realized that even with lower shelter populations, which sometimes occurred during the winter, some animals came in too young or too sick to adopt immediately. They were simply killed, a failure of passivity which contradicted Avanzino's philosophy that the shelter should be proactive in saving lives. To save these animals, Avanzino turned to his volunteers for help.

He began a foster care program, placing these animals into temporary

---

* Admittedly, this process was not completed for some time, but he gradually increased the number of animals to which it applied until he reached 100 percent pre-adoption sterilization.

homes until they were old enough or well enough or there was enough space in the shelter to bring them back for adoption. In that way, he could increase the capacity of his shelter without adding to his staff, his facility, or a budget that teetered on the edge of bankruptcy.

The volunteers accepted the challenge and the results were dramatic. Not only was the program successful at increasing the capacity of the shelter during peak periods, but the foster program had other big benefits. Foster parents and their friends, neighbors, and colleagues began falling in love with and adopting these animals—who could now be seen without having to go into the shelter. Some of the animals who went into foster care "temporarily" never came back—they were being adopted into homes instead. The pets Avanzino placed in foster care seemed to get adopted very quickly, and many of them were adopted by people who wanted a pet, but who didn't—or more, appropriately, wouldn't—come to the SPCA to avoid looking at the faces of the many animals destined to die.

There was another benefit to the foster care program. In addition to avoiding the costs of killing these animals and disposing of their bodies, having volunteer foster parents feed and care for the animals resulted in additional savings. Once the animals were adopted, the adoption fee went to the SPCA to care for even more animals. It was, as Avanzino liked to say, a "win-win" for the SPCA and the animals.

In a very short period of time, his foster program had dramatic results. If these animals were more readily being adopted because people didn't want to come to the shelter, Avanzino decided to test whether taking the animals to the people would help him adopt more animals. He called his experiment "Adoption Outreach" and he carried it out by filling a van full of dogs and cats and then setting up temporary adoption booths at locations throughout the city.

In San Francisco's financial district, in fashionable Union Square, and even beneath the Transamerica Building on the very spot where the plaque honoring Bummer and Lazarus is enshrined, throngs of San Franciscans came across SPCA adoption vans filled with dozens of cats and dogs looking for loving homes. By taking animals to where people work, live, and play, Avanzino tried to make it easy for them to adopt a shelter animal, rather than buy one from a breeder, pet store, or elsewhere. Within a few years, Avanzino had set up the nation's first permanent offsite adoption program, with temporary adoption events held daily throughout the city.

In addition, Avanzino kept the shelter open on evenings and weekends so that working people could adopt or redeem their animals, without having to miss work or go to other places to get a pet. Every innovation led to increased lifesaving, which also resulted in more revenue, donations, volunteers, and other support, which in turn allowed Avanzino to innovate further. With animals being sterilized both in and out of the shelter, fewer animals were also entering the shelter. The death rate in San Francisco was declining rapidly. Avanzino felt emboldened.

Over the next decade, he implemented additional lifesaving programs, openly defying conventional shelter practices. Instead of citations, he was providing incentives. Instead of threats, he was giving people opportunities. The SPCA was making it easy for the public to do the right thing, and in the process he was making the shelter more proactive and accountable. While some of these programs are common today (although not nearly common enough) they were non-existent at the time Avanzino began them. In most cases, Avanzino was the first to conceptualize and/or implement them. And the results—lower impounds, less killing, and more adoptions—were nothing short of revolutionary.

A REVOLUTIONARY BREAK

But not everyone shared his enthusiasm. At the then-prestigious American Humane Association conference, Avanzino led a workshop very early in his career on some of the ways shelters could save more lives. The response was a disappointment to Avanzino, but provided an important lesson about the politics of bureaucracy and indifference. One of his colleagues explains:

> *Rich [Avanzino] went to the national AHA conference ... and led a workshop on some of the ways he was trying to save lives by increasing adoptions, adoption outreach, [using] more volunteers. He said the audience didn't relate at all to what he was saying, they didn't think it made any sense. Their attitude was, "there is nothing we can do, it's impossible to change anything..."*

The audience, made up of shelter personnel, paid little attention to what he advocated in the form of increasing spay/neuter, offsite adoptions, and volunteers. Some even walked out of the presentation. To them, the status quo was fixed, there was little one could do to change it, and little reason one should try—even in the face of factual evidence to the contrary. As one shelter administrator would later put it: "The only solution to pet overpopulation is the blue solution," in reference to the blue hue of sodium phenobarbital, the drug used to kill animals in many shelters.

While the nation's animal shelter directors were not ready for what he advocated, Avanzino knew the pet loving public was. When the next decade in San Francisco saw adoptions steadily increase, the death rate steadily decline, and support for both Avanzino and the SPCA rise, Avanzino set his sights even higher. He could no longer ignore the fact that his efforts to save animals contradicted the city's mandate to run the pound. Avanzino's SPCA was wearing two hats—the lifesaving hat of the SPCA, and the other of the city pound. On the one hand, he worked to save animals by spaying and neutering them, fostering them, and taking them off site for adoption; on the other hand, his organization killed them on behalf of the city. He grew weary of the contradiction. In 1988, Avanzino signed the society's final animal control contract with the city and gave notice that he would not renew it the following year. The San Francisco SPCA was ready to sever the cord of running animal control.

Until then, virtually every major city had an SPCA or humane society that contracted for animal control services, and these shelters had become dependent on the revenue streams provided by animal control contracts, although in most cases they did not provide the level of funding needed to perform the services mandated. As a result, these agencies' private fundraising efforts, which brought in revenue above and beyond contractual payments from cities and towns for animal control services, were not being used to maximize lifesaving. Instead, they were being spent performing animal control enforcement. Animal lovers who donated to their local shelter were inadvertently paying officers to write citations, rather than fund expanding adoption services.

Avanzino was on the verge of walking away from 1.8 million dollars per year. Of more significance, he was threatening to take the San Francisco SPCA into uncharted waters. Killing unwanted pets, intentional or not, had become central to the organizational imperative of virtually every humane society and SPCA in the country. With "farm animal" slaughter laws now the subject of state and federal oversight, and draft horses replaced by cars and trains, the platforms of the late nineteenth century were now obsolete. After more than a century of service, animal control thoroughly defined the soul of the nation's animal shelters. But Avanzino no longer wanted his SPCA to be a part of it. He was going to take the San Francisco SPCA back to its roots, to the founding vision of Henry Bergh's ideal that an SPCA should be a tool for lifesaving, not killing. If a city chose to round up and kill dogs and cats, it was not the SPCA's job to do it for them. Instead, like the ASPCA of Bergh's day, Avanzino's SPCA would provide oversight to make sure that killing was done as humanely as possible, while using its resources and advocacy efforts to reduce it as much as possible.

Consequently, the "animal control" functions Avanzino saw as antithetical to the mission of an organization dedicated to advocacy on behalf of animals—impoundment of vicious animals and city ordinance enforcement (including ticketing for dog license violations, leash laws, and "pooper scooper" laws)—would go back to the city.

Because the shelter then being used was owned by the San Francisco SPCA, the city built a brand new facility, located right next door. This drastically increased the city's capacity to house animals because now there were two major shelters for the homeless animals of San Francisco.* In addition, staffing the new city department proved easy. The staff which Avanzino had inherited—schooled in the old paradigm and hostile to Avanzino's changes despite their overwhelming success—took jobs running the new animal control facility. Avanzino was now free to focus all of the San Francisco SPCA's efforts and resources on saving lives.

As the San Francisco SPCA opened its doors on July 1, 1989, it did so for the first time in nearly a century without the title of poundmaster for the City and County of San Francisco. Other than a likely handful of patrons wanting to license dogs or those with other "animal control" business, who would be directed next door to the new city shelter, few people took much notice of the change in status. Nonetheless, it was a historic beginning of an altogether different future for shelter animals—not of certain death as had been the case nationwide since before the turn of the century, but a future that held promise, protection, and a new chance at life. As the front door at 2500 16th Street in San Francisco slowly swung open that morning, the first battle flag of the No Kill revolution was symbolically being raised.

---

* In addition to the San Francisco SPCA and the newly created city shelter (the Department of Animal Care and Control), there was also Pets Unlimited, a non-profit veterinary hospital, and numerous rescue groups which also adopted out animals.

A NEW ERA BEGINS

The San Francisco SPCA immediately stopped killing healthy animals, since that task was now being conducted at the new city pound, although to a far lesser degree than in other cities because of Avanzino's spay/neuter, foster, and adoption efforts. Avanzino wasted no time expanding those programs and implementing new ones, which he believed would save even more lives. He added incentives to get more animals sterilized, such as low-cost and free spay/neuter opportunities for pets of the homeless, poor, and elderly. He expanded the infrastructure to treat sick and injured animals to make them healthy enough for adoption. He began one of the nation's first dog behavior departments. This effort both corrected behavior problems and trained dogs in basic obedience for lives as cherished human companions. Animal trainers also provided advice to people who were experiencing problems with their animals so they would not give up on them and take them to the pound.

By 1993, Avanzino's SPCA was not only saving more lives than ever before, it was gaining huge public support. In the process, it had left behind the fight with the city bureaucracy for needed revenues, ticketing of people for petty violations of city codes, and the burden of a foot-dragging staff. Once teetering on the edge of bankruptcy, the San Francisco SPCA now had an ample budget and a healthy surplus—totaling tens of millions of dollars—thanks to San Francisco's pet-loving public, which no longer felt it was subsidizing the killing of pets if it supported the San Francisco SPCA.

Having widened the safety net and built an infrastructure dedicated to lifesaving—something he could not do as long as he was subsidizing animal control services because of insufficient funding or squandering his lifesaving efforts by meeting arcane animal control mandates imposed by the city—Avanzino believed he was missing a single, unifying vision that would define his SPCA and everything for which it strived. When he relinquished the animal control contract, the San Francisco SPCA was able to pick and choose which animals to take in and even accept dogs and cats from cities throughout the larger multi-county San Francisco Bay area. Instead, he wanted all of the organization's efforts—the medical rehabilitation programs, the spay/neuter clinic, the behavior department, the adoption program—to focus on one goal: saving as many homeless animals in the City of San Francisco as possible. Avanzino wanted to take a bold leap, to make a guarantee to save each and every healthy dog and cat on death row at the city pound. He also wanted to save each and every sick and injured, but treatable one. The vision was clear and its achievement now within reach, even though virtually every shelter director and national organization in the country claimed it was impossible. Avanzino would save all the city's homeless animals who medically and behaviorally could be saved—no matter how many there were, or how long it took. He even gave it a name: San Francisco would become America's first No Kill city.

THE ADOPTION PACT

Since the majority of animals went to the Department of Animal Care and Control next door to the San Francisco SPCA, Avanzino needed to make sure the city shelter agreed to transfer all dogs and cats they would not or could not place to his SPCA. Because the city shelter was the poundmaster for San Francisco, all stray dogs and cats had to go to that facility by law. They would be held there during the stray holding period to give families looking for their lost animals a chance to reclaim them. All healthy animals who were not claimed by their families or adopted out into new homes by the Department of Animal Care and Control would be transferred to the San Francisco SPCA, instead of being killed.

Under the terms for such an agreement, the SPCA would *guarantee* to take every healthy dog and cat the city shelter could not place and would find them all homes. Avanzino eventually hoped to extend this guarantee to sick and injured, but treatable animals as well. The SPCA would take on all the costs and responsibility. In return, city shelter staff would not kill these animals, and the animals would be saved. It should have been easy to come to this agreement. But Avanzino still had one more obstacle to overcome.

With the city shelter staffed by those who had been hostile to Avanzino's lifesaving efforts when they had worked at the SPCA, it was not an easy task. In a series of private meetings, animal control leadership began throwing up one roadblock after another as to why it could not be done, why the San Francisco SPCA could not be guaranteed that these animals would be given to them rather than killed. San Francisco's Animal Care and Control Department was holding the animals hostage. Avanzino decided to go public.

San Francisco's Animal Welfare Commission (AWC) had been set up to provide a bridge between citizens and local government. Modeled after similar commissions that covered other areas of government (the Public Utilities Commission, Recreation and Parks Commission, Commission on the Environment), the AWC was appointed by and reported to the Board of Supervisors, which makes laws within the corporate limits of the city. In October 1993, Avanzino presented his case for what he called the "Adoption Act."

He wanted it to have a positive connotation: the Adoption Act would promote adoptions, instead of killing. A city ordinance, the first of its kind in the nation, would make it illegal for any "public animal control agency" to kill a healthy dog or cat so long as another "humane agency" was willing to care for and find the animal a loving, new home. Although written in broad language, the target was easy to see. The Department of Animal Care and Control was the only "public animal control agency" in the city, and Avanzino's SPCA the only "humane agency" willing to guarantee care for the animals.

On the night of the AWC's Adoption Act deliberations, individuals affiliated with animal protection organizations throughout the San Francisco Bay area filled the room. The four largest shelters condemned the plan. When it was over, each of them had spoken out against the proposed new law. Even the most esteemed national organizations—not only those that purport to speak on behalf of shelter animals, but those which preach everything from vegetarianism to ending hunting—came out against the concept, outraged that anyone would propose ending the killing of dogs and cats in San Francisco's shelters. To an outside observer, the world would have appeared to be upside down. Sadly, it made perfect sense.

When it came to other animal welfare issues like killing animals for sport by hunting, there was no debate. The goal to end hunting was a platform on which every animal welfare organization from coast to coast could agree. However, unlike with animals raised for food, used in research, or hunted for sport, the very animal protection groups formed to promote and protect animals were doing the killing of shelter animals. Without exception, the most vociferous opposition to San Francisco's Adoption Act arose from those who should have championed any means of saving animals: the leaders of animal shelters and animals control facilities who for decades turned to sodium phenobarbital, a barbiturate that ended life to manage their shelter populations under the theory that the best we could do for the bulk of these animals was to kill them.

More importantly, these shelter administrators had killed thousands of animals without much public condemnation by deflecting the blame for the killing back to the public itself. According to the Fund For Animals, one of the organizations that opposed Avanzino's plan:

> *[People] who do not spay and neuter are the greatest single cause of the companion animal tragedy… Each day an estimated 70,000 puppies and kittens are born (25.5 million a year). Six to ten million, we classify as 'surplus' and kill… The problem is simple: we have too many dogs and cats. Too many for the too few homes available.*

The buck was passed. If you blame the public for the killing, the shelter not only shields itself from public scrutiny and accountability, but the question of how to stop the shelter from killing is never even asked. Avanzino's Adoption Act threatened to expose this assumption as false. For the bureaucrats who had spent the prior decades overseeing a national infrastructure that killed millions of dogs and cats per year, the Adoption Act hit a darker, rawer nerve: if passed, the changes would mean a fundamental alteration in their public standing. Never before had killing in animal shelters really been questioned; most accepted it as a necessary evil. On the contrary, shelters had the leeway to kill most of the animals in their care and were doing little to change that policy, while their directors and presidents continued to be paid handsomely, gave national conference workshops, and were hailed as pillars of the humane movement by their colleagues.

Despite the killing, many of these organizations had also amassed impressive endowments, and some built state-of-the-art veterinary hospitals, complete with cardiologists, neurologists, and other specialists for those wealthy enough to pay, while homeless animals in their own shelters were killed behind closed doors, outside of public scrutiny, for something as simple as a cough, cold, or—even worse—being the "wrong" color, one of "too many" black cats in a shelter that already had a handful of them.

San Francisco's success, and the specter of the Adoption Act, however, was challenging all of that. Avanzino's legislation threatened to bring public scrutiny to the operations of these other shelters, with questions like "If they can do it in San Francisco, why can't we do it here?" And that could not be allowed to happen. Over the next several months, regional shelters and national organizations began a vilification campaign against the plan. They claimed it wouldn't work and, interestingly, shouldn't even be tried.

The irony, of course, is that while shelters were claiming they had no choice but to kill because of the public's irresponsibility, the city pound in San Francisco did not want a public fight that threatened to expose its own refusal to go along with a plan that would negate the perceived need to kill. To try to prevent a plan that could potentially save thousands of dogs and cats annually, at no cost to taxpayers and with no conceivable downsides, would not only be unpopular, it would be morally indefensible.

Avanzino had spent the previous two decades winning over the goodwill of the people of San Francisco. The city shelter could count on its allies in the "shelter industry" to oppose the Act based on arcane arguments, but the twisted logic made no sense to San Francisco's pet loving public, and the director of the pound knew they wouldn't stand for it.* Even the city's politicians, riding the tide of public support for the measure, were enthusiastically supportive, particularly since the expenses for the care of the animals once they left the city shelter would fall on the privately funded San Francisco SPCA.

Ultimately, the Adoption Act became the Adoption *Pact*. After months of negotiation, and the threat of a public referendum on the matter, in 1994 Avanzino forced a reluctant animal control director to sign a memorandum of understanding between the two agencies that guaranteed a home for every healthy dog and cat in San Francisco. Each and every healthy dog and cat who entered the city's pound would be saved—no matter how many there were or how long it took. Every day, a handful of San Francisco SPCA employees walked across the street with carts carrying dozens of empty pet carriers and leashes, and returned an hour or so later with all of them filled with cats and dogs one day away—and in some cases, hours or minutes—from being killed at the city shelter. The difference between life and death for San Francisco dogs and cats was the formalization of an adoption agreement that saved the lives of approximately

---

* According to Avanzino, city shelter leadership argued that an adoption guarantee would lead to increased pet abandonment because the "threat of a death sentence was what kept pets in their homes" and that "people would think pet overpopulation was solved and would no longer spay or neuter their animals." In other words, the city pound argued that they should continue to kill animals so people will be scared to surrender them to the shelter and continue to spay/neuter.

2,500 additional animals every year that the city pound could not or would not place—animals who would have been on death row without Avanzino's intervention.

After the first year of the Adoption Pact, the deaths of healthy animals in San Francisco shelters dropped to zero, and the deaths of sick and injured animals dropped by nearly 50 percent, at a time when most major urban cities were killing upwards of 80 percent of cats and over half of the dogs. Although many agencies were seeing increases in their death rates, or posting only modest declines, San Francisco's death rate had plummeted. In the first five years of the Adoption Pact, cat deaths declined by over 70 percent, kitten deaths by over 80 percent, and dog deaths by two-thirds. Of greater national significance, what the American Society for the Prevention of Cruelty to Animals, the Humane Society of the United States, and virtually every animal shelter in the country kept saying was an impossibility became a reality for the fourth largest city in the country's most populous state.

The pet loving public, of course, supported the effort enthusiastically with hearts, homes, and wallets. People adopted San Francisco shelter pets in record numbers. The number of shelter volunteers skyrocketed. The SPCA continued to amass an impressive endowment as donations soared. Five years after relinquishing the animal control contract, the San Francisco SPCA went from "the place where animals are killed" to where they were guaranteed a home—a guarantee that extended to the city pound. With a huge groundswell of support, Avanzino took a SPCA on the verge of bankruptcy in a city that took in over 20,000 animals per year, the vast majority of whom were killed, and turned it into the safest urban community for homeless pets in the United States.

Ultimately, Avanzino's most important legacy was the paradigm shift he took from the hypothetical to the real, with a series of programs and services that lowered birthrates, increased adoptions, and helped keep animals with their caretakers. His wasn't the first No Kill shelter; others had been doing it on varying scales for years. Unlike other shelters without animal control contracts, however, he focused all the resources of the San Francisco SPCA to extend their lifesaving guarantee throughout the city. So that each and every healthy homeless dog or cat, no matter what shelter they entered in San Francisco, would be guaranteed a home.

By the time Avanzino left the SPCA, San Francisco's rate of shelter killing was a fraction of the national average and over thirty times less than communities with the highest death rates. And while his successors would ultimately dismantle many of the programs that had made San Francisco into America's first and, at the time, only city saving all healthy dogs and cats, the proverbial Rubicon had been crossed. The San Francisco SPCA had fired the first volley, and with it began a revolution.

Not in My Backyard

"The only solution to pet overpopulation is the blue solution."

—Unknown shelter administrator,
symposium on 1998 California Animal Shelter Law,
Los Angeles, CA (2000)

IN 1918, like many countries around the world, the United States was in the grip of the deadliest plague in human history, the Great Influenza. In Philadelphia alone, hundreds of thousands of people were falling ill, many were dying, and the city had run out of coffins. To respond to the disease, the best scientists of the time rushed to find a cure, a vaccine, some anti-toxin that would hold promise.

As scientists, they were trained to work methodically, slowly, trying to reproduce their results over and over, before they were ready for peer review or clinical trials. But these were desperate times, and with each passing month, the body count continued to rise. Experimentation and reproducing results in the laboratory takes time. Publishing the results and peer review takes time. Clinical trials take time. And with people dying within days and sometimes hours of initial symptoms, time was something the ill did not have. As a result, scientists worked together as quickly as possible. If any endeavor showed promise, it was shared with others and rushed into the field in the hopes it might save some of the dying. In short, they acted the way people act when they are committed to saving lives.

According to a 1996 article in the *Journal of the American Veterinary Medical Association*, the killing "of healthy, but unwanted pets in animal shelters is believed to be the leading cause of death for dogs and cats in the U.S."—approximately five million lose their lives every year. In scale and scope, this killing can only be described as an "epidemic." In light of this, one would believe, predict, expect, and hope that leaders running shelters killing upwards of two hundred dogs and cats per day, or those in charge of multi-million dollar national animal protection organizations formed to aid companion animals, would try to learn about San Francisco's great success at lifesaving, and replicate its programs and services in order to stem the tide of animal killing still occurring in their own communities—animals they were pledged to protect.

One would have expected that these groups would have gone to San Francisco and brought back with them the "cure" for the disease of shelter killing. It was, at the very least, worth a try, even if they were not convinced of its potential. Since San Francisco was the first major metropolitan city in the United States that had successfully ended the killing of healthy dogs and cats, one would have expected them to seize upon any remedy that showed promise. That is what people dedicated to saving lives did during the Great Influenza. That is what ethics demanded. But, tragically, it did not occur.

Nothing was so unique about San Francisco that its success could not be replicated elsewhere, in each and every American city and county. The only difference was leadership; instead of following Avanzino's lead, many shelters and their national allies went on the defensive. The "old guard"— the presidents, vice-presidents, executive directors, and general counsels— ignored and/or denigrated the programs that made lifesaving success possible in San Francisco, while animals continued to be needlessly killed by the millions.

Historian John Barry writes that

> [i]nstitutions reflect the cumulative personalities of those within them, especially their leadership. They tend, unfortunately, to mirror less admirable human traits, developing and protecting self-interest and even ambition. They try to [create] order [not by learning from others or the past, but]… by closing off and isolating themselves from that which does not fit. They become bureaucratic.

One of the fundamental downsides of bureaucracies is their focus on self-preservation at the expense of their mission. And in the case of animal shelters and the national allies who supported them, this bureaucracy led to the unnecessary killing of animals.

These agencies—and their leadership—would ignore the success in San Francisco, would not send teams to find out how it was successful, and would not similarly reduce the killing in their own communities. They would put the interest—indeed the very lives—of the animals aside, instead promulgating an anti-No Kill rhetoric with a surprising level of venom and with no valid basis for doing so. They saw the solutions as the disease, and went so far as to call No Kill a "cancer."

Throughout the 1970s, San Francisco was impounding well over 20,000 dogs and cats annually, the majority of whom were put to death. It was nothing short of a wholesale slaughter, although typical of cities throughout the nation. As long as this practice continued, the San Francisco SPCA was not a threat and therefore was in the good graces of other shelters and national groups. When the shelter, under Avanzino's leadership, began moving in a new direction and achieved unprecedented success, the attacks began. These attacks ranged from misrepresentations to outright lies.

In 1997, for example, the Humane Society of the United States published an article attacking No Kill. In the article which admonished No Kill proponents for creating "false and harmful" perceptions, HSUS stressed the need to be "fair and truthful." In the same article, however, HSUS failed to do just that. In an article exclusively about dogs and cats in shelters, HSUS surreptitiously included wildlife numbers in their report of the statistics in order to inflate the death rate for dogs and cats in San Francisco by several thousand, making the impressive results the city was achieving in decreasing the death rate for dogs and cats appear untrue. It also refused to clarify the comparison of death rates or retract the false insinuation even after Avanzino wrote HSUS expressing dismay that the nation's largest humane organization was trying to "undermine the efforts not only of San Francisco's animal shelters, but of a phenomenal number of people who are working together to make a remarkable life-saving difference in our City."

Roger Caras, the President of the ASPCA, a position once held by Henry Bergh, called San Francisco's success "more hoax than fact." When such efforts failed to sway public opinion, he went on to claim that the success was due to the city's homosexual population, claiming that "the gay community is traditionally the most animal friendly." Others relied on more direct, though equally misleading, arguments.

The then-executive director of the Nevada Humane Society falsely claimed that San Francisco's efforts were resulting in an *increased* killing rate for dogs and cats—inflating the death rate by 450 percent. Pat Miller, the president of the California Animal Control Director's Association, and the director of operations for the Marin Humane Society, a wealthy bedroom community just north of San Francisco that was still killing savable animals, indicated the claims were "based on semantics, data distortion, and the prolonging rather than the relief of animal suffering." Miller would go on to say that she, like others who shared her views, was "disturbed by the advocacy of No Kill philosophies."

Avanzino summarized this opposition best:

> For years, there has been what seems to me a concerted, aggressive, and sometimes mean-spirited campaign against No Kill in general, and against the [San Francisco SPCA] in particular. This campaign has included statements that in my eyes go far beyond the bounds of legitimate debate, and rely instead on falsehoods and misrepresentations that demean, diminish, and disparage.... Again and again, we find programs misrepresented, motives questioned, and results and achievements ignored.

Opponents, for example, characterized Avanzino's program for offsite adoptions as nothing more than "sidewalk giveaways," which lowered the quality of adoptive homes. There was not only no evidence to support this, these claims disregarded the San Francisco SPCA's rigorous adoption screening requirements. They called his foster care program a ploy that delayed killing, or they claimed that his overall success was nothing more than "smoke and mirrors." Every effort was made to distort the city's success and diminish its potential for lifesaving in other communities.

Mostly, however, shelter directors relied on (and still often continue to rely on) two main arguments to downplay the renaissance of lifesaving, and to explain why their own shelters weren't achieving equally impressive results. The first argument is that No Kill means nothing more than keeping animals in cramped cages until they go crazy because no one will adopt all of them. This is the "animal hoarding" myth.

In 2004, ten years after San Francisco's unprecedented success, the National Animal Control Association (NACA), an industry trade group, still published such misleading attacks in an article entitled "Can No Kill Be Cruel?" Although the question was never directly answered, the slant was not hard to see. According to the article, *dogs and cats linger for weeks, sometime months, in tiny, cramped cages with barely room to move… dogs are rarely walked. They may sit in their own waste because overworked kennel workers hardly have time to clean more than once a day. Cats face a similar fate. Shelter managers can boast of decreased euthanasia rates, yet from the animal's point of view, is their suffering worth it?*

The article ends by asking the question whether it "is compassionate to force dogs and cats to live their lives in small, confined spaces for weeks or months at a time when their chances for adoption are slim to none?"

The calculus, however, is both a myth and a gross misrepresentation. First, it would be far preferable for an animal to endure a "few weeks or months" in a shelter before moving on to a loving, new home than to be killed out of convenience. Second, these animals are not in filthy, cramped cages at true No Kill shelters. While they waited for adoption in San Francisco, for example, they were housed in clean, well lighted cages/kennels, fed nutritional food, received good quality medical care, and were socialized daily by volunteers.

More importantly, animal hoarding has nothing to do with the No Kill movement. The No Kill movement seeks to end unnecessary shelter killing. Animal hoarding, by contrast, is a mental illness and a crime perpetrated by individuals who collect a large number of animals beyond their capacity to provide adequate care, and who cause the animals to suffer and, in many cases, to die. That some hoarders might call themselves "No Kill shelters" is not only an aberration, it is wholly irrelevant. If the No Kill philosophy did not exist, such an animal hoarder would just call himself a "caring pet owner." Would we condemn sharing our homes with animal companions because of that? Indeed, newspapers and television news programs periodically report stories of child abuse perpetrated by foster families. Does that mean we should condemn foster care for children? Of course not.

Avanzino's success in San Francisco has led to defensiveness and outright maliciousness on the part of the architects of the status quo to deflect blame for their own failures and/or continued killing. They perpetuated the myth that No Kill means nothing more than warehousing animals in filthy conditions because they claim some dogs and cats are too ugly, unlovable, or "unadoptable" to ever find homes, and as a result they will deteriorate in shelters until they go crazy or succumb to disease. In a 1997 article entitled "I Used to Work at a 'No Kill' Shelter," a program coordinator for HSUS wrote that she quit because she "wanted to be a shelter worker again, not a glorified collector."

In fact, No Kill is the opposite of hoarding, filth, and lack of veterinary care. In 1998, for example, No Kill advocates in California pushed a major animal shelter reform package through the legislature. One aspect of the reform was the requirement that shelters had to be open when working people could visit, work with rescue groups to place animals, and provide care to impounded animals, including socialization, nutrition and veterinary care. The law was uniformly supported by No Kill shelters and rescue groups around the state. It was, however, opposed by animal control in Los Angeles County, the Fund For Animals, and virtually every major animal control shelter in the state with a few notable and progressive exceptions. (The effort to legislate lifesaving and the response by the humane movement is discussed fully in a subsequent chapter.)

To imply that No Kill by definition means filth and hoarding, therefore, is a cynicism which has only one purpose: to defend those who are failing at saving lives from public criticism and public accountability by painting a picture of the alternative as even darker. The philosophical underpinning of the No Kill movement is to put actions behind the words of every shelter's mission statement: "All life is precious." No Kill is about valuing animals, which not only means saving their lives, but means good quality care. By denigrating No Kill as akin to animal hoarding, these groups appear to be arguing for nothing more than a nation of shelters firmly grounded in killing—a defeatist mentality that is inherently unethical and antithetical to animal welfare.

The second argument made by national organizations and shelters defensive about San Francisco's success is that No Kill is only possible because these shelters close their doors to needy animals when they are full, requiring other shelters to do the killing. This is the myth that says "open door" shelters—shelters that take in all animals without restriction—are more ethical. In a 1995 article in the newsletter of the Humane Society of Santa Clara Valley, a shelter about an hour south of San Francisco, Executive Director Christine Arnold likely felt public pressure as a result of Avanzino's success and made it clear where her shelter stood on the issue of No Kill. She wrote that:

> [t]here is a major difference between No Kill and open-door shelters: No Kill
> shelters accept only animals they believe are immediately adoptable while open-

door shelters accept all animals, regardless of health, condition or age. We are a haven for animals that otherwise might be released on the streets, unable to fend for themselves and likely to meet a cruel death.

This point of view is parroted by others. Don Reick, past president of the National Animal Control Association, published an article in *NACA News* entitled "Parting Thoughts on No Kill Delusion," where he too claimed No Kill shelters often did little more than "turn away animals every day."

Critics argued that since the San Francisco SPCA did not accept *all* animals from the public, that the agency was nothing more than a "limited admission" shelter that turned animals away. These animals were then accepted by the "open door" animal control shelter next door, which had no choice but to kill them. The argument is misleading for many reasons. First, all lost or stray animals *had* to go to the city shelter by law. Second, the Adoption Pact required the San Francisco SPCA to take every healthy dog and cat the city shelter was going to kill, making the San Francisco SPCA an "open door" for animals from the city pound. Third, the SPCA also took thousands of sick and injured animals from the city shelter as well. In reality, the animals they claimed were simply being killed anyway were being saved by the San Francisco SPCA, over 2,000 dogs and cats per year, in addition to the thousands it accepted directly from the public who surrendered their own animals to them.*

Even the director of San Francisco's Department of Animal Care and Control, the recipient of Avanzino's largesse, fed the flames of misinformation. Carl Friedman described No Kill shelters as "simply ones that can pick and choose the animals they take in, and can turn away abandoned pets when their facility is full." He also insinuated the San Francisco SPCA was not saving "unadoptable" animals; and did not admit that the San Francisco SPCA wasn't taking only "cute and cuddly" animals, as he has implied. Under the Adoption Pact, it was Friedman's shelter that had the sole authority to decide which animals would be considered "adoptable" (Friedman preferred the term "available"), which the SPCA was required to accept. The Adoption Pact further stated the pound would give the San Francisco SPCA healthy animals it would not or could not place itself;

---

* It is worth noting that the city shelter itself could have also found homes for the animals, but chose not to expand its own adoption program.

without such placement these animals would have been under a death threat.

The SPCA not only took all available animals Friedman might otherwise have killed, it took thousands of treatable sick and injured dogs and cats also, reducing the death rate for these animals beyond any other community in the nation. The end result was that the city had the lowest death rate in the country, while the city pound was subsidized by millions of dollars in reduced costs and other associated savings.

More than ten years after San Francisco's success, long after Avanzino left for other endeavors, Friedman continued his campaign against No Kill, claiming that "'adoptable dogs' are usually smaller breeds which exhibit playful personalities and good behavior" which he contrasted with "larger, unruly or hyperactive dogs. In some cases, the dogs we take in aren't even housetrained." In reality, the Adoption Pact defined "adoptable" animals in the broadest terms to include any healthy and non-vicious dogs (and cats). It did not matter if they were old, ugly, house-trained, unruly, large, hyperactive, blind, deaf or missing limbs. If they were healthy, they were guaranteed a home. Friedman knew this: his agency had been deeming such dogs as adoptable since 1994, and the San Francisco SPCA had been taking each and every one who faced death within Friedman's agency.

Moreover, every No Kill shelter that exists subsidizes the work of the local animal control agency by reducing the number of impounded animals in that community, and thus reducing the number of animals killed. But rather than receive praise and gratitude for their work, many private shelters are the subject of relentless attacks by animal control groups and their national allies. In the case of the San Francisco Department of Animal Care and Control, these attacks were disseminated and paid for by taxpayers.

By way of contrast, imagine hypothetically a Department of Social Services director attacking a private soup kitchen or homeless shelter for not having enough beds or serving enough meals, meaning the department itself has to feed or house the remainder. Every homeless person the private soup kitchen feeds or houses is one less homeless person for which city taxpayers are required to provide care. Our hypothetical director would be grateful and thankful for the private support. As a private agency, the soup kitchen or homeless shelter does what it can. The mandate to care for homeless people, by contrast, belongs with the city department. In San Francisco, however, Friedman, the director of a government agency mandated to take in San Francisco's homeless animals, used taxpayer dollars to downplay and arguably denigrate the efforts of the *private* non-profit San Francisco SPCA. Avanzino explained, "Many times I've heard the statement made that No Kill shelters can exist only because someone else down the street is doing the killing. The implication is that No Kill shelters are derelict because they refuse to kill animals." Ironically, these shelters blame No Kill shelters for not killing. According to one such group,

> *shelters that don't euthanize animals are able to do so because they admit and care for a limited amount of animals. The animals that no kill shelters don't take end up in shelters that have to euthanize. Inevitably a shelter that says no forces another shelter to take responsibility for the animal turned away.*

In a 2005 article, People for the Ethical Treatment of Animals claimed "there's not a 'No Kill' shelter in this country that does not turn animals away every single day." Another advocate of the status quo wrote that a "No Kill shelter really can't have an open admission policy. It must limit its intake if it wants to adopt out animals and not kill them." One of the top veterinarians at the ASPCA in a textbook on shelter medicine stated that

> *[b]ecause the term No Kill can be inflammatory and misleading, and many of these shelters are able to reduce their euthanasia numbers by limiting their admissions, they will from this point hereon be referred to as 'limited admission' shelters.*

By defining and controlling the language used to describe No Kill, groups mired in the philosophy of killing are attempting to control the perception of it. Once again, however, the claims are misleading. The Tompkins County SPCA, for example, is an open admission, No Kill animal control agency. (Tompkins County's success is discussed in detail in a later chapter.) The shelter provides all impoundment and animal sheltering services in Tompkins County, and so ensures that the entire community is No Kill. A shelter or community can be "open admission" and still be No Kill.

The problem is that the large national agencies have historically not endorsed No Kill or the success in San Francisco (and later Tompkins County), and so have not promoted it as a model for others to follow. They have not endorsed all the programs and services that made it possible. Nor have they used their significant resources to help other communities follow suit. As a result, it is true that many No Kill shelters are not "open admission," but given time to build the infrastructure and capacity for greater lifesaving, this can and will change. Unfortunately, it will take longer than necessary because of continued opposition from advocates of the status quo.

Moreover, the irony of the "open door" shelter crowd is that many of their facilities are little more than open doors to the killing of homeless animals. They are often so enmeshed in their philosophy that they are blind to any proactive steps that might limit the numbers of animals coming in through their doors or increase the numbers of animals adopted. In fact, when California and New York passed legislation to require shelters to spay/neuter all animals before adoption, some "open door" shelters did not respond by honoring the intent of the law or the lives of the animals in their care, but by killing animals rather than having to spay/neuter them. In the final analysis, "open door" does not mean "more humane" when the end result is death.

The claims made against the San Francisco model by local shelters and their national allies were, in the end, little more than a smokescreen, a diversion from their own failure to end the killing of healthy dogs and cats. Rather than spending time, energy, and resources trying to disparage the San Francisco model of success, they could have learned from it, emulated the programs and services that had made a lifesaving difference, and imported San Francisco's success to their own communities. Tragically, few did.

A Missed Opportunity

There are several possible reasons for their failure to do so. Unfortunately, none of them are satisfactory. In fact, most are nothing more than after-the-fact justifications. One explanation often suggested to explain why animal shelters nationwide did not embrace the No Kill paradigm is, simply, fear. Whenever a shelter kills a homeless animal entrusted to its care, it has profoundly failed. And animal shelters fail, as a general rule, fifty to eighty percent of the time. Put another way, animal sheltering is an industry whose leadership mostly fails.

Unlike any other industry, however, these directors still retain their positions, are pillars of their communities, and are tapped as "experts" by the large national groups. Some teach workshops at national conferences hosted by the Humane Society of the United States, hold positions of influence and esteem within the Society of Animal Welfare Administrators, and win awards from the National Animal Control Association. That credibility, and esteem, has been seriously threatened by the No Kill movement's widespread public support following San Francisco's success. According to Avanzino, "there was the real fear, both stated and implied, that [San Francisco's success]…would bring public scrutiny to their own operations, encouraging challenges to the status quo with comments like, 'if they can do it in San Francisco, why can't we do it here?'" In other words, animal control directors—fearful of being held accountable for failure—were putting their own interests ahead of the lives of the animals.

The second possible reason suggested for failure to follow San Francisco's lead is guilt. Having killed hundreds, thousands, or tens of thousands of dogs and cats, convinced there was no other way, shelter administrators were not able to face the fact that the vast majority of the killing they did was unnecessary. While this might have some appeal, it does not excuse it. If they were ashamed of the killing they had done, or are still doing, in light of a solution they could have adopted earlier, they should have apologized. They could have said: "We did the best we could. We did not know better, but we are going to do better going forward," and then earnestly tried to do so. That is the response one would have expected from those who truly care about animals, after seeing lifesaving success elsewhere. Instead, many continued to attack San Francisco specifically, and No Kill more generally, with vehemence—a refusal to replicate the success which resulted in more animals needlessly being killed.

The third excuse offered is ignorance. Some have suggested that we must forgive animal shelter directors because they simply do not know any better, and cannot conceive of solutions to a problem they believe insurmountable, in spite of the overwhelming evidence to the contrary provided by the San Francisco SPCA. This possibility must also be dismissed as inadequate.

In the nineteenth century, for example, Dr. Ignac Semmelweis observed a higher incidence of deaths due to puerperal fever in maternity wards associated with teaching hospitals than in births attended by midwives. In trying to figure out why puerperal fever was a hazard of giving birth in a hospital rather than at home, Semmelweis opined that students and doctors might be carrying the diseases from autopsies they performed, while midwives who did not perform such procedures were not. Semmelweis also found that rigorous instrument cleaning and hand washing could bring the fever rate down to zero. Had doctors known at the time that germs caused disease, this finding would have been unremarkable. Unfortunately, Semmelweis' discovery predated the germ theory of disease. At the time, no one knew that asepsis was important. According to Semmelweis' critics, hand washing wasn't needed when they could clearly see that their hands had nothing on them. In the end, Semmelweis lost his job for criticizing the "superiority" of hospitals to home birth. Once germ theory became known and established, however, he was vindicated for his foresight. Of course, sterility through instrument cleaning and hand washing has since become the norm.

Like the doctors of the 1800s who rejected Semmelweis' hand washing recommendations because they seemed illogical, shelter directors have also fallen prey to the lure of the seemingly obvious. A shelter director explained it like this:

> *You build a shelter with 200 cages. Today, you get 50 homeless animals and you place 10. The other 40 go into cages. Tomorrow, you get 50, but only 15 total go home. When the fictional shelter is full [people] suggest building more cages, which we do, but then those cages are quickly filled… The inflow of unwanted animals is an ongoing phenomenon. What do you do with the rest?*

But again, this excuse, to use a pun, doesn't wash. In a time of epidemic killing, any procedure—or in our case, any program—which showed potential for saving lives should have been tried, regardless of whether we know or can agree on the underlying causal mechanism. Moreover, Avanzino's national advocacy efforts for programs which he proved resulted in more adoptions, greater lifesaving, and less killing showed that the idea of "too many animals, not enough homes" was a misperception.

Rather than attack Semmelweis, doctors should have simply washed their hands, since Semmelweis pointed out that this eliminated deaths, even though, at the time, no one could explain why. Rather than attack No Kill, shelter administrators likewise should have copied its precepts because it had been shown to work in San Francisco. Historians have coined the term the "Semmelweis Reflex" to describe "mob behavior in which a discovery of important scientific fact is punished rather than rewarded." The anti-No Kill rhetoric of the nation's shelter directors and national animal protection agencies appears to be nothing more than this reflex in action.

The final possibility—and perhaps the most likely—is the most dis-turbing of all: these shelter directors didn't care enough about the animals. Killing in the face of alternatives of which you are not aware, but should be, is unforgivable. It would be like a doctor who refuses to keep pace with the changing field of medicine, treating pneumonia with leeches instead of rest, antibiotics and fluid therapy. Killing in the face of alternatives you simply refuse to implement, or about which you remain willfully ignorant, is nothing short of obscene.

The Killing Continues

When reactionary shelters opposed to No Kill could no longer argue against the reality of the massive decline in shelter killing in San Francisco, they sought ways to distinguish the city, to show that its success could not occur anywhere else. They argued, for example, that San Francisco's wealth alone made the lifesaving possible, which poor communities could not em-ulate, ignoring the fact that many urban communities had shelters with multi-million dollar endowments but were still killing healthy dogs and cats. They ignored the pockets of incredible poverty within San Francisco and that Avanzino had inherited an SPCA on the verge of bankruptcy. They ignored the fact that the San Francisco SPCA's newfound wealth was a byproduct of Avanzino's success—results which the public clamored to support—and not its cause. They also ignored the fact that many of the programs—sterilizing, fostering, or transferring animals to rescue groups—were actually cheaper than killing. In fact, adoptions bring in rev-enue, whereas killing costs money.*

So desperate were these shelter leaders to avoid comparison to their own failures that a shelter administrator from Los Angeles went so far as to state that San Francisco was only able to achieve its lifesaving rate be

---

* It can cost over one hundred dollars per animal to hold, kill, and dispose of the animal's body, for example, while adopting the animal allows a shelter to gain not only adoption fees, but future donation opportunities from those individuals. It is also less expensive to spay an animal, by way of another example, than it is to take in, hold, and kill the offspring of that animal. These representative examples cut across virtually all of Avanzino's pro-grams and services, above and beyond the huge potential for fundraising that follows a shelter's lifesaving success.

cause, as he put it, "San Francisco is surrounded by water." By claiming that San Francisco was geographically inaccessible, he argued that it prevented people from bringing more dogs and cats into that community. Yet, as the city is part of the continental United States, any map will demonstrate the fallacy of the "San Francisco is an island" argument.

An editorial in the national periodical *Animal People* summarized it best:

> *The bottom line is that too many animal control departments and humane societies have a vested interest in doing what they have always done. Going a different and more successful route would mean accepting some of the blame for causing barrels to fill, day after day, with furry bodies. Complain though many animal control and humane society people might about the stress of killing, they still find killing easier than doing what is necessary to stop it.*

Nowhere is this conclusion more telling than over a similar battle being waged across the country, with implications for the lives of as many as one hundred million animals. This war has pitted ordinary citizens against animal control agencies mired in the reactionary philosophy of killing. On one side are dedicated and compassionate animal lovers combing alleyways, neighborhood parks, backyards, and schoolgrounds, rain or shine, day-in and day-out to help animals. On the other, are animal control officers who have pursued and prosecuted these people, seeking to impound and kill the animals they work so hard to protect. And at the center of it all is a most unlikely group of creatures. To this day, this animal is "ground zero" in the battle for No Kill's hegemony. The *cause celebre* of such slavish human devotion—and such draconian backlash—are a group of animals that don't much care for the company of humans. If anything, aside from some food, they pretty much want to be left alone. They are feral cats.

Witch Hunt

"What kind of crazy town makes it against the law to feed stray cats?"

—Beatrice Zaretsky, age 69, threatened with a $2,500 fine
for feeding abandoned cats (1996)

THEY WERE REVERED as gods by the ancient Egyptians, persecuted as demons in the Europe of the Middle Ages, and have been watched over by dedicated caretakers for as long as written text prevails. They have even inspired a hit Broadway musical.

No one knows how many there are, or even exactly how to define them. They live in barns, behind restaurants, in old warehouses, wherever they can find a modicum of shelter, some scraps of food, and a place to bear their young. They are especially common wherever there are transient populations of people: on college campuses, military bases, apartment complexes, and tourist destinations.

In the lexicon of animal sheltering, they are called "feral cats." Popularly, they are known as "barn cats," "alley cats," or "wild cats." Webster's dictionary defines "feral" as "having escaped domestication and become wild," but this definition does not cover all the cats we classify as feral. Cats in our society occupy a spectrum that runs from the cherished pet to ferals who have had little or no human contact or support. Some of these elusive felines were born in parks and alleyways and will never become accustomed to people. Others may be marginally cared for, living in someone's backyard, garage, or barn, or traveling from doorstep to doorstep in search of food and occasional shelter.

Whatever one calls them, feral cats have a rich and noble history. Citing a journal from Captain James Cook, British biologist Roger Tabor writes that "At Tahiti, [Captain Cook] noted that cats from a Spanish ship that had called there three years earlier, in 1774, had 'already turn'd wild and re-tir'd to the mountains.'" The most famous group of feral cats sits in London's Fitzroy Square, about whom T.S. Eliott wrote his famous poems that inspired Andrew Lloyd Webber's *Cats*, one of the longest-running musicals in Broadway history. Some even come with an Ivy League-caliber pedigree: feral cats living on the campus of Stanford University are cared for and fed daily by the university's prestigious faculty.

There is also a dark side to their history—one of scapegoating and persecution at the hands of those who have feared, hated, and maligned them, with no legitimate reason for doing so. Cats were burned as witches, drowned as servants of the devil, and targeted by the Roman Catholic Church when, in the fifteenth century, Pope Innocent VIII issued a call to exterminate every cat in Christendom. Sadly, it is a persecution which continues to this very day and, until very recently, was championed by a very unlikely and counter-intuitive source—the Humane Society of the United States, which once called mass slaughter in our nation's shelters the only practical "solution" to their existence. It is a point of view that HSUS unleashed with such vehemence that they have even advocated the arrest and prosecution of those who believed and practiced otherwise, as one group of dedicated cat caretakers found out the hard way.

THE ENEMY WITHIN

On the eastern seaboard of the United States sit the Outer Banks of North Carolina, best known as the birthplace of powered flight. On December 17, 1903, Orville and Wilbur Wright made history at Kill Devil Hills, near Kitty Hawk, and forever changed our view of the skies. Today, the towns that make up the North Carolina coastline are a perennial favorite among easterners seeking the solace of the Atlantic Ocean. They are home to vacation residences of the wealthy, a thriving tourist economy, and a feisty group of local inhabitants—the feral cats of the Outer Banks. Despite their disposition, the cats have a dedicated core of caretakers who watch over and care for them.

Every day, members of a group of concerned North Carolina cat lovers based in Kitty Hawk wake up and head out to different spots along the Atlantic coastline, where cats are often waiting for them. Armed with food, fresh water, and other tools of the trade, these individuals are the heart and soul of the growing wave of feral cat caretakers who are helping to revolutionize animal sheltering in the United States.

Their program is a simple one. Wild cats are trapped in humane cages, and then taken to veterinarians who sterilize and vaccinate them. The stray friendly cats who may from time to time show up at these colonies are adopted into homes through local rescue groups. The feral ones are released back into their habitats, and then fed daily and watched over by dedicated cat lovers—all at the caretakers' own expense. The cat-loving citizens at Kitty Hawk call themselves the Outer Banks Spay/Neuter Fund and their program is called Trap-Neuter-Return (TNR). For feral cats, TNR is the sole alternative to the mass killing perpetrated in U.S. animal shelters. To this day, feral cats have a near 100 percent death rate in those shelters that do not endorse or have a TNR program in place. In fact, because of their unsocial disposition, they are not considered adoption candidates. As a result, there is no other animal entering a shelter whose prospects are so grim and outcome so certain. Without TNR, all feral cats who enter shelters are killed.

On February 17, 1994, the cat lovers who made up the Outer Banks Spay/Neuter Fund met with officials of the Dare County Animal Control Advisory Board to ask for assistance. They were there to introduce themselves and demonstrate how the county could save money by investing in spay/neuter rather than continuing the local practice of impounding and killing the feral cats of the Outer Banks. The Board suggested they present their plan to the Outer Banks SPCA. The SPCA director, however, told them not to bother. The SPCA had already declared "its total opposition to the spay/neuter of feral [cats]," preferring instead to kill them.

Members of the Outer Banks Spay/Neuter Fund turned to the Humane Society of the United States for help. Since HSUS was the nation's largest companion animal and humane advocacy group—and one with significant influence over local shelters—leadership of the Outer Banks Spay/Neuter Fund expected their assistance in the struggle to legitimize TNR to the local shelter. The co-chair of the Fund explained:

*We had thought HSUS would write a letter on our behalf. We thought that
HSUS would encourage the Outer Banks SPCA to stop killing these cats since
there was a non-lethal alternative. We felt that feeding and caring for these
cats was in keeping with the humane mission of the Humane Society of the
United States.*

Instead, HSUS wrote to the Outer Banks SPCA calling TNR "inhumane"
and "abhorrent," applauding the SPCA's opposition to the practice and encouraging the director to contact HSUS for assistance. The SPCA did not
have to take the initiative, however, because HSUS was not content to sit
this one out; the nation's largest self-proclaimed proponent of animal protection went even further. HSUS wrote to the local prosecutor and put
plainly its "mission" when it came to feral cats and the people who care for
them: feral cats should be taken to shelters and killed and local feral cat
caretakers were subject to arrest and prosecution. The kind-hearted citizens who took it upon themselves to feed, neuter, and care for the feral cats
of the Outer Banks area were stunned.

According to HSUS, releasing feral cats after spay/neuter—even if the
cats are fed, given fresh water, and watched over daily as these particular
feral cats were—amounted to animal abandonment, in violation of North
Carolina anti-cruelty laws, an offense that carried both a fine and jail time.
The cat lovers of the Outer Banks feared the worst—getting arrested and
being jailed for feeding and caring for homeless cats *someone else had abandoned.*

Thankfully, the prosecutor was not moved. The North Carolina
statute against abandoning pets, he stated, is

> *directed at those people who dump their pets and those individuals who move
> from an area and leave their pets behind. If an animal is returned to the area
> where it is being fed, it would be a greater injustice to find that these animals
> had been abandoned so that no action to spay/neuter the animals would be
> taken by anyone.*

The law, he said, was for people who abandon their pets on the side of
the road, not caring animal lovers who feed, spay/neuter, vaccinate, and
provide veterinary care to feral cats who do not live in a human home.
Grateful that the local prosecutor employed common sense, as well as a
dose of compassion for the cats and their caretakers, the Outer Banks

Spay/Neuter Fund went back to work. They would continue to care for the cats, just as they had always done. But they did so without the naiveté that drove them to seek help—straight into the arms of the enemy. Had they done a little research, however, the response by HSUS would not have surprised them.

Writing in *Shelter Sense* magazine, the primary device used by HSUS to influence policy among the nation's 6,000 or so shelters, Mark Paulhus, HSUS' Vice-President of Companion Animals, was very forthright about where the nation's "preeminent" animal organization stood on the issue. In May of 1992, in a column entitled "Tough Choices about Feral Cats," Paulhus made the HSUS position crystal clear. Paulhus began by asking the rhetorical question of whether HSUS could support TNR for feral cats as an alternative to death at the pound. The response was emphatic: the "answers to these questions are still, and will always be, the same: no, no, and absolutely not!" To HSUS, the answer was—*and they asserted would always be*—the same. HSUS would continue to promote the extermination of feral cats, calling mass slaughter in the nation's shelters, "the only practical and humane solution." HSUS went so far as to coin a phrase, "subsidized abandonment" to characterize the efforts of groups like the Outer Banks Spay/Neuter Fund.

In the 1994 letter to the Outer Banks prosecutor, Roger Kindler, an attorney for HSUS whose name appears on HSUS' letterhead even today, blamed feral cats for everything from plague to local budget deficits. Feral cats, he asserted "can be responsible for traffic accidents, bites, spread of contagion, and enhanced municipal expenditures to retrieve them from public space." HSUS also blamed the cats for the decimation of songbirds and other wildlife.

Unfortunately, HSUS has never stood alone in villainizing feral cats. In the 1990s, the American Kennel Club noted that "it should probably be a crime to feed feral [cat] colonies." Not to be outdone, the Progressive Animal Welfare Society in Seattle, whose administrator promised to bring the killing of shelter animals to the streets of the city, compared cats to "oil spills" and "poisons in the environment," in terms of the environmental degradation and wildlife decimation they supposedly were causing. The Association of Wildlife Veterinarians called for an "elimination of feral cat colonies" and a ban on sterilizing or feeding these animals. And People for the Ethical Treatment of Animals, legendary for its claim that when it comes to the value of life, "a rat is a pig is a dog is a boy," did not stand where compassion would dictate when it came to the unsocialized cat: to PETA, the best option for these cats was not sterilization, food, fresh water, or veterinary care, it was—in almost all circumstances—execution at the pound.

Unfortunately, many local governments were listening. On the East Coast, a town council expanded its animal control law to include a provision making it illegal for any resident to feed more than five cats. One resident, a sixty-nine year old woman who cared for homeless neighborhood cats, was threatened with fines for violating the law, even though she had sterilized and vaccinated them all. She was given two options by local authorities: turn away the cats who came to her back door looking for food and water, or trap them and turn them over to the animal control facility where they would likely be killed. For a cat lover, this was no choice at all. In San Mateo, California, an elderly couple who cared for several cats was threatened with citations and fines. Rather than risk having the cats impounded and killed at the local animal control facility, the cats had to be relocated out of county. The couple lost their beloved companions although they, too, had spayed, vaccinated, and cared for them. From coast to coast, anti-cat groups emboldened by their allies in the humane movement, moved to outlaw the care and feeding of homeless cats, and threatened compassionate cat lovers with impoundment and killing of the cats, fines and, at least in North Carolina, the potential for jail terms.

What is a Feral Cat?

The intensity with which HSUS and others have historically attacked TNR efforts was based on several assumptions about feral cats that have been promoted as undeniable truth. But how much of their view about feral cats is accurate? Do feral cats transmit diseases to humans or cause traffic fatalities? Are they really decimating bird populations? Are their lives painful and short? Most of all, why are homeless cats, many abandoned through no fault of their own, not worthy of the compassion of groups purportedly dedicated to animal welfare and animal rights?

For much of the humane movement's history, feral cats were referred to as "filthy," "vicious," "fractious," and were spared no quarter, even by those claiming to be their "advocates." As one proponent of shelter killing once remarked, "[o]wnerless animals must be destroyed. It is as simple as that." Unfortunately for the cats, it has been as simple as that.

Anti-TNR groups have long held that the feral cat is merely an unsocialized domestic animal. Domestic animals, they argue, need to live in a home in order to avoid suffering. But this belief is inaccurate; in fact, the distinctions between feral and friendly pet cats, or domestic versus wild cats, are meaningless. Even what appears to be a simple truth—one is friendly, the other is not—is not so clear cut. And since feral cats are as hardy a survivor as any wild animal, the notion that they are better off dead than living in their habitats flies in the face of the evidence.

The problem arises from the commonly held, but false, belief that a biological difference exists between a wild and domesticated animal. This misinformation has resulted in much feral cat suffering and death. We know, for example, that all cats—feral or pet—are genetically identical to the African wildcat, a wild animal by everyone's definition. Since the feral cat is biologically the same as a wild animal, it follows that the untamed feral cat born on a remote corner of a farm who never becomes accustomed to people, is a wild animal in every sense of the word.

The concepts of wild and domestic are behavioral traits. Whereas domesticated animals are animals "adapted to life in intimate association with humans," feral cats are not. They fit the dictionary definition of a wild animal: "living in a state of nature." In fact, even a domesticated cat can revert to a wild state and care for herself if necessary. Henry David Thoreau, writing in *Walden*, experienced this first hand:

> Once I was surprised to see a cat walking along the stony shore of the pond, for they rarely wander so far from home. The surprise was mutual. Nevertheless the most domestic cat, which has lain on a rug all her days, appears quite at home in the woods, and, by her sly and stealthy behavior, proves herself more native there than the regular inhabitants.

Ignoring biology, sociology, genealogy, common experience, and good sense, shelters mired in traditional philosophies argue that all cats need the same things regardless of their domesticity or wildness/ferality. To these groups, all cats are domestic animals who belong in homes, and in their view the feral cat without a human home is better off dead than living in the cat's natural habitat. They claim that an outdoor cat's life is a series of brutal experiences and shelters need to "protect" the cat from current and future suffering.

The reality, however, is that all animals living in the wild face hardship, and feral cats are no exception. The studies of feral cats by British natural-ist Roger Tabor and others confirm that feral cats survive at similar rates and exhibit behavior attributed to wild animals. Feral cats are "suffering" no more than raccoons. As humane advocates would never recommend the killing of wild animals, nor argue that to do so would be in the animals' best interest, they should also not recommend such for feral cats. In fact, the animal welfare movement has a long, noble tradition of trying to elim-inate such practices, as evidenced by its opposition to hunting.

Since no animal groups support the trapping and killing of other wild animals—raccoons, mice, fox—why is this fate reserved for feral cats? If feral cats are genetically identical to wild animals, survive in the wild like wild animals, are unsocial to humans like wild animals, share the same hardships as wild animals, and live and even thrive in the wild like wild an-imals, shouldn't animal welfare groups advocate on their behalf, push for their right to live, and protect their habitats as they do for other wild ani-mals? More importantly, why should *all* feral cats be condemned to death today because *some* of them might suffer at some undetermined time in the future? This is especially true in light of the fact that, when the evidence is gathered and examined, feral cats are not suffering as HSUS and others have historically claimed.

Opponents of TNR programs are quick to say that indoor-only cats live much longer than outdoor cats. They claim that while indoor cats typ-ically live fifteen years, outdoor cats live only a precious few. Intuitively, it makes sense and many cat lovers keep their cats inside for what they be-lieve is the cat's own good. While that still might be a good idea in appro-priate cases, is the claim true? In reality, it is not. Shelter employees who claim feral cats are better off dead need only look through their own "feral wards" where the wild cats awaiting execution are housed. Every day, shel-ters take in feral cats who have lived their entire lives outside. The vast ma-jority of these cats are healthy despite the absence of a known caretaker.

In the most comprehensive study of feral cats to date, Dr. Julie Levy, a nationally renowned veterinarian and professor at the University of Florida at Gainesville, found that feral cats had similar baselines for health to pet cats and similar rates of disease in comparison to pet cats. Furthermore, in an eleven-year study of feral cats, Levy found that the vast majority of the cats were in good physical condition, with only four per-cent killed for health reasons. By the end of the observation period, feral cats in the study had been present an average of 92 percent of the average lifespan reported for house cats, which might actually be low, since almost half of the feral cats were first observed as adults of unknown age. In other words, the lifespan of feral cats is about the same as those of house cats. Other studies share Levy's findings. One study found that ten- to fifteen-year-old feral cats were common in TNR colonies, while another found that feral cats had an "A+" rating for coat, muscle, teeth, and weight gain post-neutering.

It appears that not even a cataclysmic hurricane can change this calculus. Following the devastation caused by Hurricane Katrina in the greater New Orleans area in 2005, officials for St. Bernard Parish Animal Control reported that "feral cats did surprisingly well after the hurricane. They were not thin or sick."

There is no question that cats living outside face risks. But life is about risks.* The contention of TNR opponents that we stop the cat from *possibly* suffering or *possibly* dying by killing the cat ourselves is an irreconcilable contradiction. Life, by its very definition and common experience, is a mix of easy and hard, good and bad, happy and sad. We experience it as humans. Deer experience it, too. So do birds, fox, mice, and rabbits, which does not lead to the conclusion that these creatures should face mass slaughter. In a call for mass extermination, the feral cat stands alone. But the contradiction goes deeper, because while traditional shelters argue that all cats are the same and have the same needs, they themselves treat them very differently.

In the shelter, the feral cat meets a deadly double-standard: once there, a friendly cat is capable of adoption; a feral cat, by contrast, is killed outright. The distinction between the two is real and obvious, and is made daily by the very shelter professionals who, on the one hand, make the claim that all cats are the same and require the same things in order to lead happy, healthy lives and, on the other, condemn feral cats to death because their temperament is that of a wild animal, which makes them unsuitable for placement as pets.

---

* Indoor cats face risks as well, albeit different ones. While people who confine their cats indoors can provide their pets with needed exercise and socialization, as a general rule, a cat who is allowed to play outdoors is friendlier, healthier, and happier. This is because an indoor cat is more likely to be bored and obese than an outdoor cat, and fat cats are a recipe for a host of health problems. In addition, chronic boredom can lead to unsocial behavior like biting, scratching and inappropriate elimination. Roger Tabor, perhaps the world's foremost cat biologist, relates the rise in obesity and behavior problems in cats to the move by the humane community to indoor-only cat practices.

In the final analysis, however, feral cats are not being wiped out because of disease. They are not starving. It is not predation by coyotes or wild dogs that is killing the cats. (These are all arguments HSUS and others have in the past, or currently make, against TNR.) The number one killer of healthy cats in the United States is the local animal shelter. If groups like HSUS are truly concerned about the safety of feral cats, the focus should be on keeping them out of shelters through TNR.

VICTIMS OF DOGMA

Convoluted "humane" concerns are not the only or perhaps even primary reasons why HSUS and other groups have historically opposed TNR programs. In North Carolina, as in other places, HSUS has claimed that the elimination of feral cats was necessary to protect people—that, in fact, the cats are a threat to the health and safety of human beings. In March of 2006, HSUS provided a "Guide to Cat Law," "Cat Care Basics," and a pamphlet on cats to shelters from across the country at its national conference. In those documents, HSUS accuses cats of:

- being a public rabies threat: "cats are now the most common domestic vectors of rabies;"
- decimating wildlife: "free-roaming cats kill millions of wild animals each year;"
- being invasive, non-native intruders: "cats are not a part of natural ecosystems, and their predation causes unnecessary suffering and death;" and,
- causing neighborhood strife: "they also cause conflicts among neighbors."

As a result, HSUS instructed shelters and humane activists to "document public health problems that relate to cats. Include diseases that are spread from cat to cat as well as those spread between cats and other animals." But where are the facts and studies to support such claims? Statements are not facts. They are not arguments. They are not proof of anything. It is important, if TNR opponents are going to make such claims, that they show proof. They must answer the fundamental question: how do you know all this? Unfortunately, the assertions seem to stand on their own, as nothing more than "received wisdom," where—to the objective observer—facts, experience, studies, complexity, nuance, and analysis appear to have no place. It is what it is. See? It says so here, *in the annals of the Humane Society of the United States.**

There is no doubt that rabies from stray animals has long been of concern to public health authorities. However, this is not a fact upon which to support the systematic rounding up and killing of cats, or dogs for that matter, for it is an inflated concern. In 1869, for example, Henry Bergh fought New York City's attempt to kill dogs based on the groundless fear of rabies after his detailed review of data showed no cases of humans catching rabies from the bite of a stray dog.

That does not mean cats cannot get rabies. In 2004, there were 281 cat rabies cases reported in the United States. However, in a country where the population of feral cats has been estimated at about sixty million and an additional ninety million housecats, only 0.00002 percent of cats were found to have been rabid. More importantly, there has not been a case of a cat transmitting rabies to humans in the United States since 1975—*over thirty years ago.*

Of more significance, there has never been a reported case of rabies in a cat who has received at least one rabies vaccination, which is a standard aspect of virtually all TNR programs. In the last fifteen years, for example, while there have been five reported cases of rabies in humans in Washington State, there have been no reported cat rabies cases at all. Perhaps if anyone is at risk of getting rabies, it is the cats who should be worried about getting it from us.

In fact, while Upstate New York is considered by public health officials to be rabies endemic, county health departments in at least two such coun-

---

* These statements are not isolated. HSUS, for example, has long maintained that an unspayed cat and her offspring will lead to 420,000 cats in seven years. This ludicrous claim has been repeated so often that even as esteemed an institution as Columbia University cites it on their website. But is it true? A review by veterinarian Dr. Christine Wolford, in conjunction with the mathematics department of the University of Washington in Seattle, found that, in fact, at best this situation would yield less than 200 cats. Even that number is too high, however, when one takes into account the fact that some of the cats will get adopted by people, get spayed, and/or become indoor-only. If an unaltered cat could produce 420,000 cats in seven years (even theoretically), society would be completely overrun with kittens and people would have to shovel them out of the way like people in the Northeast have to shovel snow during winter months!

ties have endorsed TNR. In one case, the health department paid the local SPCA to administer a TNR program. In addition, New York State Department of Public Health regulations endorsed TNR in order to encourage spaying and neutering. Ironically, some humane organizations—which were founded to protect *animals* from *people*—oppose TNR, whereas a state health department—which was founded to protect *people* from *animals*—endorses it.

Where Have All the Songbirds Gone?

The final argument the Humane Society of the United States has made to oppose TNR is that cats are not "native" and are killing native birds and other species. Others have also joined this chorus. According to the ASPCA's policy on cats and wildlife:

> There is no denying that free-roaming cats, including feral cats, kill large numbers of birds and other wild animals, including endangered ones. For this reason, among others, the ASPCA is strongly in favor of keeping all pet cats indoors or in escape-proof enclosures. .. [The ASPCA] does not support [feral cat] colonies in areas where...their presence presents a threat to endangered populations of wildlife.

In a joint campaign called "Cats Indoors" established by the American Humane Association, the American Bird Conservancy and the Humane Society of the United States, the organizations claimed that "scientists estimate that cats kill hundreds of millions of birds each year and three times as many small mammals." The coalition's resulting *Cats Indoors* campaign would later go on to say that

> [s]cientific studies actually show that each year, cats kill hundreds of millions of migratory songbirds. In 1990, researchers estimated that "outdoor" house cats and feral cats are responsible for killing nearly 78 million small mammals and birds annually in the United Kingdom.

> University of Wisconsin ornithologist, Dr. Stanley Temple estimates that 20-150 million songbirds are killed each year by rural cats in Wisconsin alone.

Both of these claims fly in the face of the evidence, and neither of the studies cited stands up to scrutiny. In the British study, a bird advocate asked a small number of people living with cats who allowed the cats outside to record any birds and small mammals their cats brought home. The researcher then took that number, multiplied it by how many cats he guessed lived in England, and came up with the astonishing number of seventy-eight million. The methodology, to put it mildly, is unscientific; the "study" is nothing more than an oversimplified formula of multiplying a guessed number of cats in England by how many birds a small number of cats brought home. Since the world is not that simple, statistical models are not created by merely multiplying two numbers. The study's formulation is, in the words of one reviewer, "irresponsible and reflects a feeble understanding of basic science."

Science, by contrast, asks qualitative questions: How did the birds die? Did the cats kill them? Were they road kill or fledglings who would have died anyway? Was there any indication of disease in the prey? Was the catch freshly killed or were the birds dead for days? All of these answers could have been found with very little effort, but the author ignored them. More importantly, the study also ignored the fact that several hundred birds in the village where the study was conducted must die each year to maintain a stable population and that the village's bird density was nine times higher than the rest of Britain! These latter facts lead to Jeff Elliott's inescapable conclusion after he analyzed the study:

> Taken together, these elements suggest another interpretation: cats are simply weeding out birds from an overcrowded population. Nor are they apparently catching healthy birds at their peak of winged life; wintertime is most stressful on birds that are old or sick, and fledglings tumbling down from nests could account for the high count in early summer. And with only 130 dead sparrows recorded... the cats kill—or find—less than half the numbers that must be annually culled to sustain their population.

The Wisconsin study cited by these groups is simpler to debunk because it is not a "study" at all. In "Cats and Wildlife, a Conservation Dilemma," Dr. Stanley Temple states, "recent research suggests that rural free-roaming domestic cats in Wisconsin may be killing between 8 and 217 million birds each year." That "recent research" turned out to be his own citation, an article called "On the Prowl." In that article, he states, the estimates of bird predation by cats are his "best guesses" by using the same quantitative (and discredited) formula from the British study. In a subsequent interview with Elliott, Dr. John Coleman (Dr. Temple's pro-tégé and co-author of the articles) commented that

> the media has had a field day with this since we started. Those figures were from our proposal. They aren't actual data; that was just our projection to show how bad it might be.

That has not stopped anti-TNR groups, however, from citing it as factu-al. Belief, supported by bad science, is a hard opponent to defeat. According to Elliott, "we trust science. We put our faith in the writings of scientists. We trust that in the scientific pursuit of discovery, truth will hold sway." But that is not always the case. Scientists can bring their own biases to the table, throwing a spin on results to make them best reflect preconceived notions. Data that points to a different conclusion can be ig-nored. Statistics can be manipulated to make results seem alarming.

Science can be pursued honestly, with integrity, at the same time it is in error. When we trust science, and it subsequently fails to live up to the rig-ors of comparative scrutiny, we take refuge in the process, the unfolding of what we call "the learning curve." Private agendas pursued under the cloak of science pose a different problem altogether: they are, quite simply, an af-front to the intellectually honest pursuit of knowledge. This is unforgiv-able, particularly when it comes at the expense—indeed calls for the end—of a vital humanitarian endeavor. A hidden agenda masquerading as science is especially appalling in light of the fact that it could potentially re-sult in millions of cats slated for eradication.

The divide between the above studies and independent, well-designed, and methodical ones looking at the impact of feral cat predation on birds is glaring. Several more reliable studies found the presence of cats to actu-ally be good for birds. In one study of cat predation in New Zealand, it was found that "cats suppress populations of more dangerous predators such as rats and thus allow denser populations of birds than would exist without them." Another study looked at the impact of feral cat predation in Australia and came to the same conclusion, like virtually all non-partisan studies, that the "common belief that feral cats are serious predators of birds is apparently without basis."*

---

* For more information, see Roger Tabor's *The Wild Life of the Domestic Cat* (Arrow Books 1983) and two books by Ellen Berkeley, *Maverick Cats* (New England Press 1987) and *TNR Past, Present and Future* (Alley Cat Allies 2004).

While bird species' decline is evident, the vast majority of studies on the issue point to a different culprit: *habitat destruction caused by humans*. Pesticides are also recognized as a major culprit in bird decline—particularly the effect of toxic lawn care products, insecticides, fungicides, and rodenticides. A 1994 World Watch Institute study showed that four primary factors are responsible for bird declines: habitat loss, over trapping, drought, and pesticides. A 1993 study by the Center for Conservation Biology at Stanford University found environmental loss was responsible for the decline of the songbird. In 1998, the University of Georgia blamed forest fragmentation across the southern United States. An article in *National Geographic* in 1993 blamed poisons in the environment, particularly lawn care and farm products. Of course, Rachel Carson's seminal work, *Silent Spring*, shared this conclusion. Unless we conclude that predation studies on four continents (fourteen studies in Europe, twelve in North America, nine in Australia, and one in Africa) are all wrong, feral cats should no longer be unfairly implicated in any decimation of bird populations.

Even Dr. Coleman himself admits that birds in Wisconsin who used to live in prairie lands have since lost their habitat to human encroachments and now only find refuge on farms. Farms, of course, are notorious for using significant amounts of pesticides. If they are truly in decline, the answer to why birds are disappearing from Wisconsin is not hard to see, if the question is being asked without a predetermined agenda.

BIOLOGICAL XENOPHOBIA

Even if we were to wrongly conclude that feral cats are decimating birds, however, the conclusion as to what to do about it is not self-evident. To say "if cats kill native birds, we must kill cats because the cats are non-native" comes from a troubling belief that the value of an individual animal comes from lineage and that worth as a species stems from being at a particular location first. This belief is called "nativism." The notion that native species have more value than non-native ones finds its roots historically in Apartheid South Africa and Nazi Germany, where the notion of a garden with native plants was founded on nationalistic and racist ideas and "cloaked in scientific jargon." This is not surprising. The same arguments that were being made for biological purity of people in these reactionary regimes are exactly the types of arguments made for purity among animals and plants. This is not to say that the nativist movement is inherently racist, but its antecedents cannot be denied.

In the United States, nativists believe that certain plants or animals should be valued more than others if they were here first, although the exact starting point is difficult to ascertain and is in many cases, wholly arbitrary. Indeed, all plants and animals were introduced (by wind, humans, migration, evolution, or other manner) at some point in time. For example, wild ponies currently live on the Assateague Island National Seashore, off of the coast of Maryland and Virginia. One theory is that they are the descendants of the horses that survived the shipwreck of a Spanish galleon in the 1500s. Another theory is that pirates put horses ashore on Assateague to be used as food when they passed through. Yet another theory is that the ponies are the descendents of escaped horses placed there by American colonists in the 1600s to avoid British taxation. Still another theory is that they may have been there for even longer. While their actual origins are unknown, what is known is that they can be traced with some accuracy back to 1671. But even if it were 1971, should it matter to the question of whether they are protected or killed by the National Park Service (NPS), which has jurisdiction over Assateague lands?

From a humane standpoint, the horses are there, and they are as worthy of our compassion regardless of when and how they came to Assateague. From the "nativist" standpoint, however, since there is no direct evidence to show that they were there in 1491 before Christopher Columbus set sail and European colonization brought "exotic" or "non-native" plants and animals to the continent of North America, they should be eradicated. They argue that any plant or animal introduced after this time period must be destroyed, especially if *they* determine that it potentially interferes with one that was here before. The NPS agrees, having taken the position that the horses are "non-native" and using our tax dollars to round up and sell them, in many cases for slaughter. The Assateague wild ponies are not alone. In Northern California, for example, two kinds of deer live on NPS jurisdiction lands. The deer are almost identical in all respects, except one has a black tail and the other one a white tail. The NPS is set on slaughtering one and protecting the other, for no other reason that one can trace its roots to the area before the other.

To nativists, the point is clear: these animals do not have value and are not worthy of compassion. They can—and should—be killed to return the continent to some vague, so-called idyllic, past. Trying to hold the world to a mythical state that we can never return to, however, is both irrational and unattainable.

It is irrational because the belief that some species of animals are "better" than others lacks a coherent moral or logical foundation. According to the San Francisco SPCA, many of these nativists

> *have long rallied to label cats as "pests" of our cities and "invasive non-native" intruders in our parks and countryside. But cats aren't the only ones to be targeted for slaughter in the name of protecting other species or preserving "native" habitats. They have been joined at different times and in different places by red foxes, gulls, cowbirds, elk, sea lions, coyote, mountain lions, ravens, skunks, raccoons, wild horses, the list goes on. Referred to as "garbage animals," "alien" species, "weeds," and "vermin," these creatures have become scapegoats for the massive habitat destruction, environmental degradation, and species extinction caused by one species and one species alone: humans. For nativists, the point is clear: the lives of these animals don't count, and therefore they can and should be eliminated to protect more important species and to preserve "natural" environments. Had we honored and preserved life, had we treated all animals—cats, birds, and every other creature who shares our planet—with the respect they each deserve, we might have spared many of the species now lost forever. To us, there are no "garbage" animals, and slaughter and death aren't the tools we need to preserve life.**

The nativists' ideal is unattainable because nature cannot be frozen in time or returned to a pre-European past. No matter how many so-called "non-native" animals (and plants for that matter) are killed, the goal of total eradication will never be reached. As far as feral cats are concerned, they will always exist. To advocate for their eradication would be to propose a massacre with no hope of success and no conceivable end. Nonetheless, as TNR inevitably reduces the number of cats by eliminating their reproductive capacity, nativists—by their own logic—should therefore support it.

Equally inconsistent in the nativist philosophy is its position—or, more accurately, lack of a coherent position—on humans. If one accepts

---

* In fact, despite claiming that the non-native animals have a well established negative impact on native plants and animals, new research actually reveals that nature is far more resilient than native species proponents would lead us to believe.

the jingoistic attitudes that only native plants and animals have value, the biggest non-native intruders in the United States are human beings. With 300 million of us altering the landscape and causing virtually all of the environmental and species decimation through habitat destruction and pollution, shouldn't nativists demand that non-native people leave? Of course, non-profit organizations which advocate nativist positions would never dare say so, or people would stop donating to them.

Finally, if we follow the argument that we should kill cats because they supposedly kill birds, where does it end? What about a campaign to save worms and caterpillars by killing birds? It sounds preposterous, but is based on the same logic used to justify the killing of cats, and stems from the same attitude: *biological xenophobia*. In 1949, for example, Illinois Governor Adlai Stevenson considered this very issue when he vetoed a bill that would have made it illegal for cats to be outdoors:

> *We are all interested in protecting certain varieties of birds. That cats destroy some birds, I well know, but I believe this legislation would further but little the worthy cause to which its proponents give such unselfish effort. The problem of cat versus bird is as old as time. If we attempt to resolve it by legislation who knows but what we may be called upon to take sides as well in the age old problems of dog versus cat, bird versus bird, or even bird versus worm. In my opinion, the State of Illinois and its local governing bodies already have enough to do without trying to control feline delinquency.*

SEEKING POLITICAL COVER

Eventually, the voices of compassion in North Carolina and elsewhere drowned out the anti-feral cat vitriol of HSUS and other groups. In the intervening period, cats overtook dogs as the most popular pet in America, millions of compassionate people feeding stray cats joined the Internet revolution and discovered that they were not alone in caring for feral cats, and two volunteers turned their fledgling organization promoting TNR into one of the nation's fastest growing and most influential animal organizations. Alley Cat Allies took No Kill out of the shelter and brought it to the streets, parks, and alleyways, legitimizing the practice of TNR all over the country. With feral cat groups increasing in numbers and influence, and winning converts at shelters, municipalities, and health departments nationwide, HSUS' endorsement of mass killing for feral cats in our nation's shelters was becoming politically untenable and increasingly seen for what it always was: a viewpoint grossly out of step with a nation of cat lovers. In response, the organization sought to modify its position.

After several previously failed attempts to change its rhetoric, HSUS issued a new feral cat position statement on March 20, 2006. In the statement, HSUS acknowledges that TNR is "the most viable, long-term approach available at this time to reduce feral cat populations." It also urged communities to work together toward non-lethal "approaches to feral cat management." These statements are significant improvements from prior policies. However, in light of other contradictory language in the statement, as well as against the backdrop of other equally contradictory HSUS policies and literature, it is very far from a powerful and positive vision of the future as some of its proponents claim. It is less than one page in length, vaguely worded, and replete with a myriad of limitations.

In fact, HSUS' endorsement of TNR continues to come with at least three major restrictions:

+ TNR efforts must be limited if someone says that feral cats are a threat to wildlife;
+ feral cat caretakers must respect the "limitations" of other groups in the area, including those who may not share their views about feral cats; and,
+ killing of feral cats can continue for an undefined "interim period."

Taken to their logical conclusion, these "limitations" are so severe they effectively nullify any ostensible support for TNR in the 2006 statement. There is no feral cat colony anywhere in the United States, for example, where wildlife is not also present. HSUS asks us to make the decision "about whether to maintain a particular colony" after a determination of "the potential negative impact on local wildlife." To make this determination, HSUS asks feral cat caretakers to "respect" the views of all interested parties—which potentially includes animal control and nativist proponents who do not support TNR.

The unspoken converse to deciding whether to maintain a particular colony is deciding whether to eradicate it. That is the choice presented, providing a powerful tool to the enemies of TNR. Taken to its logical conclusion, it means that feral cats can be excluded from locations whenever someone says wildlife is impacted, which could potentially happen everywhere. In fact, these are exactly the types of claims being made all over the United States today, and while HSUS says it no longer favors eradication, what is the alternative to TNR? Since it is very difficult to relocate colonies *en masse*, the most likely outcome is that the animals will be trapped and killed.

Furthermore, what does HSUS mean when it says that feral cat advocates must "respect" the "limitations" of other "interest groups"? Animal control and the American Bird Conservancy would consider themselves interested groups on the issue of feral cats. Why should feral cat advocates accept the "limitations" that the cats be away from wildlife, including birds, if other groups say they are a threat, when hard facts say they are not? It is the ethical duty of feral cat advocates to utterly reject and rally against all these points of view.

Finally, HSUS says killing is acceptable for an "interim period" in places where TNR cannot be implemented. If TNR cannot be implemented, however, it is only because animal control or local government has put in place laws and roadblocks to prevent it—all of which HSUS has historically promoted. The limitation is self-imposed by animal control, but nonetheless HSUS is asking feral cat advocates to respect those limitations. Therefore, there is no need for killing to continue for *any* period, much less the one HSUS proposes: an interim period, which in some locations conceivably has no end.

In short, the limitations to TNR proposed by HSUS appear to contradict the statements preceding them that express support of TNR. As a result, HSUS argues to this very day, in spite of a wave of public sentiment moving in the opposite direction, for cat confinement laws, mandatory cat licensing, mandatory cat registration, pet limit laws, and requiring the release of colony locations to animal control. All of these positions threaten the lives of feral cats nationwide.

If, as HSUS claims, cats kill wildlife, are a rabies threat and an invasive non-native species, and cause neighborhood strife, does this mean that TNR is acceptable so long as the cats are kept away from neighborhoods, people, birds and other wildlife? Because these conditions exist nowhere, it would appear to mean that TNR is acceptable so long as the cats are not allowed outdoors—a logical absurdity.

If history is any guide, it is enticing to consider the notion that the less HSUS says about feral cats, the better. But from the largest and wealthiest animal protection organization in the country, a group that not only claims to be committed to a respect for life and compassion for all animals, but which also wields tremendous national influence, No Kill advocates must demand more. There must be clarity as to what those limitations are and to what policies they would have feral cat caretakers agree. These are questions that HSUS' 2006 TNR statement does not answer. More importantly, HSUS must state, in no uncertain terms, that feral cats have a right to live, especially in light of an experiment at one of the most prestigious universities in the United States, which definitively put the issues to rest once and for all.

AN EXPERIMENT IN COMPASSION

In November 1769, Captain Gaspar de Portola left Spain for the Americas as part of an expedition to the northern part of the Spanish territory in Las Californias to fortify the port of Monterey. He instead landed at what is now San Francisco Bay. The party worked its way down the peninsula and camped on the bank of San Francisquito Creek near a giant redwood tree that stood well over one hundred feet high and was visible for miles. Later travelers came to call the old redwood El Palo Alto ("the high tree" in Spanish), a name it retains to the present day.

Over a century later, former governor and railroad magnate Leland Stanford purchased 650 acres of Rancho San Francisquito for a country home. He later bought adjoining properties to bring his farm to more than 8,000 acres, land that ultimately became the Stanford University campus in Palo Alto, California. From Stanford's beginning, El Palo Alto has been the university's symbol and the centerpiece of its official seal.

Today, on the campus sitting adjacent to El Palo Alto, not too far from the very spot where Captain de Portola scouted terrain to claim in the name of the King of Spain, sits a small wooden box. It rests on its side, a makeshift shelter. Inside the box is a bowl of water and a paper plate with remnants of a meal. It is a feeding station, one of several, for the feral cats who make their home at Stanford University. These cats came from a variety of sources, but the vast majority were from students who turned their pets loose after the school year when they left for the summer.

During the spring of 1989, just like every previous spring, the feral cats living on campus gave birth to kittens. As they became old enough to forage, moms and kittens would wander to populated areas in search of food. That year, however, after quietly looking the other way for years, Stanford University announced plans that it was going to hire a trapping company and exterminate what it estimated were up to 1,500 mostly wild cats living throughout the 8,100-acre campus.

In response, a small group of women who worked at Stanford met in the one-room office of the neighboring Palo Alto Humane Society and tried to come up with a plan to stop the university. With the support of the Palo Alto Humane Society, the women decided to trap the cats, sterilize them, vaccinate them against disease, find homes for all the kittens and the friendly cats, and then release the remaining ones back to the largely wooded campus.

When Carole Miller, Carole Hyde, Dolores Arnold, Hildegard Taleghani, and others allied themselves to fight for the Stanford cats, they didn't expect to play a significant role in changing the way feral cats were treated throughout the United States. Their only goal was to save the feline campus residents who called Stanford their home.

To do so, they realized they would need to convince the university that TNR was a good idea, a better idea than killing the cats. Without documentation and supporting data that Stanford demanded showing the cats did not pose a health risk to students, the administration predictably balked, but with Miller, Hyde and the rest of the team gaining converts, the university agreed to look into the matter. That same year, the Stanford Department of Environmental Health and Safety, in consultation with the Stanford Medical School and the Santa Clara County Health Department, found that the proximity of the cats "posed virtually no health or safety risk" to individuals on campus. The Stanford Cat Network was born.

Within a few years, the Stanford Cat Network sterilized all the cats on campus, placed hundreds of friendly cats and kittens in loving homes under the auspices of the very progressive and feral friendly Palo Alto Humane Society, and set up official feeding sites throughout the campus. By 1992, no new kittens were born on campus. A few years later, after friendly cats were adopted out and because many of the feral cats were much older in years, the number of cats was down to 150 and continued to decline. If new cats showed up at feeding locations, caretakers responded immediately to spay and put up for adoption the friendly ones before they had a chance to give birth to what would otherwise become feral kittens. If they were feral, they were sterilized to ensure they never reproduced. As a result, there are fewer than fifty cats remaining today.

At Stanford, feral cats roam throughout the university. Roads and cars criss-cross every conceivable part of the campus. Owls, birds of all kinds, rats, raccoons, skunks, opossums, and other wildlife do, too. There are tens of thousands of people entering the campus on any given day. There are pet dogs, fleas, ticks, and viruses. If outdoor cats faced a litany of risks, they would face them here. But the cats do not show up to their feeding locations injured and wounded. And they are growing old, when conventional wisdom says they should be dying young, and dying tragically.

Stanford's resulting success with TNR is not unique. In San Francisco, roughly three out of four kittens received by animal control in the early 1990s were found to be from feral moms. In order to reduce the cat and kitten death rate, Avanzino believed the city would need to embrace a TNR initiative. The San Francisco SPCA put the plan to work. By the year 2000, the number of feral cats killed in the city dropped by 73 percent and the number of kittens killed declined over 80 percent. San Francisco animal control officers were also taking in fewer stray cats, and getting fewer complaints about stray cats despite an increase in the human population. At a time when the number of animal control officers on the job was increasing, which should have increased the numbers of feral cats impounded, the number of cats seized declined significantly, a sure sign that TNR was working.

At Stanford, as in San Francisco, TNR was the key not only to reducing feral cats as demanded by some, but doing so in a non-lethal, humane, and effective (though long term) way. At roughly the same time frame, other universities like Sonoma State and Georgetown went the traditional route, trapping and killing the feral cats that lived on campus, year after year, with the end nowhere in sight. More broadly, while San Francisco was experiencing substantial declines in the killing of cats because of TNR, cat deaths were rising in other metropolitan areas which adopted the historical HSUS position on feral cats.*

---

* A 2006 study of animal shelters in Ohio published in the *Journal of the American Veterinary Medical Association* found that cat deaths in shelters were generally increasing from 1996 to 2004, with the feral cat most at risk for being killed. The researchers found a strong correlation between an agency having a spay-neuter program and a lowering of the kill rate, but reported only one animal control agency having a TNR program.

Despite TNR's proven success, there are many organizations to this day that remain mired in the animal sheltering methods—*and failures*—of the past. They continue to unfairly blame feral cats for perceived decimation of birds and wildlife based on shoddy science and the misleading pronouncements of nativist organizations. They claim that TNR perpetuates suffering based on mistruths. They continue to regurgitate clichés about all cats belonging in homes. As a result, too many shelters continue to cling to "catch and kill" policies for feral cats.

Despite the advent of TNR as an alternative to killing, however, success in other communities proved elusive. San Francisco's lifesaving results remained an aberration. And nationally, a wholly unnecessary body count continued. As the nation entered the new millennium, shelter deaths continued in the multi-millions annually. What was needed was someone to take the whole package—not just TNR, but all the other programs that San Francisco pioneered and concentrate them on an animal control shelter in one community. If that occurred, a community could save not only all healthy dogs and cats the way San Francisco did, but all those who are sick, injured, traumatized or feral, something San Francisco had not yet accomplished. As a result, the achievement of No Kill could cross the threshold from the theoretical to the real.

This is where the story becomes personal. As director of operations for the San Francisco SPCA, I knew that to get to No Kill, a shelter needed to implement a fundamental shift in policy. It required an agency to stop blaming the so-called "irresponsible public" and to embrace the community instead. It required an agency to stop waiting for people to come to a shelter and to be proactive about adoptions. Most of all, it required comprehensive implementation of several key programs and services that I have come to call the *No Kill Equation.* (These programs are outlined in detail in appendix II.) These include TNR, comprehensive adoption programs, an active volunteer base, partnering with rescue groups and foster homes, medical rehabilitation, behavior socialization, and low-cost spay/neuter, the very programs that brought San Francisco's rate of shelter killing to national all time lows.

It was the full implementation of these programs, at an open admission animal control shelter, that I believed could create a No Kill community. And I would have to drive 3,000 miles in a rented RV with two kids, two dogs, and twenty mostly feral cats to prove it. It was time to take the show on the road.

The Road Less Traveled

"Be bold and mighty forces will come to your aid."

—Johann Wolfgang Goethe (circa 1800)

THROUGHOUT THE 1990S, one of the chief criticisms about San Francisco's lifesaving success was that it could only be achieved in a wealthy, urban community. Saving animals on that scale was said to be impossible in rural America. The reasons advanced for this argument were many—fewer adoptions, more poverty, less education, antiquated attitudes, and the type of frontier mentality that allowed animals to be viewed as mere property. But are these assertions true? In fact, they are not.

First, the fact that a community is rural does mean that it has special challenges, but most animals are being killed in the urban centers, not rural ones. If there is a problem in America, it most certainly is in the urban core. Even in this context, however, San Francisco, the second most congested urban area of the country outside of Manhattan and one of the most ethnically and economically diverse cities in the United States, proved that it could be done. Moreover, as a general rule, rural shelters take in and kill fewer animals per capita than their urban counterparts. Despite what some bill as their "behind the times" attitudes toward animals, people in rural America are readily accepting of less-than-perfect animals.

Second, while rural communities might have fewer overall resources, they also take in fewer animals. Urban communities may have more animals, but there are also more resources potentially available—whether homes, volunteers, dollars, or other support. In the end, the issue is relative.

Third, and most importantly, Tompkins County in Upstate New York is predominantly rural. And since 2001, the community has not killed any healthy or treatable dogs and cats, and has a 100 percent rate of TNR in its shelter. In short, the home of the nation's first truly No Kill community is in rural America. This achievement, and the response to it by animal sheltering's old guard, lays the groundwork for the next chapter in No Kill's unfolding history.

San Francisco Veers Off-Course

By the year 2000, six years after the city's historic achievement, new San Francisco SPCA leadership tragically, though deliberately, began moving in another direction. At the time, San Francisco was a whisper away from saving all medically treatable sick and injured dogs and cats, and with feral cat deaths dropping at a significant rate, the city was well on its way to becoming the first to provide a lifesaving guarantee for all but irremediably suffering animals. It was on the verge of fulfilling the legacy of Henry Bergh—to achieve No Kill, the agency simply needed to seize the opportunity. It failed to do so.

After Avanzino's departure, the San Francisco SPCA suffered a series of setbacks. In reality, the issue of a No Kill San Francisco was settled beforehand: Avanzino would always challenge the status quo, but in the face of absolute entrenchment, he was unwilling to go to war. With the city pound continuing to publicly downplay San Francisco's success and refusing to fully embrace the opportunity for No Kill and Avanzino not willing to call upon the significant endowment, political capital and public goodwill he amassed, the goal of zeroing out the deaths of sick and injured but *treatable* dogs and cats was abandoned.

Instead, the San Francisco SPCA began taking in a larger number of young healthy animals from other communities, while the city pound preferred to hire more officers rather than expand adoption opportunities. Although it was still saving all healthy dogs and cats and the numbers of treatable animals continued to decline, sick and injured dogs and cats, motherless neonatal kittens, and feral cats would continue to be killed in the city. True, the SPCA was still saving over 2,000 dogs and cats from the city pound annually, but the dream of a truly No Kill San Francisco was left in abeyance.

In late 1998, nonetheless, Avanzino left the San Francisco SPCA with a strong infrastructure, departments that had become the envy of the growing No Kill movement, and a fundraising apparatus that had amassed an endowment of over forty million dollars. His successor would not fully leverage the opportunity he was given. In a short period of time, with money being wasted, fundraising opportunities missed, deficits created, an increasingly bloated bureaucracy developing, and key programs gutted or eliminated, the SPCA finally abandoned all pretensions toward No Kill in San Francisco.

The final straw came on a Monday morning in October, 2000. Starting at about 7:00 a.m., people lined up outside the doors. All had one thing in common: they had spent their weekends trapping feral cats in their back-yards, alleyways, neighborhoods, or local parks. They came to the San Francisco SPCA spay/neuter clinic, where feral cats were spayed every weekday morning for free, day after day, so they could be re-released with-out breeding, while their caretakers fed and watched over them for the re-mainder of their lives. By 7:30 a.m., at least twenty people had lined up outside with traps that held feral cats and kittens for surgery.

This was the linchpin of the San Francisco SPCA's feral cat assistance program, and it was key to reducing the death rate by an astonishing 73 percent for feral cats and 81 percent for kittens at the city pound, at a time when some cities were seeing the death rate for cats rise. The program in-volved the coordination of seventy field volunteers to handle feral cat issues, each of whom was responsible for a different section of the city. It involved an agreement with the San Francisco Housing Authority to put a TNR program in place in nearly a dozen housing projects in the city. It involved a TNR program on neighboring Treasure Island, the first such program in the nation on a U.S. military installation. It involved the daily rescue of feral cats from death row at the city pound and a foster care program that saved the life of every kitten that came through the doors. By far, however, the cornerstone of San Francisco's success was the free spay/neuter clinic for feral cats, which was so popular that over 1,100 feral cat caregivers and thousands of others had used the program.

But things had taken a bad turn at the San Francisco SPCA, and for the first time since the program began, after seven years and over 8,000 sur-geries, the order came to turn the cats away. The president had "temporarily" closed the spay/neuter clinic. It wasn't the first cutback in the program since Avanzino's departure, but it was for me personally the most painful one. After fighting the changes to programs and services, and futilely trying to keep the SPCA focused on its core mission of saving homeless animals, I left the agency as its director of operations.

Exporting the San Francisco Model

In 2001, I took over as the executive director for the Tompkins County SPCA, a full-service animal control agency in rural Upstate New York. It was time to prove that the No Kill model, which had worked so well in San Francisco, would work anywhere and everywhere. I wanted to prove that the naysayers were wrong, that the question of urban or rural, affluent or poor, public or private, city or county, was not relevant. That the only relevant issue was whether a community embraced the programs and services that once made the San Francisco SPCA so successful. In a rented RV, with two children and our pets, my wife and I left the San Francisco Bay area to make our home near Ithaca, New York. In addition to a number of cats and two rescued dogs, I also brought with me the lessons learned from San Francisco's success.

Before my arrival, the Tompkins County SPCA was an animal control agency like many others. Although it was completely independent, with no ties to any other SPCA, for the most part, it—like the others—was a somewhat typical SPCA, geared to overkill. The shelter was built in an old house that had been converted to a kennel, away from populated areas of the community. Since its inception, right through the year 2000, for example, the Tompkins County SPCA routinely killed animals when the cages got full. In fact, it killed animals to clear out cages in anticipation of the cages getting full. It killed for space, minor illnesses, fixable behavior problems, or if shelter leadership felt there were too many black dogs or adult cats.

To its credit, unlike many shelters, it dabbled in alternatives—a volunteer-led effort was responsible for periodic offsite adoption venues, and it had established a token-level foster care program. (The program was cancelled after an uproar when the shelter killed kittens a foster parent had spent several weeks caring for and then brought back for adoption). However, it was clearly not doing enough to save lives.

When I arrived, I found a filthy shelter where animals were standing in their own waste, employees were rude and disrespectful, and sick kittens in what they called an "isolation room" were hovering around empty water bowls and getting substandard care. The agency was routinely fining people for technical violations of leash laws, and cats were being killed, rather than adopted, only because potential adopters wanted to let the cats out of doors. And in what is clearly the height of hypocrisy and poor strategy, it declared the importance of spaying and neutering but then adopted out unspayed animals, which would lead to the unenviable position of potentially taking in—*and killing*—the offspring of these adopted pets. This was the local Society for the Prevention of Cruelty to Animals, but it was by no means an anomaly or an aberration in the United States. This was the status quo, with one major exception.

Rather than circle the wagons in response to community criticism as most shelters often do, the Board of Directors wanted to create a No Kill community. They declared their desire to do so in 1999, with the caveat that the agency retain its animal control orientation—in other words, remain an open admission facility. They hired me to do it.

I started my job on June 11, 2001. As I drove into the parking lot for the first time as the agency's new chief, I was met at the front door by a truck driver with five kittens he didn't want. Spaying his cat was not a priority. To him, the kittens were no longer "his problem." Whether they lived, died, or anything in between was not his business. By handing them over to us, in his estimation he had done his duty. He had brought them to the Tompkins County SPCA, the animal control authority for the entire county, and they were now our responsibility.

For most shelters, this is the point at which the breakdown that leads to killing occurs. The current view is that killing the kittens is, in large part, a *fait accompli*, and that the fault for the killing belonged to the truck driver at the front door. It was *his* failure to spay his cat, *his* failure to make a lifetime commitment to the kittens. But this view, while endemic to the culture of animal control, is not accurate.

First, it is because of this irresponsibility that shelters exist in the first place. Second, it is often the practices of the shelter itself that lead to killing. If a shelter does not maintain adequate adoption hours or has poor customer service, refuses to work with volunteers, foster parents, or rescue groups, fails to treat and rehabilitate sick, injured, or traumatized animals, or does not offer TNR as an option, the shelter is not doing much to prevent killing. If an employee cuts corners and does not clean and sanitize water bowls daily, it may lead to an outbreak of parvovirus, a deadly and highly contagious disease in dogs and puppies in unclean shelters. If an employee does not scrub cat cages, leading to spread of upper respiratory infection or panleukopenia (feline distemper), a highly contagious and deadly disease for cats, large numbers of animals will be needlessly killed. These problems plague shelters nationwide, and the Tompkins County SPCA was no exception.*

Thankfully, on June 11, 2001, the truck driver did not live in a community whose shelter still subscribed to those views. On that day, the Tompkins County SPCA explicitly rejected the policies legitimized and championed by most shelters nationwide. Having been director of operations for the most successful SPCA in the country, I knew what worked and what didn't work. Clearly, killing those kittens was not going to be an option. Not surprisingly, we found all of them homes.

The day after my arrival, my staff informed me that our dog kennels were full and since a litter of six puppies had come in, I needed to decide who was going to be killed in order to make space. I asked for "Plan B": there was none. I asked for suggestions: there were none. It was time for my first staff meeting.

I introduced myself formally, told them about my background and experience, and shared my view of what constituted a successful shelter. Success, I said, is defined by how many animals go home alive, period. Of course, we want to make sure they are going into responsible, loving homes; anything less would mean that they would come right back to the shelter, taking us further away from, not closer to, our goals. However, finding homes, I emphasized, was the bottom line, and everyone would be measured by results. The rest would fall into place: community support, new resources, and the programs that follow. To get the results, we needed the desire to succeed, the creativity to come up with solutions, and the flexibility to implement them. My words were direct:

> *Volunteers who work with animals do so out of sheer love. They don't bring home a paycheck. So if a volunteer says "I can't do it," I can accept that from her. But staff members are paid to save lives. If a paid member of staff throws up her hands*

---

* There will always be *individual* cases of parvovirus or panleukopenia in shelters, but epidemics or spread of such diseases is almost always a result of sloppy handling and poor cleaning practices by staff.

and says, "There's nothing that can be done," I may as well eliminate her position
and use the money that goes for her salary in a more constructive manner. So
what are we going to do with the puppies that doesn't involve killing?

And a solution was found: horse troughs for puppies in the lobby next to the front desk. What better way to showcase those little gems, while simultaneously giving them much needed socialization that would lead to happy, permanent placements? The next weekend, seventy kittens were relinquished to the shelter, above and beyond the regular number of incoming dogs, cats, and other assorted animals (including sixteen mice left out by our dumpster). When the humane officers informed me that they had just raided a residence and were bringing in about thirty sick cats, I overheard one staff member say to another, "Maybe now he will euthanize some animals." Back to square one. I explained that killing for space was no longer an option. Again, creative life-affirming alternatives were found, and nobody was killed.

Like so many shelters with animal control contracts, the Tompkins County SPCA had relied on the fiction that the only solution to the influx of homeless animals was killing. Staff would shake their heads and continue to blame "irresponsible owners" for the fact that so many animals would go out the door in body bags rather than in the loving arms of families. Like so many other shelters, the team that made up the Tompkins County SPCA upon my arrival never once saw the killing as its own failure to find solutions, meet its real mandate to be an animal welfare organization, or live up to the very real but often ignored shelter credo that "every life is precious."

Not all staff was supportive of the new order. In the first six months, over half of all employees moved on or were fired, eventually replaced with new coworkers who shared a vision of a No Kill Tompkins County. Together, we developed a flurry of programs to increase the number of available homes, reduce birthrates, rehabilitate injured animals, and keep animals with their loving, responsible caretakers. We approached every veterinarian in the community for a partnership to increase spay/neuter, treat sick and injured animals, and improve animal care at the shelter. We went to Cornell University's Veterinary College for support: emergency care, development of vaccination protocols, behavior rehabilitation, and treatment for sick or injured animals. We relied on the local media to help us showcase our animals and promote our mission.

When I started, the staff did not want volunteers around. The then-shelter manager informed me that, "Volunteers are more trouble than they are worth." Once we adopted our new philosophy and the shelter manager was fired, we went very quickly from a handful of volunteers to about 140. By the time I had left, we had nearly 200. From 2001 to 2004, these dedicated volunteers came through time and time again. They fostered nearly 800 pets a year, put in over 12,000 annual volunteer hours, walked the dogs four times a day, socialized and groomed the cats, did offsite adoptions, maintained the website, and helped with adoptions.

All I did was to create the framework in which they could do so—and ensured that staff supported, rather than impeded, those efforts. Volunteers not only helped us care for, adopt out, and place the legions of kittens and puppies who made their way to the shelter every spring and summer, they helped us save blind pets, pets missing limbs, animals hit by cars, and those with behavior problems.

The animals who came to us also found homes because we were supported just as passionately by the public: adopters who took home older pets with special impediments because they believed in our lifesaving mission, donors who helped us double the average gift, and the media who told our story 406 times in one year alone.

In 2003, for example, our humane officers raided a trailer park and seized dozens of cats, five of whom were blind. Some of their eyes were so infected, they had to be surgically removed in order to save the lives of the cats. We named one of the older ones "Justine." We put the call out to the public, in the form of Justine's plea for a home:

> *What does it mean to be loveable? What makes us worthy of compassion? These are the questions I ponder as I wait for someone to find me loveable. I am not looking for philosophy. I am looking for something real and tangible. For me, that truth is a loving home. I am blind. I also had to have one eye removed. My last home didn't take care of me and I lost my sight. But I am very loveable and every bit as worthy of compassion as the hundreds of little kittens who get adopted in a day, while I sit and wait... and wait... and wait.*

The response was overwhelming. Not only did Justine and her four blind brothers and sisters get adopted the afternoon after the ad appeared in the local newspaper, we raised enough money to pay for all their veterinary care. Nor was Justine an isolated instance.

That year, we also impounded fifty-nine dogs from a "backyard breeder." Every dog had medical problems: rotten teeth, blindness, neurological damage, or tumors. Once again, a public call for help was issued. Once again, every one found a home, including Foxfire, a nine-year-old blind dog who had lived inside a crate his entire life.

Each and every time we appealed to the community, the community rallied. The community rallied when we found a dog hit by a car with fractured rear legs who needed multiple surgeries to walk again. They rallied when we asked them to help us erase a deficit of greater than $120,000 per year I inherited when I arrived (and allowed us to finish the year with an operational surplus). They rallied when the county eliminated funding for cat care and control in a round of budget cuts by forcing the legislature to restore the money, and they rallied when we sought to raise the money to build a brand new pet adoption center.

We didn't eliminate public irresponsibility. Our cages and kennels were still filled to capacity, especially during the spring and summer. We just didn't use it as an excuse to kill, even though this was in rural America, where I was told that No Kill could not happen because of reduced affluence and a supposedly antiquated view of animals. In the end, it was the public's support that created No Kill in Tompkins County, *the same public that is vilified by traditional animal sheltering proponents.*

How does a traditional shelter make a community No Kill? In Tompkins County, we did it with a simple yet highly effective three-step process: 1) Stop the killing; 2) Stop the killing; 3) Stop the killing. I am not joking. No Kill starts as an act of will. If there is a lesson here, it is not hard to see: There is enough compassion, caring, kindness, and love for animals to overcome human irresponsibility in any community, despite the thousands of dogs and cats who find themselves abandoned in any given shelter each year.

We went from excuses to answers, blaming to solving, in the process becoming the nation's first—and only—No Kill community, saving 100 percent of healthy dogs and cats, treatable animals, and healthy and treatable feral cats.*

---

* We also saved all the mice, hamsters, rabbits, goats, chickens, gerbils, and horses who made their way to our shelter. While the focus of this book is the movement to save dogs and cats because they represent the vast majority of animals killed in shelters, the arguments apply with equal force to all other species of shelter animals.

We did lifesaving surgery and behavior rehabilitation, amputated limbs when necessary, and spent thousands of dollars and months of tender, loving care to save the animals. We did not do it with a big shelter or a large endowment. We succeeded because of a simple, unwavering commitment to stop the killing and the flexibility to see it through.

We became the safest community for homeless animals in the United States—saving 93 percent of all dogs and cats who came through our doors, returning "euthanasia" to its dictionary definition for animals who were hopelessly ill, injured, or irremediably suffering.* In the end, we realized the dream of the humane movement since its founding and electrified the community. Our success became their success, a source of pride for Tompkins County, that saw bumper stickers all over the county announcing that we were the "Safest Community for Homeless Pets in the U.S." But, once again, the national groups had an altogether different view.

The Great (Non-)Achievement

The large national animal protection groups should have shared our community's pride, and helped promote the model nationwide in order to accelerate lifesaving in other communities. The impact would have been tremendous: if every community in the United States did as well as Tompkins County had in 2003 by adopting all the programs and services of the No Kill Equation and implementing them as comprehensively, 4.1 million of the five million dogs and cats killed in shelters that year would still be alive today—*four out of every five of them.* Unfortunately, that did not occur.

When Tompkins County proved that No Kill was possible in rural America, shelters in urban communities seemed to be overcome with a case of collective amnesia. No Kill, they said, might have been possible in a rural community, but it could not happen in an urban community—*exactly the opposite of what they argued about San Francisco.* Mostly, however, the achievement in Tompkins County was simply ignored.

That same year, the ASPCA began research for an article about the

---

* A very small number of dogs, who were irrevocably vicious and whose adoption would have been a threat to public safety, were also included. A detailed discussion of aggressive dogs is provided in a subsequent chapter.

future of No Kill. They interviewed me about our success in Tompkins County. At the end of the interview, the writer told me that we were the only animal control agency she had found which was No Kill, but we did not appear in the final story. The ASPCA decided to ignore our success by focusing on communities that were trying—*perpetually trying.* Other national groups were simply silent. To this day, for example, the Humane Society of the United States—the largest companion animal advocacy organization in the nation—has never published a single article about Tompkins County's success in any of their publications or reported that a No Kill community has actually been achieved.

One of the most unfortunate aspects of continued opposition or failure to fully embrace the No Kill philosophy by national organizations like the Humane Society of the United States is the lost opportunity to profoundly influence animal shelters in a life-affirming way. We can imagine, for a moment, what the future would look like if HSUS embraced the notion that animals in shelters have a right to live, No Kill philosophies should be implemented everywhere, and used its vast wealth to provide shelters with the training and tools they need to succeed in those endeavors. No other agency has the ability, resources, and influence to bring about a No Kill nation faster. No other agency is poised to hasten the day when feral cats and homeless animals find a new beginning in shelters, instead of reaching the end of the line there. Yet they refuse to do so.

Every day that HSUS or any other group denigrates or fails to fully and unequivocally embrace No Kill, delays that potential future.* Instead, animal lovers have to fight pet limit laws, mandatory registration laws, and

---

* In 2002, HSUS rallied around the New York City animal control shelter even after the comptroller's audit found "a number of allegations of animal neglect and abuse." The report found that not only were animals wrongly killed, but "many animals didn't have regular access to water and were often left in dirty cages." Despite nearly 70 percent of dogs and cats being killed, HSUS defended the shelter, which called those statistics "useless." In 2003, HSUS supported an animal control shelter at a time when a No Kill agency was poised to take over sheltering operations in Rockland County, New York, even after an auditor substantiated allegations of high rates of shelter killing and other deficiencies that were not corrected after a year. According to No Kill advocates, HSUS excused the failure of the agency "to correct the worst deficiencies noted by an outside inspection the year before [despite that such] deficiencies [also] violate[d] each and every one of Defendant HSUS' own published program and policies for 'Every Animal Shelter.'" In 2003, HSUS also opposed a rescue group's efforts to get pre-killing notification from animal control in Page County,

(continued on next page)

other destructive policies promoted by these organizations. Instead of turning to these organizations for support and guidance, No Kill groups have to spend time trying to overcome the obstacles they lay in the path to lifesaving. As a result, *and because of the cost in animal lives that this potentially entails*, these groups continue to fail miserably in terms of moving this country away from traditional, reactionary, "adopt some and kill the rest" sheltering practices.

To this day, animal shelters continue to ignore their own culpability in the slaughter, while professing to lament continued killing as entirely the fault of the public's failure to spay/neuter or make lifetime commitments to their animals. Instead of following San Francisco's and Tompkins County's lead, many shelters are still not sterilizing animals before adoption or providing the public with affordable alternatives. Some do not have foster care programs and do not socialize and rehabilitate dogs with behavior problems. Still others do not take animals offsite for adoption, have not developed partnerships with rescue groups, limit volunteerism, are not practicing TNR, and still retain adoption hours that make it difficult for working people or families to visit the shelter, the very people they should be courting to adopt the animals they are charged with protecting. The failure to implement these programs is mostly the result of one fact: they believe a certain level of killing is acceptable. Indeed, some would go as far as to deny they are even killing.

In March of 2006, at the largest national animal sheltering conference in the United States, the Humane Society of the United States held a workshop on "euthanasia." In the workshop, their featured speaker and expert on "euthanasia" flatly denied that shelters were even killing animals, "we are not killing [animals in shelters]. We are taking their life, we are ending their life, we are giving them a good death… but we are not killing." Any agency that thinks there is a difference between "killing" animals and

---

(continued from previous page)

Virginia, so that they could save the dogs, calling the request unreasonable. In 2005, it said No Kill was impossible in Philadelphia unless Pit Bulls were given to dogfighters. They also labeled feral cat caretakers "closet hoarders." In a September 27, 2006, speech at a Eugene, Oregon, town hall meeting on the issue, HSUS sent a representative who claimed No Kill was a sham, killing was necessary, and the blame belonged with the irresponsible public. One of the activists in attendance wrote that "[the HSUS representative] spent all her time slamming [the] No Kill philosophy, defending a shelter's need to kill animals, and blaming it on the irresponsible public."

"taking their life" is out of touch with reality. It is only by the deepest self-delusion that an argument can be made that the millions of dogs and cats exterminated in U.S. animal shelters are not being "killed." When you sugarcoat the words, you do not make the act more palatable.

This intentional misrepresentation of reality, however, isn't limited to the apologists associated with HSUS. In a study of shelter workers, two graduate students at Tufts University identified how shelter workers avoid blame for the killing. According to the authors:

> Sociologists have long documented a variety of techniques such as vocabularies of motive and accounts that people use to protect themselves psychologically when they consider their own acts immoral, strange, or untoward. To avoid real or anticipated negative attributions of others as well as self recriminations, people seek to present themselves in a favorable light by constructing explanations— excuses, justifications, apologies, and absolutions.
>
> Guilt feelings, in particular, may spur people to construct these accounts as they try to minimize the perceived blame of others and/or self-blame. Forced to manage ensuing guilt, they rely on after-the-fact, damage-control tactics or blame-management strategies.

In other words, they blame the public and, furthermore, also deny that what they are doing is in fact *exactly* what they are doing. In some shelters, they put animals in a chamber and turn on the gas until they are dead, a barbaric and inhumane practice.* In other shelters, they hold the animal down and administer an overdose of barbiturates until the heart simply stops. Whatever the mechanism, they still deny that they are killing. "By viewing killing as an act of mercy, shelter workers absolved themselves of their guilt" cite the study's authors, quoting a shelter worker as follows:

> I'm not actually killing the animal. I'm just giving it an injection. I'm just helping the process speed up. It—I really feel that most of these animals are dying as we speak. Um, sitting in those cages, the kennel stress that goes on, the frustration

---

* Gas systems take time to kill—during which animals experience distress and anxiety, and can struggle to survive. They can result in animals surviving the gassing, only to suffer more. And they take longer to kill if animals are young, old, or have respiratory infections, which can be common in shelters. They are designed for the ease of shelter workers, not care and compassion for the animals and should never be used.

> *. . . the fear, loneliness, and boredom. I mean, I—I can't call it living. Um, so by euthanasia, I think that we're only helping the process along. It's already started, long before we decided to.*

Once again, the authors are instructive:

> *This outlook made euthanasia a morally neutral action, if not an act of kindness, in the minds of the shelter staff. By stripping euthanasia of its negative connotation, shelter workers reduced their own feelings of guilt about killing.*

Shelters workers in the study further ignored the fact that over 90 percent of animals who enter shelters can be saved and with a small amount of free intervention by volunteers who walk, groom, and socialize the animals, shelters can easily eliminate any "frustration…fear, loneliness, and boredom." What is truly remarkable about this viewpoint, however, is the fact that it eliminates the impetus to stop killing.

As late as 2005, even the nation's most ardent animal rights group, People for the Ethical Treatment of Animals, called shelter killing "often the kindest option for animals admitted to sheltering facilities." They claim, despite San Francisco's and Tompkins County's success,

> *that all open admission shelters must euthanize healthy animals. According to the Humane Society of the United States (HSUS) Seven Basic Policies for Every Animal Shelter, "Euthanasia of shelter animals to make room for others is a tragic necessity that prevents animal suffering."*

In fact, killing is neither kind nor necessary, nor will it prevent animal suffering. Indeed, it is population control killing that itself is the root cause of animal suffering in our nation's animal control shelters. Wrote an observer:

> *It may seem surprising that People for the Ethical Treatment of Animals, a group that often comes to the defense of rats, euthanized more than 1,300 cats and dogs last year. But PETA President Ingrid Newkirk says it was the only humane thing to do.*

In 1999, while PETA was spreading its message around the globe and spending millions of dollars annually to protect chickens, cows, and other animals, it killed 1,325 of the 2,103 dogs and cats it claimed to "rescue."

Despite what appears to be a No Kill policy for other animals, PETA claimed that killing 63 percent of the dogs and cats in its care that year was an act of kindness. By 2005, nearly 2,000 dogs and cats—over 90 percent of those it "rescued"—were killed. What kind of rescue is that?

By making shelter killing a morally neutral action on the one hand (the reaction of the shelter employees in the Tufts study), denying that this is what you are in fact doing (the statements made in the HSUS "euthanasia" workshop), or asserting that killing is kind to the animal (PETA's viewpoint), the contradiction—*we protect animals by killing them*—disappears, as does the abhorrence of the systematic practice.

In Tompkins County, by contrast, our rejection of the consensus of killing started with six puppies in a horse trough. By the time I left, it involved hundreds of animals in foster care, hundreds more traveling to off-site adoptions, a coalition of breed-specific rescue groups, local veterinary participation, and a community that had faith in its shelter and wanted to support its lifesaving results. In the end, 93 percent of the animals were either returned to their responsible caregivers or found loving, new homes, an achievement unparalleled anywhere in the country. There were no excuses, no blame shifting. The animals came, were cared for, and were saved. It is, after all, what an SPCA is there to do.

Like the San Francisco SPCA before it, the Tompkins County SPCA has shown what can happen when one leader believes it is time to stop the killing and sweeps away the employees, policies, procedures, and defeatist mentality that seek to give legitimacy to the killing. There are those, particularly directors running shelters, who continue to kill the bulk of their occupants, who will nonetheless say "that what happened in San Francisco or Tompkins County can't happen here." But if No Kill isn't happening in their city—anywhere and everywhere that killing is the primary method for achieving results—it is not because of some singular trait that makes that community different from a San Francisco or Upstate New York. To imply such is a misrepresentation of the highest order. If a community is still killing the majority of shelter animals, it is because the local SPCA, humane society, or animal control shelter has fundamentally failed in its mission. And this failure is nothing more than a failure of leadership. The buck stops with the shelter's director. That is what No Kill requires. There is no doubt about it.

The first step toward No Kill is taking responsibility. Do shelters behave consistently with their claim that each life is precious? Only if they acknowledge that at the end of the day, every death of a healthy, sick, or in-jured treatable animal in American shelters is a profound failure—and only if the shelter director acknowledges that the responsibility for the death is his or hers alone.

Part II

AT THE CROSSROADS

Lost in the Wilderness

"With friends like these, who needs enemies?"

—American Proverb (unknown)

TOMPKINS COUNTY'S No Kill achievement, the first of its kind in the United States, should have had dramatic consequences around the country. It should have been the model that finally pushed failed ones aside and cleared the way for a No Kill nation. Had it been so, over four million of the dogs and cats who are killed in shelters every year, their bodies disposed of in landfills or rendered into pet food, would instead find a new life in the loving homes of American families. Tragically, this did not occur. To this day, the business of killing continues as usual in shelters nationwide.

Although shelter directors continue to kill in appalling numbers and ignore No Kill alternatives, they are doing so under ever greater scrutiny and criticism from the media, the public, and local animal activists.* With news of the No Kill success in Tompkins County spreading like wildfire, a light of hope has been kindled for animal rescuers and activists. Armed

---

* These activists have little power over shelter operations. Generally, they do not work in shelters but are part of TNR organizations, breed rescue groups, private shelters, or do animal rescue on their own. They see what happens because they visit shelters regularly in an effort to rescue animals from death row. Despite having no formal power, they have the power of numbers on their side and the "hearts and minds" of the citizenry.

with the revelation that an alternative to mass killing of homeless pets exists, and hoping to improve the appalling death rates faced by the animals in their own communities, they have begun to organize and clamor for change. Throughout the country—from Austin, Texas to New York City, from Kansas City to Los Angeles, and many points in between—animal lovers are joining together to begin laying the groundwork to build No Kill communities. But none have achieved success.

While emboldened by No Kill in Tompkins County, activists have almost uniformly failed to heed the central lesson: never mind the laws, reform the shelter. While they are demanding San Francisco- and Tompkins County-level success in their own communities, they fail to demand that local shelters either replicate the programs that eliminated the deaths in Tompkins County for all but irremediably suffering and non-rehabilitatable animals, or to insist upon the removal of directors who refuse to implement them. Instead, many seek No Kill through traditional models like LES. The end result is not hard to predict.

Until its low-cost spay/neuter clinics were closed, for example, the City of Los Angeles had begun the march toward No Kill with its municipally funded program that provided affordable access to spay/neuter services and incentives to increase the number of animals sterilized. At its core, the Los Angeles experiment was a community-based model that tried to eliminate the obstacles preventing people from acting in ways the shelter wanted them to. In other words, the city made it easy for people to do the right thing. It was the model that Avanzino embraced wholeheartedly and incorporated into a wide range of programs in San Francisco.

After the Los Angeles clinics closed, the City of Los Angeles was again the target of criticism for killing tens of thousands of dogs and cats annually. Unfortunately, rather than revisit the program that had been successful, the old school mentality of blaming the public found a champion in a group of animal activists called the Coalition to End Pet Overpopulation. They proposed a public straightjacket in the form of legislation seeking to make failure to license or spay/neuter an animal a misdemeanor on par with weapons possession or domestic violence.

The consequence of their effort was to divert focus away from establishing vital programs such as offsite adoptions, TNR, and foster care in favor of a more traditional enforcement orientation: hire more officers, do more sweeps of stray dogs, write more citations, impound more animals. While the final version of the proposed ordinance was less draconian than originally proposed, the end result was predictable. That a group con-cerned with high levels of shelter killing would actually seek legislation to empower its dysfunctional animal control bureaucracy to impound—and thus kill—even more animals, was a contradiction that was ignored. The law passed.

An editorial in the national periodical *Animal People* summarized it best:

> On March 22, 2000, the Los Angeles City Council at the urging of the Coalition to End Pet Overpopulation adopted what In Defense of Animals spokesperson Bill Dyer called "the nation's strongest spay/neuter ordinance." ... Los Angeles Animal Services Department manager Dan Knapp and local activists celebrated victory. They should have mourned a self-inflicted defeat.

Unfortunately, the viewpoint that the public, *rather than the shelter*, is to blame for the volume of killing has been internalized by animal activists all over the country. And the tool they use to make the public responsible is a resurrection of the failed LES model. Since the very "solution" they propose makes the goal impossible, however, they are forced to seek more citations, greater penalties, more animals subject to impounding, and more dracon-ian laws, increasing the divide between the shelter and the public, and tak-ing themselves further and further away from the goal of true lifesaving with each piece of punitive legislation.

Sadly, it is a pattern played out by animal activists throughout the country, over and over again. Despite animal control's dysfunction and overkill, animal activists continue to ignore and apologize for the shelter's failures by blaming the public, rather than those who are directly respon-sible: the very staff and administrators who fail every time they inject an animal with an overdose of barbiturates in the face of alternatives like fos-ter care, offsite adoptions, working with rescue groups, or TNR.

These activists fail to see the real causes and solutions to shelter killing because the bar or "industry standard" has been set so low, and because the national agencies to which they look for guidance reaffirm this point of view again and again. In a 2002 article reflective of this mentality, HSUS liberally quotes Baltimore's animal control chief about lack of adequate funding and public irresponsibility leading to a high rate of shelter killing. Yet the article ignores blatant practices in the Baltimore shelter that con-tribute to the death rate, such as poor adoption, cleaning, and handling protocols, practices that HSUS itself documented in an assessment of the agency two years earlier (which included many recommendations for change that were ignored).

In June of 2005 after I left the Tompkins County SPCA to start the No Kill Advocacy Center, a non-profit organization dedicated to the creation of a No Kill nation, I was hired by a local rescue group to do a review of operations in the Baltimore animal control shelter. Contrary to the excuses I heard while I was there (not enough money, not enough staff, public irresponsibility), the biggest impediments to lifesaving that I observed were internal.

The shelter had an overwhelming smell that made it difficult, if not unhealthy, to breathe. The floors were filthy and animals were standing in their own waste. Although it was early in the day and staff had not cleaned all the rooms, I did walk into two rooms that had already been "cleaned." Instead of the sanitary environment I should have found, I observed that the cages were not cleaned thoroughly, and were caked with dried bodily fluids and discharge. Staff was not operating with the awareness (or, if they were, they did not appear to care) that when they fail to clean properly, animals will get sick, the shelter will not be inviting to the public, and lives will be needlessly lost.

I observed a dog with an obvious injury, probably a broken hind limb, as he was not bearing weight on his leg. I was told by shelter leadership that the shelter did not provide treatment of any kind. I was also told the dog would be held for five days and then killed, but that an animal could be killed before the expiration of the holding period if he was "suffering." I was also told there weren't written or evaluative standards to make this determination, no written pain or treatment protocols, and often no action taken in these circumstances until the animal was simply killed at the expiration of the legally mandated stray holding period. Allowing a dog to stay in that condition with no treatment or pain control, only to be killed days later, is cruel.

Another disturbing practice I observed was dog kennels being cleaned with high-pressure hoses and chemicals while dogs were left in the same space. All of the dogs were wet and shivering. This was not only unnecessary, it too was cruel. I was told that dogs in the adoption room were removed from the kennels first, but that "stray" dogs posed a staff safety risk. I had contact with most of the dogs in this stray room, including allowing them to sniff and lick my fingers, and none of them was aggressive towards me.

Even defenders of outdated shelter practices like HSUS have condemned this practice

simply because it is a matter of routine, convenience, speed, and for employees who fear the animals with no objective basis for doing so. The repeated use of cruel practices cannot be a substitute for professional animal handling, restraint and transport skills.

I saw many empty adoption cages and kennels, yet animals continued to be killed. I saw animals in rooms scheduled for lethal injection labeled as "unadoptable" even though they were friendly, young kittens who were free of ocular and nasal discharge. I was also told it could take up to twenty days to investigate neglect cases reported by the public even though all shelters have the ability to respond virtually right away. (In Philadelphia, for example, the public was upset that it took three days to respond to a call for service, despite twice the population and overall fewer field services staff than Baltimore.)

The problem in Baltimore was the same problem I have observed in the last two years doing similar assessments of shelters nationwide, in Henry, Georgia, in Montgomery County, Texas, in Philadelphia, Pennsylvania, in Kansas City, Missouri, in Eugene, Oregon, and elsewhere. It was the same problem that existed in San Francisco before and after Avanzino, and the same problem that plagued Tompkins County before June 11, 2001. What plagued all these shelters can be summarized in two words: *poor management.*

Many of the deficiencies I saw in Baltimore were reported by HSUS in their own assessment of the shelter five years before I visited. Unfortunately, the fact that Baltimore failed to address deficiencies which compromised lifesaving HSUS itself noted years earlier did not stop HSUS from claiming that Baltimore's leadership was "committed to bringing change, one step at a time, for an agency that has for years been at the bottom of the list of priorities for city managers." In reality, the agency has not been a priority for its own leadership.

This lesson is perhaps nowhere more stark than in comparing Tompkins County's tremendous success with neighboring Cortland County, New York, which still had an unacceptably high kill rate compared to Tompkins. In 2003, as head of the Tompkins County SPCA, I offered to take up to thirty adult cats from Cortland County and place them into our adoption program if they would bring them to our facility—*a short twenty-minute drive door-to-door.* We were told it was "too far" to drive the paltry sixteen miles even though the Cortland County SPCA routinely killed healthy cats, ostensibly for space.* By contrast, the president of their Board of Directors did make the drive to our shelter some time afterwards, but not to save the lives of cats. Rather, he made the drive to complain that the Tompkins County SPCA's successful publicity was making them look bad and to request that public relations efforts not be focused on their county.

None of these shelters is an aberration in the United States. Nonetheless, activists in communities throughout the United States who are seeking to decrease killing are focusing their energies on legislation aimed at the public.

A MISGUIDED PREMISE

Legislation is often thought of as a quick solution to high rates of shelter killing. "If only we had a law," the argument goes, "all the bad, irresponsible people would have to take care of their pets properly, and shelters wouldn't have to kill so many animals." If this were true, given the proliferation of punitive mandates nationwide, there should be many No Kill communities. That there are not, is because experience has proven that legislation is far from a cure-all. In fact, it often has the opposite effect. Communities that have passed such laws are not only far from No Kill, many are moving in the opposite direction.

Studies show the primary reasons people do not sterilize their pets are cost and lack of access to spay/neuter services. The same is true for licensing. The higher the cost, the lower the rate of compliance. As a result, lower-income households with animals, those who are unaware of these laws, and truly irresponsible people will not comply in significant numbers. Punitive legislation will only discourage people from caring for homeless pets or drive disadvantaged people "underground," making them even harder to reach and help. If a person is feeding homeless cats, they will be loathe to turn to the shelter for low-cost spay/neuter help or other support be-

---

*In the end, I sent my staff to Cortland to pick up the cats and bring them back.

cause doing so risks putting the cats in jeopardy for some technical violation of a community's pet limit, licensing, or leash law. Compounding the problem is the fact that enforcement of ordinances, such as pet limit laws, cat licensing, mandatory spay/neuter, confinement/leash laws, and "nuisance" laws, is often selective and complaint-based, leaving people who care for animals vulnerable to retaliation from neighbors and others, even when the animals are healthy and well cared for.

As indicated earlier, legislation may be worded so that the result of non-compliance is the impoundment and death of the animal. Many jurisdictions have seen their impound and death rates increase following passage of laws which give agencies *carte blanche* to round up and kill outdoor animals. If a shelter has high rates of shelter killing, it makes no sense to support the passing of laws that give them greater power and more reasons to impound—and subsequently kill—even more animals.

Finally, in most jurisdictions, licensing revenues go into a city or county's general fund, not directly back to the animal control agency. As a result, even where licensing rates increase, it has no direct impact on shelter finances. In the end, the shelter is diverting money from needed programs to hire more officers to write more citations, only to raise money for the city or county, at the expense of its own needs.

When Fort Wayne, Indiana, San Mateo, California, and King County, Washington, passed their animal control legislation, for example, these laws were hailed as "national models." To this day, animal activists use these as examples of "success" in order to convince their own communities to adopt similar approaches. A hard look, however, reveals they are a dismal failure. Historically, Fort Wayne's aggressive enforcement of cat licensing yielded only single-digit compliance and a steadily increasing death rate for several years following mandatory cat licensing. In 2003, two decades after passage of that legislation, animal control still killed 76 percent—*three out of four*—of all domestic animals.*

The unincorporated county of San Mateo adopted its mandatory cat licensing program in the first quarter of 1992 and noted a higher level of killing than the previous four years. The number of cats killed increased by 54 percent following the implementation of cat licensing, and 60 percent

---

* Fort Wayne only identified "domestic species" in its annual report. While this category would include rabbits, hamsters, and other animals, the vast majority are dogs and cats.

in year two. This represented the first ever increase in cats impounded and killed in San Mateo County. By contrast, in the City of San Mateo—which did not implement the law—the number of cats impounded and killed that same year followed the predictable downward trend of 14 percent fewer cats impounded and 14 percent fewer killed.

The shelter claimed a decrease in the kill rate for cats of 24 percent two years after implementation, citing the licensing law as the reason. But this still represents a 42 percent increase from the year preceding cat licensing. In fact, adjusting for the fact that cat licensing did not go into effect until the end of the first quarter of 1992, the actual decline was closer to about five percent, significantly lower than the 24 percent claimed, and low compared to the decline of 29 percent experienced in the City of San Mateo which had not implemented cat licensing.

No legislation has been more heralded or more promoted as a national model, however, than the 1992 ordinance that passed, with great fanfare, in King County, Washington. Animal control in that community claims that because of the ordinance, they are now saving the vast majority of "adoptable" animals. Closer scrutiny reveals just how overreaching this claim is.

First of all, despite being billed as a lost pet's ticket home, redemption rates—the number of stray animals who are actually reunited with their families—have either remained flat or declined since King County's ordinance went into effect. In 1990, two years before the ordinance, 1,775 stray animals were reclaimed by families looking for their lost dogs and cats. In 2004, only 1,766 were. In real numbers, there is a decline in redemptions, so the claim made about cat licensing (and dog licensing for that matter) increasing reclamation rates is not borne out by the data. If anything, most of these redemptions are dogs, and despite the doubling of dog licenses sold, overall redemptions are still down. These rates are also consistent with other jurisdictions where such laws are not in place.* The only other

---

* The reason why licensing fails to help most cats is simply because the vast majority of cats entering shelters do not live in homes with people. They are either feral cats, homeless strays, or surrendered to shelters by individuals who no longer want them and therefore have no one to claim them. While obvious, this fact is conveniently ignored by animal control agencies and other groups to push for more punitive and expansive laws.

argument is that it leads to greater spay/neuter rates because of declining impounds, but there is no evidence of that either. In addition, jurisdictions that have simply made spay/neuter affordable, have achieved greater declines in impounds and greater rates of lifesaving, since they did not divert animal care dollars to bureaucratic enforcement of laws.

Second, for the three years prior to implementation of the ordinance, King County was already experiencing declines in cat killing of 13 percent, 9 percent, and 15 percent, respectively, declines that were more significant than the declines for the six years following passage of the law. In fact, the law may have limited the actual decline and therefore reduced lifesaving rates because animals impounded were not redeemed. More recently, the trend is toward greater declines in killing and King County is now saving more lives than ever before, but the reason for this is far from a law of dubious value. King County began sterilizing all animals before adoption rather than sending them out unspayed, adopting out Pit Bulls rather than having a policy of 100 percent killing, treating cats and kittens with respiratory infections rather than killing them, offering a foster care program, working with rescue groups, and working with feral cat caretakers who practice TNR rather than killing all feral cats.

Although the implementation of lifesaving programs is not being done as rigorously as it could be and almost half the animals are still losing their lives, declines in impounds and killing perfectly track changes in programs—spay/neuter of adopted animals, making Pit Bulls available for adoption, treating illnesses, working with TNR groups, and more progressive policies in adoptions. In short, King County began implementing some of the non-punitive, non-legislative programs and services of the No Kill Equation, the very same programs that made San Francisco and Tompkins County successful. It is this effort—and not their 1992 law—which accounts for the decline.

Third, as an animal control agency, the Tompkins County SPCA typically took in more than three times the number of animals than available cages/kennels in the shelter, but did not kill a single animal for space. Success wasn't achieved with legislation requiring the public to spay/neuter their animals on threat of impound or fines, nor was it accomplished by licensing cats. In fact, it wasn't done through laws at all. As seen time and time again, these other approaches are largely a distraction, increasing the power of animal control to impound and kill yet more animals, targeting the wrong people, and diverting resources from programs that do work so that agencies can hire yet more officers to write yet more tickets, to no avail.

No better proof exists for this proposition than Long Beach, California, which has had a breeding ban for over thirty years. If legislation is the answer, Long Beach should be a No Kill community by now. But it is far from it, as many homeless animals have discovered who have had the misfortune to enter that animal control shelter system. The same is true of Fort Wayne, Indiana, San Mateo, California, and even King County, Washington. By contrast, the three most successful communities in the nation with the highest percentage of animals going home alive—San Francisco, Tompkins County, and, as we shall see, Charlottesville, Virginia (discussed more fully in a subsequent chapter)—have no mandatory cat licensing or spay/neuter laws.

Nonetheless, local activists and national groups—even those who embrace No Kill and are sincere in their desire to end killing—continue to champion the legislative approach. The National Humane Education Society, for example, has a position paper called *The Killing of Healthy Animals*, which states:

> Companion animals are sentient creatures who have intrinsic value in and of themselves. Therefore, our stewardship includes sanctity for their individual lives, and we will not participate in the killing of one animal in order to make room for another animal. But rather, we will remain committed to each animal that comes into our care until such time as an appropriate adoptive home can be found, because this is part of the humane solution to ending animal suffering.

The viewpoint is laudable. But the conclusion that follows is a *non sequitur:*

> Ultimately, the humane solution to the overpopulation of unwanted animals is responsible pet ownership and legislatively imposed mandatory spay/neuter ordinances in every county of our nation.

They could not be more wrong; such an approach has never worked. In 2006, however, Los Angeles *County* activists turned out in droves to champion just such an ordinance, even though it was similar to the failed legislation the City of Los Angeles passed six years earlier. "We believe that all attempts to curtail pet overpopulation require a three pronged approach," a local activist exclaimed after the county law passed by unanimous vote, "legislation, education and a low-cost sterilization program. This is indeed a welcomed cornerstone."

In a democracy, animal lovers are free to believe whatever they want. But believing something doesn't make it so, and never will. Meanwhile, animals continue to be killed in appalling numbers and reform efforts are squandered on an agenda that has no hope of achieving success. Moreover, the animals are paying the ultimate price for the false beliefs of animal activists. They are the ones being slaughtered *en masse* because of it. With animals being killed every day in Los Angeles County shelters because shelter leadership has not embraced a comprehensive TNR program or the other programs and services of the No Kill Equation, activists must move beyond the empty hope that LES will ever be anything but a failure. Los Angeles activists are still championing a nineteenth century model of sheltering rooted in defeatism and failing to demand the real changes necessary for No Kill to succeed, while ignoring over a decade of No Kill success in San Francisco and Tompkins County. And they are not alone.

While some activists simply do not know better and mean well, others obstinately ignore facts, experience, and history and continue to push these types of laws. They will do what they have always done—facts, logic, and history be damned. They will continue to blame the public and they will continue to fight for more and tougher laws. They will argue that their community is different, that their situation is unique, that citizens in their community are particularly—or peculiarly—irresponsible. None of this is true, but they do not care.

While they claim to be motivated by saving lives, there is something much more powerful driving them: *the desire to punish.* An activist truly focused on lifesaving, who subsequently learns that punitive legislation is not only a dismal failure, but that it has the opposite results (more impounds, more killing), would end their support of such methods and begin to push for regime change at animal control or the programs and services of the No Kill Equation.

By contrast, those who are intent on pursuing their own agenda are being driven by other imperatives. In the end, they so want to punish the public for not taking care of their pets as much as they think they should, they are willing to ignore all the evidence about legislation's true results or about how to truly save lives, and instead empower animal control to kill animals in the process. Unfortunately, animal control is generally more than willing to oblige and do just that. In the end, these activists become that which they claim to most despise—people whose actions result in the impound and killing of animals. They become the "irresponsible public."

FAILURE IS THE NEW SUCCESS

After decades of being bombarded with the false message that shelters are not responsible for high rates of killing, the fault belongs to the public, and we must pass more laws to empower animal control to impound more animals, activists have come to believe these claims. Rather than champion the No Kill Equation, the only course of action that has created a No Kill community, they are chasing shadows. They are, to put it bluntly, going after the wrong enemy.

As San Francisco proved, shelters that implement the programs of the No Kill Equation substantially increase lifesaving. Yet virtually no shelters nationwide have comprehensively done so, remaining content to blame the public for their own failure to end the killing and promoting a legislative approach that fails to achieve results. In turn, activists have developed a culture of defeatism, a sense of helplessness that No Kill cannot be achieved.

As a result, many in the humane community have internalized the belief that killing is necessary, and have grown forgiving of poorly performing shelters. They become apologists for the status quo, championing mediocrity and failure, when they should be demanding the resignation of shelter leadership. In her 1998 book *Lost & Found: Dogs, Cats, and Everyday Heroes at a Country Humane Society*, author and animal lover Elizabeth Hess elevates this phenomenon to an absurd level. Though praised by book reviewers and even animal activists, the book is a series of irreconcilable contradictions, as if the author and all those readers who lauded its message either ignored facts, or failed to recognize incompatible propositions.

Hess tells the story of the Columbia-Greene Humane Society in Upstate New York which, she states, occupies "a series of ramshackle buildings and a shabby trailer" with "no money" and a "tiny staff [which] struggles just to keep the doors open and the animals alive." She then goes on to say that this paltry situation "is as good as it gets for homeless animals." With such a low threshold of expectations, is it any wonder that we have accepted the notion that the best we can do for homeless animals is to adopt a few and kill the rest? Is it any wonder that national groups have been able to fool the public into believing that killing is done at the hands of caring shelter workers who would do everything in their power, leave no stone unturned, implement any program that had a glimmer of hope, if it held any promise of something different?

By the time Hess published her book, the San Francisco SPCA had medical, behavior, foster, public relations, fundraising, volunteer, and adoption programs that made Columbia-Greene Humane Society, as described in the book, look positively medieval. The City of San Francisco had not killed a healthy homeless dog or cat in four years, had a lifesaving rate that was the best in the nation, and had just opened the Maddie's Pet Adoption Center. This new facility replaced traditional cages and kennels with homelike apartments, spacious rooms, and large, picture windows—a far cry from the crumbling infrastructure and ramshackle buildings she describes for Columbia-Greene.

Like many animal lovers, Hess could not grasp the notion that Columbia-Greene was failing because of its own actions or, more accurately, for its own failure to act. Instead, she parroted the fiction that insolvency and lack of success were imposed on Columbia-Greene from outside, while the agency failed to implement the programs and services that not only made San Francisco successful, but which the San Francisco SPCA promoted from coast to coast.

The contradiction does not stop there. Despite the success of TNR, the national ascendancy of programs like the Stanford Cat Network, the San Francisco SPCA's Feral Cat Assistance Program, and the nation's largest and most vocal feral cat advocacy organization, Alley Cat Allies, Hess goes on to say that the director "doesn't participate in any programs to save feral cats or release them into controlled colonies; they are all euthanized after their five days of stray time." Despite the fact that San Francisco demonstrated the absolute necessity of a foster care program to save the lives of animals, especially for young animals not yet ready for adoption, Hess writes that "there's no time to begin hand-feeding the kittens. '[The director] doesn't encourage us to keep them alive if there's no mother and they are too small to eat on their own,' she says sadly. 'Kittens under six weeks old are usually euthanized.'"

Hess also goes on to describe how "unwanted pets [are] prematurely transformed into smoke and ash. When I first smelled the crematory at Columbia-Greene, I thought the whole place was on fire. Eventually everyone learns to live with this odor." But why should they have to? We could excuse the apologia, even the contradictions, the *non sequitur* from facts to conclusion, if San Francisco had not existed. Or maybe we could excuse it if Hess was not familiar with the No Kill paradigm. But she was. She not only ignored No Kill's success—or failed to research the issue adequately— she also implied that No Kill was akin to substandard care or "living year after year in cages." She also seemed to indicate that when private shelters turned animals away, traditional shelters had no choice but to kill—to, as she put it, "pick up the slack." After dismissing the promise No Kill held out for the animals of Columbia-Greene, Hess concludes by saying:

> The power in every shelter ultimately lies with the person who has the authority to determine who lives and who dies…. referring to four nearby litters (fifteen kittens) that are scheduled for euthanasia because they are too young, sick, or were simply born the wrong color. People don't realize that kittens are so plentiful that they are frequently selected for euthanasia on the basis of their color. Black cats, for instance, are more common than calicos; if there are already three black cats up for adoption and a new one arrives, he or she might not even be given a chance.

In other words, animals are dying based on arbitrary criteria determined by the director, who can choose not to implement the proven, life-saving programs and services of the No Kill Equation. Consequently, animal deaths at Columbia-Greene had nothing to do with being feral, unweaned, or "born the wrong color." The failure to embrace the No Kill paradigm is the culprit; the fault lies with the shelter itself.

If we are ever to achieve a No Kill nation, we must stop ignoring shelter failures. Failure to implement TNR, comprehensive adoption programs, foster care programs, medical rehabilitation programs, and engage in modern public relations and fundraising efforts to pay for it all, kills. These are the lessons given to us by the No Kill movement Hess dismisses too easily. In Hess' ideal humane society, as personified by Columbia-Greene, killing is kindness, and failure is success—a point of view the No Kill paradigm utterly rejects. In Tompkins County, black kittens, sick cats, wild cats, and hand-fed motherless neonatals whom Columbia-Greene killed were all saved—at an animal control shelter also situated in rural Upstate New York, a three hour drive from Columbia-Greene.

Pet lovers like Hess are not the only ones who have accepted the mass killing of dogs and cats by people who claim to be the animals' protectors. Even ardent animal rights activists have—championed by the largest of them all, People for the Ethical Treatment of Animals.

In a 2005 article it published called "The Disturbing Facts about No Kill Shelters," PETA claims that it is more ethical to spend money on spaying and neutering than on trying to save the animals who have already been born. But Jeff Lydon, who took over as executive director of the Tompkins County SPCA after my departure, exposes the fallacy of this argument:

> *PETA claims that it is more ethical to spend money on spay/neuter than on warehousing dogs and cats already born. But are these really the only two choices? Hardly. PETA's readers in general and people in the sheltering business in particular have a right to know that there's another possibility, a choice less draconian than mass murder to finance mass sterilization (as PETA ironically if not directly advances).*

Nonetheless, many animal rights activists blindly follow PETA's lead, whitewashing killing even in the face of No Kill alternatives and widespread incompetence in shelters. They do so because they see PETA fighting for the right to life of other animals—animals in circuses, on factory farms, in research laboratories, and in other places.

When it comes to eating animals for food, PETA's argument is unassailable ethically: why is a pig called dinner but a dog is a pet? Why is one animal more worthy of our compassion than another? Side-by-side, pigs may be smarter, more trainable, and would make as loving a companion as a dog. Despite the comparison to dogs when it suits their agenda, PETA treats dogs very differently than it does pigs. They have two entirely different standards. They not only call for the deaths of dogs in shelters, they kill dogs (and cats) themselves—nearly 2,000 per year.

In 2005, two PETA employees were charged with over thirty counts of felony animal cruelty in North Carolina after investigators found that PETA was killing animals and throwing the bodies in a shopping mall dumpster. A deputy sheriff involved in the investigation told reporters that PETA employees assured the shelters "they were picking up the dogs to take them back to Norfolk [Virginia, PETA's headquarters] where they would find them good homes." In addition, a local veterinarian told CNN and other reporters that the "cat and two kittens I gave [PETA] last week were in good health and were very adoptable, especially the kittens." He also stated that "these were just kittens we were trying to find homes for. PETA said they would do that, but these cats never made it out of the county."

The manager of the supermarket whose dumpster was used stated that the PETA employees "just slung the doors [open] and started throwing dogs ... beautiful cats. I saw a [dead] beagle last week that was pregnant ... last week it was 23 or 24 dogs ... it's happened to us nine times ... they drove straight from there, straight here, and disposed of the dogs in 30 seconds."

But the biggest travesty in PETA's view that No Kill is a movement to be condemned rather than embraced is the larger effect this has on the validity of the animal rights platform to the American public. Millions of Americans have a very deep relationship with their pet dogs and cats. It is that relationship that can provide a springboard to larger animal rights issues. In their daily interactions with their dogs and cats, people experience an animal's personality, emotions, and capacity both for great joy and great suffering. They learn empathy for animals. It is not a stretch that someone who is compassionate—and passionate—about their pets would over time and with the right information be sympathetic to animal suffering on farms, in circuses, in cosmetic research facilities, and elsewhere.

If groups like PETA openly champion the killing of dogs and cats in shelters, if they do not take the position that killing dogs and cats is inherently unethical and should be condemned, how does PETA expect to convince the public that pigs, chickens, and other animals with whom Americans do not have a close relationship should have a right to live? How can PETA expect to convince the public that animals should not be killed out of convenience, infliction of suffering and death is unacceptable, and animals should be valued for their own sake, irrespective of their relationship to humans when they openly claim that these values should not be applied to the five million dogs and cats that shelters kill every year? If the animal rights community, which claims to be the standard bearer for what our relationship to animals should be, does not champion No Kill (and tacitly approves or legitimizes the killing) doesn't that undermine their ultimate goals? Once again, Jeff Lydon is instructive:

> It has long been a simple yet compelling argument for activists to ask – how can you justify treating a pig this way when you would never treat a dog this way. PETA ... threatens to turn that argument on its head – you shouldn't kill pigs but it's important to kill dogs. Companion animals provide the bridge for many by which to make a connection with broader animal issues, such as the plight of farm animals. Why is PETA burning that bridge?

One possibility is that PETA's founder, Ingrid Newkirk, previously worked at the Washington Humane Society in Washington, D.C., a shelter that has historically been the subject of public criticism for high rates of shelter killing. In fact, at a time when Stanford University was having great success with its TNR program, the Washington Humane Society opposed Alley Cat Allies' efforts to create a similar program on the Georgetown University campus. In the end, Georgetown sided with the Washington Humane Society, which embraced a campaign of extermination.*

Few activists who follow PETA's lead on the companion animal issue are probably aware that the founder's former job was to kill homeless dogs and cats in a shelter that had a poor record for saving lives. So while Lydon's question is important, the more imperative ones become: Why are the most ardent defenders of animals supporting killing? Why are they embracing the type of hypocrisy they would not accept for pigs, cows, and chickens? If animal rights supporters turn their backs on dogs and cats in shelters, how can we expect the public not to also? In short, *why are animal advocates listening to PETA?***

REFORM IN CALIFORNIA

In 1998, while Hess was whitewashing Columbia-Greene's failures in New York and groups like PETA were demeaning No Kill success, a dedicated California animal rights lawyer was attempting to "redraw the playing field" for shelter animals with one fell swoop. University of California at Los Angeles (UCLA) law professor Taimie Bryant was assisting State Senator Tom Hayden, from the greater Los Angeles area, who wanted a statewide legislative solution to a political and practical problem California's animal

---

* It should also be noted that the national headquarters of the Humane Society of the United States is in Washington, D.C., and both the Washington Humane Society and Georgetown University cited HSUS and PETA for its position that the cats should be trapped and then killed at the local pound.

** Except for a few notable exceptions, the salient question for animal rights groups and activists who do not support mass slaughter of dogs and cats in shelters is, why are they silent about it?

control shelters would not address, particularly those shelters in his home district of Los Angeles.

It was not cat licensing, mandatory spay/neuter, pet limit laws, or any other artifact of the failed LES model. Bryant actually took her lead from San Francisco, which at the time was saving seven out of ten cats (and most dogs) entering its shelters, while Los Angeles shelters were killing that many. She was directing her aim not at the supposed "irresponsible public," but at those truly responsible for the killing—the shelters themselves. It had the potential to become the most significant piece of companion animal protection legislation in years. Bryant explains:

> *With some notable exceptions, shelters have failed to provide hours the working public can visit the shelters for adoptions or redemptions of their companion animals. They have failed to provide adequate lost/found services. They have failed to keep records adequate to find pets within the system. They have failed to use freely offered microchip scanning services. They have failed to provide adequate veterinary health care for many animals. They have resisted working with the rescue/adoption community. They have failed to raise funds aggressively to promote lifesaving methods to spare the lives of placeable companion animals. They have used tax dollars to kill animals they didn't have to accept in the first place ("owner-relinquished" pets) and to kill animals whose companion humans never even had a chance to locate them.*
>
> *Our shelters have a very bad track record when it comes to adoption. In California in 1997 with a statewide human population of close to 33 million, only 142,385 cats and dogs were adopted from our shelters. The vast majority—576,097— were killed.*

The legislation required, among other things, that animal control shelters in California give animals to rescue groups and No Kill shelters instead of killing them; provided incentives for shelters to have either evening or weekend hours so that working people and families with children in school could reclaim lost pets or adopt a new one; set a statewide preference for adoption rather than killing; and sought to end the practice where animals surrendered by their "owners," including healthy and highly adoptable kittens and puppies, were killed within minutes of arriving. It also modestly increased the time shelters were required to hold *stray* animals before killing them so that lost animals had an opportunity to be reunited with their families. In other words, Senator Hayden was trying to legislate some of the programs and services of the No Kill Equation.

Shelters mired in killing, afraid of public scrutiny, and unwilling to work with rescue groups predictably opposed the measure. In addition to their desire to avoid being held accountable, their main objection was that the law made it illegal to kill an animal if a rescue group or No Kill shelter was willing to guarantee that animal a home through its own adoption program. This threatened to open up shelter killing and other atrocities to public scrutiny. According to Bryant:

> As frequent visitors to the shelters, rescuers saw systemic problems and inhumane treatment of animals, but their access to animals was tenuous and many times hinged on not publicly disclosing concerns. Under the 1998 Animal Shelter Law, …[t]heir right to take these animals is no longer legally premised on silence as to shelter practices and violations of the law.

Despite the opposition of shelters and their allies, it made no sense to state legislators that taxpayers were spending money on killing animals when No Kill shelters and other private rescue agencies were willing to spend their own money to save them. Not surprisingly, the proposed bill passed the legislature with overwhelmingly bipartisan support—ninety-six to twelve—and the state's Republican governor signed the measure into law.

The reaction was strong and swift. The Fund For Animals joined Los Angeles in fighting the measure through a regulatory challenge, replete with bloated figures and misleading claims. They claimed that it would be too expensive to implement, a claim debunked by the California Department of Finance. They claimed that the "longer" holding periods, which would give people a chance to find their lost pets or for the pets to be adopted into new homes, would lead to the increased killing of other animals. That argument was also a red herring: the law did increase the holding period from a paltry seventy-two hours from the time of impound to four days if the shelter was open one evening a week or one weekend day. But as Bryant points out:

> When California's holding period was 72 hours, there was only one state with a shorter holding period—Hawaii, with a 48-hour holding period. Now that California has increased the holding period, it has joined the bottom six states in the country in terms of holding period. By national standards, California's current holding period is far from generous.

The Humane Society of the United States parroted the claim that the new law "leaves little leeway in California" as shelters struggled to accommodate what it termed "lengthy" holding periods, which in California was shorter than HSUS' own long-standing recommendation of five days.

Shortly after the law went into effect, Dan Knapp, the General Manager of Los Angeles Animal Services, blamed it for the city's over-crowded, and poorly managed facilities which existed before the law passed and were the reason Senator Hayden sought the legislation in the first place. The law and a companion piece of legislation, the 1998 Shelter Spay/Neuter Law, provided authority for Knapp to send very young kittens and puppies to rescue groups rather than kill them even before they were old enough for spay/neuter. Knapp refused, choosing to kill the animals instead, despite experienced rescue groups ready, willing, and able to save the tiny babies. According to Bryant,

> [t]he horrible fact is that the vast majority of companion animals die in our shelters regardless of their status. Some of our worst shelters protest that they want to kill unadoptable pets so that they can keep the adoptable ones, when, in fact, they kill almost every animal and do little to help owners find lost pets or would-be owners adopt pets. Secondly, this argument totally ignores the statutory obligation to be first and foremost a bailee for people's lost pets. A dog or cat may not look like a good adoption candidate to a particular shelter employee, but these animals may very well be family members whose owners miss them and love them regardless of their age, infirmities, or lack of objective beauty. Moreover, these complaining shelters avoid comment on the embarrassing fact that the overwhelming majority of states in this country provide far more time for owners to claim their lost pets and for would-be owners to adopt.

Unfortunately, while full and vigorous implementation of the 1998 Animal Shelter Law could have provided the basis for success, some shelters failed or refused to implement either the letter or spirit of the new law. As a result, the hoped-for renaissance of lifesaving has had mixed results, while city governments and shelters continued killing in direct violation of the law.

Kern County's municipal animal control shelter, an agency tasked with enforcing animal-related laws, for example, was itself in violation. There, killing illegally continued until a local activist filed a lawsuit to stop it in 2004, six years after passage of the 1998 Animal Shelter Law. Full implementation continues to prove elusive. Unfortunately, Kern County does not appear to be an isolated incident; Sacramento County animal control was also the target of a lawsuit for illegally killing animals before their care-takers could find them, for not making them available for adoption, and for failing to keep records on thousands of others. There is mounting evidence that other communities are also routinely violating the law.

A Call for Change

Nonetheless, despite the widespread preference of animal activists to fight for laws with no hope of success, their desire for No Kill is often very real. By the early 2000s, with No Kill rhetoric sweeping the nation, shelter administrators who once openly attacked No Kill realized that it was becoming politically untenable to continue doing so publicly. With the pressure for change mounting, these directors needed a new public image. In a few communities where they dug in their heels, they were forcibly swept aside.

Most directors, however, found another way. They began to say one thing, while they did something else. In short, they learned the art of po-litical double-speak. The supposed effort to save animals deemed "adopt-able" began, even by those who were No Kill's fiercest detractors. These old guard institutions began to use "new" language and promote "new" pro-grams. Leaders who once pledged to stop what happened in San Francisco from spreading to their own hometowns were now seeking to save all "adoptable" animals. In reality, they did nothing of the kind. Instead, they narrowed the definition of "adoptable" to the point of meaninglessness.

The real race was not to save lives, but to end public scrutiny and crit-icism by co-opting the No Kill movement. Business would continue as usual, but it would come with new terminology. "There are three kinds of lies," an old saying goes. "There are lies. There are damn lies. And there are statistics." The move to co-opt the No Kill movement has encompassed all three.

Co-option

"Ethics and honesty demand avoiding euphemisms. The challenge is not to do away with the troubling words 'No Kill,' and to white wash killing; rather the challenge is to do away with killing, which requires ceasing to pretend—to oneself and to the public—that it amounts to anything else."

—Merritt Clifton, Editor, Animal People (1997)

IN 1974, the Humane Society of the United States, the American Humane Association, the ASPCA, and other animal welfare groups had an opportunity to take a decisive stand. Had they endorsed and succeeded in promoting municipally funded low-cost spay/neuter nationwide, the lifesaving results could have been dramatic. Sadly, they failed to do so. After more than 7,000 copies of the recommendations of the Chicago conference were sent to animal shelters throughout the country, another conference was held in Denver, Colorado two years later. Once again, defeatism and special interests won the day.

Despite two more years of indisputable proof that high volume spay/neuter clinics in Los Angeles were having a decisive impact on lowering shelter deaths, a fact presented in detail at the conference, the participants again failed to support municipally funded low-cost spay/neuter programs for fear of alienating veterinary business interests. In addition, instead of using the Los Angeles model—and later, the one provided by the San Francisco SPCA—some of these groups continued, and continue to this day, to push for punitive measures that blame the public, when fault lies with the shelter's failure to do what is necessary to stop the killing.

The incentive-based and community-based approaches of the No Kill Equation are the keys which will forever slam shut and lock the door of population control killing. Nearly thirty years after high-volume, low-cost spay/neutering was introduced in Los Angeles, and over a decade after San Francisco's success, such efforts have still not been implemented in many communities. Had these leaders taken a principled and decisive stand, what might have been the result? If the success achieved in San Francisco and Tompkins County is any indication, we might be a No Kill nation today. But the humane movement did not take the road of principle, the road less traveled, and, unfortunately for the animals, that has made all the difference.

By the middle of the current decade, however, with the attacks on No Kill by local shelters and national groups failing to convince activists that the paradigm should be abandoned, shelter directors found their agencies' kill rates the subject of mounting criticism. Many directors were facing a choice: abandon the traditional platform, which relied on killing, or be pushed out of the way.

Although many of them were not moving to implement the philosophy, programs, services, or culture of lifesaving that No Kill represents, they nonetheless began to promise their constituents that, in time, they would make their shelters—and communities—No Kill. It has become common to hear shelter directors proclaim their shelters will be No Kill in five years, or ten years, or, in some cases, even claiming that they are very nearly there already. It is a strategy of self-preservation.

In those communities that claimed "success" or near "success," such as Maricopa County animal control in Phoenix, Arizona, a review of their statistics from 1998 to 2003 showed little change in the levels of killing or, at best, only modest declines consistent with other communities. After claiming at national conferences that Maricopa County shelters had not killed a treatable dog or cat in years, that the costs for No Kill initiatives were not being borne by taxpayers, that Maricopa County was a model of lifesaving, and that it would be No Kill within two years, its director left the agency in disarray. At the time, the shelter was still killing over 29,000 dogs and cats a year, had a structural deficit in excess of a half-million dollars, and was nowhere near No Kill. In fact, according to former shelter

managers, animals were being intentionally misclassified and poorly cared
for and the agency was near financial ruin.

Likewise in 2005, the local humane society in Harrisburg,
Pennsylvania, claimed that it achieved No Kill despite having killed over
half of all incoming cats. Meanwhile, after publicly announcing a plan to
make the City of San Antonio No Kill by 2012, animal shelter leadership
quietly continued rounding up and killing stray cats. It also continues to
issue citations to people who spay/neuter and care for feral cats by clam-
ing they are, according to a local newspaper account, "allowing the cats to
roam without wearing a county license and a rabies tag."

Shelter directors have found a new way of doing business. Prior to San
Francisco and Tompkins County's success, shelter administrators openly
killed for reasons such as lack of space, antipathy to certain breeds, because
the cats were feral, the animals had (highly treatable) illnesses like upper
respiratory infection and kennel cough, or because the director felt there
were too many black dogs or cats in the shelter. Most savvy shelter directors today would never be so blatant, so unapologetic for the slaughter.
They still kill at an alarming rate (roughly five million dogs and cats every
year) but many are now doing it with a difference. They are now doing so
under the cloak of scientific legitimacy: the dogs and cats they kill, we are
now told, are "unadoptable."

For well over a century, the killing of dogs and cats has been a central
strategy of most private SPCAs, humane societies and animal control facilities which contract with cities and towns to run shelters for animals
who are stray or no longer wanted. They even created a euphemism—
"putting them to sleep"—to make the task of killing easier. In the end,
that's exactly what the humane movement has become: a movement of "euphemisms"—euphemisms such as "putting them to sleep," "euthanasia," and
"humane death." These euphemisms have been created to obscure the gravity of what is actually occurring and to avoid accountability for it. In the
age of No Kill, add one more euphemism: "unadoptable."

To shelters mired in nineteenth-century philosophies, an "unadoptable"
animal is interpreted very broadly. Some shelters, for example, consider a
kitten with a minor cold or a dog older than five years old to be unadoptable. In Tompkins County, by contrast, the animal control shelter routinely adopted out blind dogs, pets missing limbs, traumatized cats, and other
animals most communities would have killed as "unadoptable" without
ever giving them a chance. It has proved there are no animals supposedly

"too old" or "too ugly" to be adoptable, so long as they are not vicious or hopelessly ill.

In 2003, for example, the Tompkins County SPCA's animal control officers impounded a stray geriatric dog who was nearly deaf and losing his eyesight. They named him "Grandpa." When no one came forward to claim him as their lost stray, a plea was put out in the local newspaper:

Hello. I am a little old man. I like to sleep a lot. And I don't cause too much trouble. I don't hear so good so if you sneak up on me and touch me, I get a bit spooked and flinch. So you need to make sure I see you when you want my attention. I am older in years, and maybe not so much fun. I know kids today like a dog who can chase a ball and stuff. I'd like to play but I don't really have the energy. Someone left me here to die. But I don't want to. I want to live. I want to sleep inside for a little while. Do you have space in your heart and in your home for me? I promise not to be too much trouble. All I want is a little dignity at the end of my days.

Like the call for Justine and Foxfire before him, the response to Grandpa's plea was overwhelming and he was adopted within days. The shelter had the same success with Oliver, a cat with a broken jaw and one eye. It had the same success with a cat who had neurological problems and could not use stairs. It had the same success with a blind dog. It had the same success with a three-legged dog. It had the same success with a cat who defecated with no control.*

Shelters that use an overly broad, meaningless definition of "unadoptable" ignore the fact that some adopters want older animals who are less excitable and more sedate to match their lifestyle. They ignore the fact that if shelters let people know how they can help, the public responds. And they ignore the importance of people wanting to be heroic by saving the life of an animal who someone else failed to love. Making the mental leap that the public is capable of such great compassion, unfortunately, conflicts with the shelter viewpoint that sees the public as the source of the problem.

---

* It is worth noting that the vast majority of dogs and cats entering shelters are young and friendly animals, with no injuries, illnesses, or behavior problems. The aforementioned should not be read as meaning that most shelter animals have problems. Some do, however, and good homes can just as readily be found for them as the thousands of cute and cuddly kittens and puppies and adult animals who make their way to a shelter every year.

However, the restrictive definition of what constitutes an "adoptable" animal is not simply a failure to overcome a personal bias. It also has an intentional and dark side: the label of "unadoptable" allows shelters to appear to be doing a better job than they actually are.

To the public, "unadoptable" implies a commonsense definition of the word—a dog or cat who is hopelessly sick or injured or, in the case of dogs, who may be vicious and therefore pose a real and immediate threat to public safety. That is what many of these shelters expect the public to believe: that they are, in fact, already meeting the dictionary definition of euthanasia ("the act or practice of killing *hopelessly sick or injured* individual animals in a relatively painless way for reasons of mercy") when they call a dog or cat "unadoptable." But that is not the criteria they are using to make those determinations. As a result, while shelters claim they are saving "most adoptable animals," they are still killing as they have always done but only after unfairly labeling the animals "unadoptable."

At its conference in 2002, the American Humane Association held a "leadership forum" on the issue of what constitutes an "adoptable" animal. One of the national "leaders" they selected to present was Jane McCall of the Dubuque Humane Society in Dubuque, Iowa. She described the considerations involved not only for determining "adoptable" animals, but "treatable" animals as well. "Frequently," she wrote, "our staff also considers *resources, space, time…* to help them decide whether an animal is adoptable" (emphasis added). Under this type of reasoning, an animal can be "adoptable" at the beginning of the budget year when there is plenty of money and cages, but perhaps not at the end when resources may be in shorter supply.

Moreover, using this model means a kitten with an upper respiratory infection would potentially be "treatable" in February when there is plenty of cage space, but not in August because of "mating season" when numerous puppies and kittens enter the shelter. If the shelter chooses not to budget any money for medicine, this would potentially mean that the community does not have any "treatable" animals. As absurd as this is, the conclusion appears inescapable. By this definition, every shelter in the country is saving 100 percent of adoptable or treatable animals because when they run out of cages or money or otherwise fail to find the animal a home, the animals killed simply become "unadoptable." In other words, rather than use a common sense definition based on the individual animal's health, shelters are defining "adoptable" based on their ability or failure to find the animal a home. The end result is a tautology: "if we find the animal a home, the animal was adoptable. If we kill the animal, the animal was not adoptable." But that is not what the No Kill revolution envisioned. A shelter does not achieve No Kill by re-categorizing animals, it achieves No Kill by saving their lives.

Other shelters have been less open about their standards for adoptability. In 2002, New York City's animal control shelter killed over 70 percent of incoming dogs and cats—more than 41,000 of the 61,000 they received, a dismal failure by any standard. Indeed, overall killing had increased by four percent from the prior year according to Shelter Reform, a group that has been trying to bring a No Kill orientation to New York City's abysmal animal control system. Nonetheless, shelter leadership went on the New York State conference circuit to help other shelters achieve similar "success" just by claiming the agency was saving most "adoptable" animals, a claim contradicted by the staggering level of killing.

In Los Angeles, a memorandum from animal control to the Board of Supervisors in 2003 stated that for a three-month period that coincided with the start of the busy spring season, county shelters were saving 91.7 percent of adoptable animals, a dubious figure in light of the fact that nearly 80 percent of cats and about half of all dogs were being put to death annually.

To claim the animals being killed are largely "unadoptable," many shelters have broadened the term to the point of absurdity. And the mechanism they use—at least as it relates to assessing behavior—is a process called temperament testing.

Temperament Testing in the Age of No Kill

Temperament testing is a series of exercises designed to evaluate whether an animal is aggressive. The goal of the test is to simulate the experiences a dog might encounter in the home and evaluate whether a dog responds aggressively. For example, a dog is given food and then staff pulls it away to see how the dog reacts. Does he allow it? Does he growl? Does he bite? Or a staff member will knock on the door and pretend to be a stranger walking into a room, the way someone might at a house, and then gauge whether the dog is friendly.

To be effective, the ideal temperament test needs to do three things.

First, it should accurately evaluate a dog's behavior. If a shelter is going to label a dog as "unadoptable," kill the dog, and publicly say that it had no choice, the test must be accurate. In courtrooms across the country, DNA testing is used to determine if a defendant is guilty of a crime based on samples found at crime scenes. In the case of capital murder cases, a positive DNA match could result in a suspect or defendant being sentenced to death if convicted. The reason such tests are used is because they are incredibly accurate. Imagine for a moment if the test were not accurate. Could we justify a guilty verdict and death sentence based on a shoddy test that was wrong more often than it was right? The question, of course, answers itself: we simply could not.

Second, the test should be repeatable at different times and in different environments. If two different people test the same dog, they should get the same results. Going back to our analogy, imagine a DNA sample on a murder suspect that was sent to two different laboratories for analysis, with one test result indicating the defendant was the perpetrator of the crime and the other indicating he was innocent. Such a situation would be intolerable as a basis for making life-and-death decisions.

Third, the test should accurately predict the dog's behavior in the home. If a dog is friendly at the shelter, the test should be able to determine that the dog will be friendly in the home. If a dog is aggressive in the shelter based on this test, we would expect the dog to be aggressive in a home. In other words, a friendly dog who is scared in the shelter should not be killed.

Unfortunately, none of the standardized tests routinely used across the country today have been able to accomplish all of these goals; most do not even achieve one. To put it mildly, temperament testing requires skill and training that is not often a priority for shelters; the results vary depending on the environment in which the test is conducted and, because its predictive validity has not been established, it can and often does result in dogs being executed when they are not really aggressive.

As a result, in many—if not most—shelters across the country, dogs are being killed as unadoptable based on deeply flawed test results that are wrong more than they are right, where different shelter staff could easily get different results, and with very poor predictive validity in the home. Not only are the chances of a dog being saved in a shelter reduced by under-performing management or lack of effective policies, but often dogs must first "pass" this test of dubious value. Add to that the pressure to provide a publicly palatable reason for killing ("aggression"), and the obstacles to getting out alive are formidable.

Despite these severe limitations, HSUS published an article in the September/October 2003 issue of *Animal Sheltering* magazine, in which it created the impression that these tests generally had predictive validity. HSUS suggested that some shelters had good results with temperament testing because their return rate had declined for adopted dogs with aggression cited as the reason. Unfortunately, while this may mean fewer aggressive dogs are being adopted out, it does nothing to reduce the concern that friendly dogs are being wrongly killed. It is not enough that "no dogs" or "fewer dogs" have been returned because of aggression to a shelter that has implemented formal temperament testing, because this does not address the important issue of whether the test overreaches and is killing too many dogs.

In order to be fair, a temperament test must do two things. It must screen out aggression *and* it must ensure that friendly, scared, shy, sick, or injured dogs are not wrongly executed. By focusing on the first prong, traditional shelters have ignored the second, a violation that goes to the core of the No Kill ideal: *animals are to be judged and treated as individuals.*

Part of the problem stems from the fact that temperament testing is still in its infancy. Its development is in the gray area between laboratory analysis and clinical trials, and has a long way to go before it gains the stamp of scientific legitimacy. There are also other reasons why temperament testing is so problematic.

One reason is that dogs are highly contextual, and we can't recreate life experiences in all their complexity. We can put a doll in front of a dog, but not a little child, cooing, with arms outstretched, who wants to run up to and hug the dog. If a dog reacts badly when we attempt to look at his teeth, we can't always differentiate whether the dog is aggressive, or just in pain from lack of good dental care. Stray dogs or dogs seized from cruelty situations who are underweight and have not eaten steadily sometimes growl or snap when someone tries to take their food away (one of the tests to determine "food aggression"). If you had not eaten for a couple of days and someone put out a plate of your favorite meal in front of you but after two bites tried to take it away, you might growl, too.

Another part of the problem is the unnatural environment of the shelter from the dog's perspective. It would be difficult to design a more frustrating environment for a dog than a typical shelter: dogs thrive on socialization, familiarity, and routine, while shelters are unfamiliar places filled with strange smells, unknown people, and barren kennels. Since they can't talk and say, "Leave me alone, I am scared and don't understand what is happening to me," they communicate in the only way that biology allows—by backing up, barking, growling, and, when all else fails, snapping.

Today, in shelters across the country, staff is offering underweight and hungry stray dogs food-filled bowls, allowing the dogs to taste the food, and then removing the food. If the dog tries to prevent the food from being taken away, the dog "fails" and is killed as "unadoptable." Hunger is not aggression, but that is not recorded in final disposition logs after the dog is killed. Employees bang on the sides of kennels, and if a dog shows fear, they are "failed" and killed as "unadoptable." Being scared or shy is not aggression, but those facts are ignored. Injured dogs are being tested, and if they react—perhaps out of pain—they are killed as "unadoptable." Being injured or sick is not aggression, but that is also not considered.

THE STATE OF TEMPERAMENT TESTING

To promote temperament testing in shelters, groups like the Humane Society of the United States and the National Animal Control Association have turned to the person they call the temperament testing "expert," Sue Sternberg, who has held workshops at conferences hosted by both these groups. Sternberg was featured in an HBO special about her methods. Her test, or a variant of her test, is done in many—if not most—shelters, which employ a formal temperament testing process.*

In 1999, however, the San Francisco SPCA invited Sternberg to give a seminar on her methods in which she demonstrated them on actual shelter dogs. According to Jean Donaldson, the Director of the Academy for Dog Trainers at the San Francisco SPCA, Sternberg tested eight dogs at the shelter. Of the eight, she failed five of them or 62 percent. This is consistent with her past statements that the majority of shelter dogs are "unadoptable."

The San Francisco SPCA, finding the dogs friendly by its own standards,

---

* While some shelters claim not to temperament test, this is inaccurate. All shelters screen dogs for aggression. Where a formal test is not used, shelters rely on the casual observations of staff—also a recipe for inaccuracy and unnecessary killing.

overruled Sternberg and adopted the dogs anyway. Of the five dogs she failed for aggression, at a follow-up two years after adoption, all were still in their homes without a single incident of aggression and without any significant behavior issues. Of the three dogs she passed, one came back two weeks later with reports of inter-dog aggression and a bite of the caretaker. In simple terms, the nation's supposedly foremost expert was wrong six out of eight times (five out of five false positives, where she said the dogs were unadoptable, and one out of three false negatives, where she said the dogs were adoptable.)

San Francisco's shelters adopt out nearly 80 percent of impounded dogs annually, Tompkins County typically adopts out over 90 percent, and Charlottesville, Virginia, saved 87 percent of dogs in 2005 and 92 percent in 2006. If Sternberg is correct about the extent of aggression or unadoptability in shelter dogs, these communities would have been adopting out hundreds, if not thousands, of vicious dogs who, if temperament testing were accurate, should be attacking people or other animals in the community. In fact, they are not, and the reason is simple: *the vast majority of dogs entering shelters are friendly.*

From 2001-2004, while I was executive director of the open-door Tompkins County SPCA, all dogs in our shelter who were at least five months of age were tested for aggression against people, dogs, and cats. Staff members conducting the test were trained by the Department of Behavioral Medicine at the Cornell University College of Veterinary Medicine. A veterinary resident seeking Board Certification in Behavior Medicine reviewed staff determinations in many cases, and if aggression was noted, the dog was rehabilitated, sent for further testing, or killed, depending on the prognosis.

As the animal control authority for all of Tompkins County, the Tompkins County SPCA took in dogs of all breeds, ages, and circumstances. The shelter seized or took in aggressive dogs under New York State dangerous dog laws, all strays, dogs people no longer wanted, dogs that scratched or bit, and dogs of every conceivable history and temperament. Yet in 2003, 93 percent of all the dogs impounded passed the temperament evaluation. The Tompkins County SPCA has proven that more than nine out of ten dogs who enter an animal control shelter are not only savable, they are safe to place into homes with children and other animals—results verified over a one-year period after the dogs were adopted out. Based on telephone interviews with adopters at two weeks and six months, and a study of dogs returned to the shelter over a period of one year, only three dogs out of all who were adopted during this period exhibited true aggression in the home. This is a false negative rate of less than half of one percent (0.3 percent to be exact). A shelter—including an animal control shelter—can be fair to dogs and also cognizant of public safety.

To be fair to the dogs while keeping truly vicious dogs out of a shelter's adoption program, shelters need to thoroughly train staff, make sure that rehabilitation efforts are comprehensive, and embrace a pro-dog culture of lifesaving. In other words, they have to adopt the central tenet of the No Kill philosophy: *accountability*. The elements of a fair aggression evaluation include an opportunity for a dog to acclimate to the shelter before being screened, a medical review to ensure the dog is healthy and at least of normal body weight, a culture of lifesaving among the staff, a socialization and training regimen, retesting by highly skilled professionals, a discussion about prognosis if aggression is noted, rehabilitation for aggression issues with a fair prognosis, and the liberal use of foster care. These elements, while generally missing from current standardized tests and traditional kill-oriented philosophies, were all embraced by the Tompkins County SPCA during my tenure.*

In Tompkins County, dogs entering the shelter were given three days to feel comfortable in the shelter environment, during which time they were given a thorough medical screening and were walked and treated kindly. After they were evaluated, dogs who demonstrated perceived aggression were put through a series of follow-up tests, including review by a veterinarian from the Cornell University Veterinary College Department of Behavior Medicine. In the first year, despite a staff dedicated to the No Kill paradigm, Cornell overruled the staff's assessment that a dog had failed a temperament test over 70 percent of the time. Instead, they recommended the dog be adopted because the dog was not actually aggressive, or, in a more limited number of cases, that the dog be put through a behavior rehabilitation protocol and then retested before being made available for adoption. In the vast majority of cases, this recommendation was followed

---

* Finally, an effective and fair aggression screening process must also *exclude* one important element: shelters need to stop looking for reasons to fail a dog. A formal, fair, and thorough process will *increase* the number of dogs who are deemed "adoptable" because over 90 percent of dogs entering shelters are friendly. Unfortunately, temperament testing is misused by shelters to find reasons to kill dogs.

and the dog subsequently "passed" and was adopted into a home with no incidents of aggression.

To be accountable to the animals, furthermore, the shelter did not temperament test cats. In most shelters, cats are relegated to tiny cages. This not only precludes species-typical behavior, but requires them to sleep, eat, and defecate in the same space, something so contrary to feline behavior that it is nearly impossible to accurately assess a cat in that environment. Truly feral cats aside, many friendly cats appear shy, fearful, and defensive in the shelter ("aggressive" is almost never the proper term for a cat with behavior problems), but then blossom after placement in foster or after adoption in a home. In Tompkins County, moreover, cats were never killed for behavior reasons during my tenure. Feral cats were sterilized and returned to their original habitat or released elsewhere, such as barns or other suitable locations. Since semi-social cats with behavior issues do not pose the kind of threat to public safety that would preclude adoption or alternative placement like a barn or feral colony, these cats were placed as well. The terms "fractious cat," "aggressive cat," or "feral cat" meant only that shelter staff employed different strategies for placement or adoption—they were not a death sentence for any cat.

Except for long-term holding facilities in sanctuaries that are in short supply, however, there are currently no such options for vicious dogs. As a result, a truly vicious dog faces a death sentence. The decision to end a dog's life is extremely serious, and should always be treated as such. No matter how many animals a shelter kills, each and every one is an individual and deserves individual consideration. A dog may appear aggressive, but in reality he may simply be frightened by his new surroundings and by being away from the only family he has ever known. Being able to determine whether a dog is truly aggressive or merely frightened can mean the difference between life and death. A fair policy helps ensure the decision is reached correctly.

Implicit within the No Kill philosophy is the understanding that some animals, such as those who are irremediably suffering or hopelessly ill, will be killed for reasons of mercy. A sick, injured, or traumatized animal with a behavior problem, however, can have several possible prognoses, one of the complexities a shelter should consider in determining a strategy post-temperament testing. If the prognosis for rehabilitation is good to guarded, a No Kill shelter is obligated to provide treatment. In the No Kill paradigm, the only animals who are killed are those with a poor prognosis for rehabilitation. Conditions such as upper respiratory infections, broken bones, and, in the case of behavior, food-related guarding, are usually treatable. In three years of the Tompkins County SPCA's temperament testing protocol, a dog was never killed for food guarding because the prognosis for rehabilitation was always good, and *none of these dogs ever bit anyone after adoption.*

The No Kill philosophy's break from traditional methods of sheltering is underscored by fundamental fairness to the animals. This commitment to fairness is echoed in the mission statement of virtually every humane society and SPCA in the country that claims to cherish animals, enforce their rights, and teach compassion. These goals can only be achieved if shelters judge, treat, and devise a plan for each and every animal with all the resources they can muster. But that is not the process being advocated by most shelters and national groups. This disparity—an animal control shelter saving more than nine out of ten dogs while most are claiming that the majority of their dogs are "unadoptable"—is striking. But the contradiction rises to absurd levels when one considers the fate—and Sternberg's view—of the "dreaded" American Pit Bull Terrier.

Failing the American Pit Bull Terrier

There is no breed of dog in America more abused, maligned, and misrepresented than the American Pit Bull Terrier. There is no breed of dog more in need of the humane movement's compassion, in need of a call to arms on its behalf, and in need of what should be the full force of a shelter's sanctuary. Many shelters, however, have determined that these dogs are not worthy of their help. They have determined that Pit Bulls do not deserve to live.

The more circumspect among them might not say so publicly. They may couch it in more benign terms, shifting the blame to others, claiming that no one will adopt them, convincing themselves that only a ban *and death* will keep them out of harm's way, but the end result is exactly the same. By their actions, words, policies, and failure to speak out positively on behalf of Pit Bulls, they stoke the fire that has at its core only one end: *their mass killing.* To a breed abused for fighting, victimized by an undeserved reputation, relegated to certain death in shelters, add one more torment: those who should be their most ardent protectors have instead turned against them. The humane movement has joined the witch hunt. The very agencies whose officers seek out dog fighters and abusers in order to "save" Pit Bulls often relegate the dogs to locked and barren corridors away from public view with no hope of adoption, regardless of their temperament. Ultimately, all of them—the healthy and friendly ones, side-by-side with the hopelessly sick or vicious—are put to death.

In Multnomah County, Oregon, Pit Bulls are killed *en masse* in a shelter that claims it is near No Kill by using temperament testing to find reasons to fail Pit Bulls, creating a virtually *de facto* ban on the breed. In Denver, Colorado, they have simply been outlawed and executed. And People for the Ethical Treatment of Animals, the nation's most outspoken animal rights group, has joined the battle to exterminate these dogs—demanding that all cities ban the breed, and that all Pit Bulls who enter shelters seeking sanctuary be killed. According to Ingrid Newkirk, PETA's founder and president,

> [m]ost people have no idea that at many animal shelters across the country, any *"pit bull"* who comes through the front door goes out the back door—in a body bag. From San Jose to Schenectady, many shelters have enacted policies requiring the automatic destruction of the huge and ever-growing number of *"pits"* they encounter. This news shocks and outrages the compassionate dog-lover. Here's another shocker: People for the Ethical Treatment of Animals, the very people who are trying to get you to denounce the killing of chickens for the table, foxes for fur, or frogs for dissection, supports the pit bull policy...

Ending the tragic plight of the American Pit Bull Terrier should be among the humane movement's most ardent goals. Humane groups must remind people that the Pit Bull's misfortune is in finding itself the favored breed of the dog fighter at this time in history—a distinction shared at one point by the German Shepherd, Doberman, and Rottweiler. This is a distinction that will shift to another breed if Pit Bulls are banned but the scourge of dog fighting is not ended.

Rather than rally against an injustice which condemns an entire breed of dogs to death—literally hundreds of thousands of dogs a year—shelters have failed the Pit Bull completely. And one of those leading the charge is none other than the dog behavior expert championed by HSUS and NACA, Sue Sternberg. In her training video, *The Controversial Pit Bull*, Sternberg claims most Pit Bulls are aggressive to other dogs and cats and perhaps even children, a statement that flies in the face of Tompkins County's experience. Sternberg goes further, claiming that even if they are friendly, they should not be adopted into homes with children because they are

> *very strong, very powerful, the tail alone will cause bruises on a small child. And they have no boundaries, so when they go to kiss you, as my friend who used to do Pit Bull rescue [found out], knocked her front tooth out [and caused] $500 worth of bonding. Just saying hello.*

Due to a strong, swishing tail and a freak accident involving her friend, the woman considered to be the foremost temperament testing expert by shelters nationwide says Pit Bulls should not be adopted by families with children. This point of view would be ludicrous if the end result—the slaughter of healthy, friendly dogs nationwide—were not so tragic.

In Tompkins County, by contrast, if one isolates "Pit Bulls," a breed condemned by Sternberg as generally being aggressive to cats and other dogs and otherwise dangerous to kids, nearly nine out of ten of them—86 percent—passed temperament testing and were adopted in 2002. It is also worth noting that Sternberg's shelter, where she claims the Pit Bulls who come in are "unadoptable" is also in Upstate New York—a three-hour drive door-to-door from the Tompkins County SPCA. The point is worth underscoring. In Tompkins County's animal control facility, 86 percent of all Pit Bulls impounded were found to be friendly to kids, other dogs, and cats, and were all adopted. This occurred in the same region of the country, in the same state, a few short hours drive from the shelter of the nation's expert who says the vast majority of Pit Bulls in her shelter should be killed. It is a contradiction that can only be reconciled one way—Sternberg is wrong.

Not only does the experience of Tompkins County prove this point, national outside-the-shelter testing does, too. According to the American Temperament Test Results for 2004, the three breeds commonly referred to as "Pit Bulls"—the American Pit Bull Terrier, the American Staffordshire Terrier, and the Staffordshire Bull Terrier—had a combined passing rate of 86.6 percent, virtually the same as found in Tompkins County, and, interestingly, a pass rate higher than the Golden Retriever.

The hypocrisy of this kill-oriented sheltering philosophy finds no better example than in Denver, Colorado, where in 2005 local authorities began enforcing a law making it illegal to have a Pit Bull as a pet. Banning Pit Bulls or any breed of dog is geared to overkill by definition because—media hysteria to the contrary—the vast majority of dog bites occur within the home by many breeds, with the dog biting a member of the family after some provocation, a different causal mechanism than the false image presented: an epidemic of free roaming Pit Bulls attacking unknown children or the elderly. As a result, a breed ban won't stop the vast majority of dog bites. Nonetheless, Denver newspaper reports describe police officers seizing friendly pet Pit Bulls from homes on threat of arrest, again putting the lie to the claim that shelters are killing because of public irresponsibility.

While groups like the Fund For Animals whitewash the truth, saying that shelters are doing the "public's dirty work," the truth is more sanguine: the work is dirty, but it is not the public's. In the case of Denver's Pit Bulls, the lie is two-fold because people are not discarding them: government animal control and police agencies are taking cherished family members on threat of arrest—only to put the poor creatures to death. This is *your* American animal shelter, the one that blames *you* for the killing.*

In shelters throughout the United States it doesn't matter if dogs are healthy, friendly, scared, sick, or injured, they can be classified as "unadoptable" and killed. As a result, the public is misled into believing that shelters are doing the right thing. In turn, the moral hypocrisy of telling the public it shouldn't treat animals as disposable by dumping them in shelters, and then having the shelters treat them exactly as if they were disposable by killing them, disappears.

No one wants hopelessly ill or injured dogs and cats kept alive while irremediably suffering, because that is cruel. No one wants truly vicious dogs placed into the community, because that is dangerous. But over 90 percent of dogs entering shelters are neither hopelessly suffering nor vicious, yet they are being labeled as such. They have only one thing going against them, which today is punishable by death: they have entered a shelter that has not embraced a culture of lifesaving.

With temperament testing, traditional shelters found a tool to maintain their leadership position in the humane movement by claiming they

---

* It is worth noting that some families chose to move out of the city to avoid having their dogs killed.

are on their way to saving adoptable animals. They only had to do one more thing to cement their positions: silence the voices that remained openly critical. In 2004, ostensibly to find ways to reduce shelter killing, the self-proclaimed national "leaders" met for a third time, as they had twice before, once in Chicago (1974) and two years later in Denver (1976). The faces may have been different, but many of the same groups were represented, most notably the Humane Society of the United States, the ASPCA, and the American Humane Association. Several local shelters and animal control agencies, along with the National Animal Control Association, joined them. Like before, the stated goals were lofty and, once again, the effort was doomed to failure from the start.

Backlash

"The definition of insanity is doing the same thing over and over and expecting a different result."

—Various attributions

IN 2004, the Humane Society of the United States, the American Humane Association, the ASPCA, local animal control shelters, and a few new players on the national scene met in Asilomar, California, on the Monterey Bay Peninsula. Like the meetings in Chicago and Denver of the mid-to-late 1970s, the stated goal was to find "solutions" to the killing of dogs and cats in shelters—as they put it, "creating goals focused on significantly reducing the euthanasia of healthy and treatable companion animals in the United States." The roadmap to the future they came up with was christened the "Asilomar Accords." These were a series of guidelines of how shelters and others in the humane community should operate. Almost immediately, they pledged to promote the *Accords* and achieve their national acceptance and have been working to do so ever since.

Had they been truly looking for a path to No Kill, it would not have been hard to find. The programs and services that made San Francisco the first city to end the killing of healthy dogs and cats were the same programs that allowed Tompkins County to become the nation's first No Kill community. In addition, this meeting should have brought with it the lesson of two prior failed attempts (Chicago in 1974 and Denver in 1976) that success could not be achieved with a focus on consensus so long as individual groups participating could thwart effective remedies, the way the AVMA did with low-cost spay/neuter three decades earlier. Leadership, by definition, leads; it never waits for consensus.

But they did not lead. With consensus once again the stated goal, and with the participation of groups hostile to the No Kill paradigm invited, there was no hope for success. Efforts to advocate for national promotion of TNR for feral cats, for example, were considered and voted down, despite decades of proof that it was not only humane, but that significantly reducing the killing of cats was simply impossible without it. In order to avoid alienating groups opposed to them, the programs that San Francisco and Tompkins County proved were necessary to save lives, like TNR, were simply left to "local decision-making." This effectively legitimized inaction by local shelters opposed to implementing the programs necessary for No Kill.

In other words, a shelter can still kill feral cats, keep volunteers out of the shelter, fail to spay/neuter their own animals, pass punitive laws to punish compassion, and more without running afoul of the *Asilomar Accords*—all in direct contravention of the programs vital to No Kill success, and all policies that result in unnecessary killing. The *Asilomar Accords* give truth to the adage that "the definition of insanity is doing the same thing over and over and expecting a different result." By seeking consensus and ignoring a track record of success in San Francisco and Tompkins County, the national groups once again promoted a plan that not only legitimized shelter killing, but offered no hope of doing anything about it.

While many animals are left without protection under the *Asilomar Accords*, no animal potentially suffers more—or is given such short shrift—under this "new" vision for animal control than the feral cat. Not only do the *Accords* fail to mention TNR or require groups to accept TNR, they classify feral cats as "untreatable" or "unhealthy." According to the *Accords*, feral cats fall into the category of those animals who "suffer from a behavioral or temperamental characteristic that poses a health or safety risk or otherwise makes them unsuitable for placement as a pet." Under the *Accords*, feral cats share the same category as hopelessly ill or irremediably suffering pets, and the same fate: *death*.

While feral cats are not generally suitable for placement as pets, this should not mean they do not have an equal right to live, or that the humane movement isn't obligated to put in place non-lethal alternatives. A commitment to both of these principles requires identifying feral cats as their own category—feral cats—and then making an equal commitment to TNR and pro-feral advocacy to bring an end to their killing. The *Accords* do neither.

The bias is not hard to see. While the *Accords* demand very little of traditional shelters, they do make one demand of No Kill groups—that they cease using the term "No Kill" because it makes kill-oriented shelters look bad. In January of 2005, for example, HSUS sent a representative to Atlanta to meet with local shelters and rescue groups. At the meeting, HSUS chastised the groups present, demanding they cease using the word "kill" to describe the killing of shelter animals and "No Kill" to describe the alternative, claiming that this was required under the *Accords*.

From a historical perspective, No Kill shelters and rescue groups have been vilified by the proponents of the status quo, their successes misrepresented from coast to coast. Attacking No Kill advocates for hurtful language that is supposedly "inflammatory and misleading" as some of the Asilomar participants claimed, therefore, is a classic case of the pot calling the kettle black. In addition, such a position cannot be reconciled with other misleading terms of which these shelters are fond, terms like "euthanasia," which is a euphemism that obscures the gravity of killing, or the term "untreatable" to define healthy feral cats.

DOES LANGUAGE MATTER?

Webster's dictionary defines euthanasia as "the act or practice of killing or permitting the death of hopelessly sick or injured individuals in a relatively painless way for reasons of mercy." Using the term "euthanasia" when a shelter is killing for population control, because it has run out of cages, or because the shelter is opposed to TNR or other progressive programs is misleading and an incorrect usage of the term. The killing in these cases has nothing to do with the animals being "hopelessly sick or injured" and it is not merciful when applied to healthy or treatable pets.

Nor is it always entirely painless, as anyone who has witnessed the killing of animals in a shelter can attest. With some animals there is fear, disorientation, nausea, and many times even a struggle. A dog who is skittish, for example, is made even more fearful by the smells and surroundings of an animal shelter. He doesn't understand why he is there and away from the only family he has ever loved. For this dog to be killed, he may have to be "catch-poled" with a device that wraps a hard-wire noose around the dog's neck. These dogs often struggle to free themselves from the grip, which results in more fear and pain when they realize they cannot. They often urinate and defecate on themselves, unsure of what is occurring. Often the head is held hard to the ground or against the wall so that another staff member can enter the kennel and inject him with a sedative. While the catch-pole is left tied around the neck, the dog struggles to maintain his balance, dragging the pole, until he slumps to the ground. Slowly—fearful, often soiled in his own waste, confused—he tries to stand, but his legs give way. He goes limp and then unconscious. That is when staff administer the fatal dose.

If any word in the vernacular of animal sheltering is misleading, it is the term "euthanasia." Shelters should no more use it when reporting statistics or when discussing killing than they should in their interactions with the public or each other. "Euphemisms are misnomers used to disguise or cloak the identity of ugly facts," wrote one commentator. To which the noted writer Albert Camus added, "The truth is the truth, and denying it mocks the cause both of humanity and of morality." A more fitting description of the use of "euthanasia" to describe shelter killing could not have been written.

These euphemisms, however, served a purpose for the participants at Asilomar, while the term "No Kill" did not. They were trying to co-opt No Kill and reclaim control of sheltering politics by eliminating the moral high ground of the words themselves: ban "No Kill," call it something less appealing to the public ("limited admission") and reassert control. This tactic was not surprising, given that some participants and signatories had a long, dismal history of lifesaving: Fort Wayne, Indiana, animal control, for example, killed 76 percent of all impounded domestic animals in 2003 (the vast majority of whom were dogs and cats), while the Southeast Area Animal Control Authority in Southern California killed more than 90 percent of cats it impounded the same year. What is surprising, however, is that the *Accords* found support in Richard Avanzino.

According to Avanzino, if the large national groups and local shelters supported the one element of the *Accords* he believed in—transparency in statistics—the rest would follow over time. In other words, by getting agreement from these organizations to make their life and death rates open to anyone who was interested in them, Avanzino was betting that the animal advocates in the community would demand more lifesaving when they realized how poorly many of their shelters were doing. He believed that this grassroots uprising would compel the shelters to embrace No Kill over time. As he put it, "the American people will insist that the killing ends."

Avanzino uses the analogy of our founding fathers for this proposition. He argues that when the framers of the Declaration of Independence signed the historic document, they were not committing themselves to an egalitarian society. Nonetheless by subscribing to a document that stated "all men were created equal," the disparity between claim and reality became the focal point for the suffrage and civil rights movements that followed. In the end, there was no choice but to acknowledge equality under the law. Avanzino explains:

> *The Asilomar Accords were a compromise to get buy-in. We had to make concessions in order to get transparency of statistics. It is a flawed document, imperfect. It isn't what we wanted in total. But it is a starting point. Because without a collaborative, community-based process, there is no way to achieve No Kill.*

There are significant problems with this viewpoint. First, Avanzino was only one vote among many of the ultimate signatories. And under the reporting system which was ultimately approved by the groups in attendance, shelters are not required to provide raw data. Rather, in tallying final results and for reporting to the public, the *Asilomar Accords* allow shelters to report numbers that do not include entire categories of animals, including those they deem unhealthy and untreatable, animals who have died in the kennel and feral cats. The result is a skewed figure that literally sweeps these animals under the rug. They simply do not count. Their lives are erased from public records.

A shelter succeeds at saving all healthy and treatable dogs and cats, including feral cats, when it is saving roughly 90 to 95 percent of all impounded animals. Unfortunately, a small percentage (well under 10 percent) tend to be irremediably suffering, hopelessly ill, or, in the case of dogs, vicious with a poor prognosis for rehabilitation. To make it easy for animal advocates to determine whether their shelter is doing a good job, Avanzino should have insisted on publishing both raw intake and disposition data and the live release rate (the percentage of all animals who leave the shelter alive). Since deciphering shelter statistics is difficult, simply requiring signatories like Fort Wayne, Indiana animal control to say "we killed some 9,000 dogs and cats in 2003 and only 26 percent of all domestic animals were saved" would give community advocates the information they need to judge how lousy a job at saving lives its shelter is doing. Instead, the *Accords* report lifesaving only after the deaths are filtered through a subjective and often self-serving categorization of "adoptable" versus "unadoptable."

As a result, the *Accords* are using categories to "spin" the numbers to make it appear a shelter is doing a better job than it actually is. While the *Accords* claim to seek transparency and "the open sharing of accurate, complete animal-sheltering data and statistics in a manner which is clear to both the animal welfare community and the public," the model advanced and agreed upon for collecting that data is far from "accurate" or "complete." The categories they agreed to, for example, are vague in and of themselves, leading to misuse and misapplication. Many shelters call kittens with ringworm "untreatable," or say that a dog who is scared or shy has a "temperamental characteristic that poses a health or safety risk or otherwise makes them unsuitable for placement." These results are entirely consistent with the *Accords*, even though ringworm is not only highly treatable, it is self-limiting, meaning that it can resolve on its own, while shy dogs can be readily adopted.

Second, unlike a document such as the United States Constitution, the agreements in the *Asilomar Accords* are not enforceable. In fact, my efforts to get statistics from some of the signatories were ignored. As a result, the call for "transparency" by Avanzino has not been heeded by all its signatories. This should have been no surprise to Avanzino since many of the signatories were the San Francisco SPCA's most vociferous and misleading critics during his tenure. Integrity has not historically been their strong suit.

Third, why should any more animals have to die unnecessarily? Shelters know how to save lives. They know how to end the killing. What are they waiting for? More importantly, why agree to a document that undermines the programs and services that make No Kill possible? Why not simply agree to an accord on record keeping? By narrowing the scope of the document, Avanzino could have avoided alienating those who had been his strongest supporters.

Fourth, over two years after the *Asilomar Accords* were signed, the document continues to be used to avoid public accountability, with some of its signatories adhering only to those passages which shield them from public criticism and accountability, exactly the opposite of what Avanzino envisioned. Otherwise, how could one explain why some of the groups refuse to provide statistics when requested to do so?

Fifth, in his defense of the *Accords*, Avanzino argues that each commu-nity should have the power to determine what the lifesaving expectations should be for their local shelter. In other words, community consensus should determine the level of commitment to the No Kill endeavor. This view is reckless. Shelters have always had this power and the results have been an appallingly high death rate. For the last several decades, shelters all over the United States have made the choice to kill in the face of No Kill alternatives. A document that claims to seek an end to unnecessary shelter deaths but then allows shelters with historically high death rates to deter-mine their own level of commitment to ending that killing is analogous to asking the Southern states immediately after the Civil War to interpret for themselves the thirteenth and fourteenth amendments to the Constitution.

Sixth, just because these groups agree to something in writing does not mean they will ultimately embrace it in practice. In the mission statement of virtually every humane society or SPCA, for example, is some variant of the statement that "all life is precious." Despite 100-year-old mission state-ments of this kind, shelters continue to ignore the credo daily every time they kill a dog or cat in the face of a No Kill alternative. The Humane Society of the United States has a mission statement which, among other things, claims to "celebrate the benefits of the bond between people and an-imals who live with us or in our communities, and teach people how to solve human/animal conflicts humanely." How can this be reconciled with their support for the killing of healthy dogs and cats in shelters every year? Or with their claim that mass killing of feral cats was the only "practical and humane" solution? How can this be squared with their call to deni-grate cats by encouraging shelters to "document public health problems that relate to cats. Include diseases that are spread from cat to cat as well as those spread between cats and other animals"? Or, the claims that cats decimate wildlife, are a public rabies threat, are invasive, non-native intrud-ers, and contribute to neighborhood strife?

Seventh, at the time the Declaration of Independence and U.S. Constitution were written, the world was a series of monarchies based on the arbitrary rule of a few. Ancient regimes notwithstanding, modern democ-racy was non-existent and these documents were a radical step *forward* for society. By contrast, San Francisco had stopped killing healthy dogs and cats ten years before the *Asilomar Accords* were signed, and Tompkins County had been No Kill for two years. One does not negotiate a vision for the future of sheltering that is a radical step *backward* from what the No Kill movement has already achieved.

Finally, animals in shelters are being killed because local shelters continue to cling to kill-oriented practices. Sanctioning or allowing for local practices that permit killing to continue is no way to bring an end to the killing. As a result, the No Kill paradigm and the *Asilomar Accords* are irreconcilable. When two philosophies are mutually exclusive, as No Kill and the voices of the status quo are, agreement can only come about when No Kill's hegemony is firmly established and the old philosophies and practices are abandoned. In the end, this is not a war of "ideas." It is a life-and-death struggle for saving shelter animals. Either they live or they do not. No Kill demands that they do.

As a result, Avanzino's goals for the *Asilomar Accords* are incompatible with the actual document. His view is misinformed because it continues to ignore a vital truth: *most of the time, animal control and large private shelters vested in the status quo do not feel compelled to change.* As long as this is true, any effort that is predicated on collaboration with these groups will fail. While the *Accords* focus on building collaborations, they allow shelters to work actively against No Kill by killing rather than sterilizing feral cats, keeping volunteers out of the shelter, and using temperament testing to unfairly label dogs "unadoptable."

Collaboration is Not Always Key

To the extent a shelter isn't implementing the No Kill Equation, animals are needlessly being killed. Since No Kill advocates must represent the interests of the animals, they must first demand and then fight for these programs. Throughout the United States right now, however, there is a major roadblock to this occurring: the old guard of shelter directors who will not implement these No Kill solutions because they are content with the status quo. They have accepted killing even in the face of lifesaving alternatives. No list of excuses can change the simple fact that the biggest barrier to No Kill success in any given community is often the individual who runs animal control or the large private shelter in a community; this single person can make or break No Kill success.

While achieving No Kill is certainly made easier if all shelters in a community are willing to work together, collaboration only works when

animal control or private shelters are dedicated to the No Kill endeavor.*
If they are not, a focus on collaboration can actually delay lifesaving efforts
or even doom them altogether. In such cases, the effort at coalition building detracts from the real impediment to saving lives: reforming the animal
shelter or forcing regime change within those agencies whose directors
continue to cling to outdated models of sheltering.

In short, a community that comprehensively implements each and
every program and service of the No Kill Equation will succeed. Those
communities that focus on collaboration instead will fail as long as leadership of the major shelters is not committed to the No Kill paradigm. If collaboration is so important, why hasn't it created No Kill? In fact, there is
not a single community in the United States where collaboration has actually led to No Kill success. It has utterly failed and will continue to fail for
the simple reason that while large national organizations like the Humane
Society of the United States continue to push the idea that all humane societies and animal control agencies are interested in the same goals, the
facts frequently tell a different story, one of intransigent, reactionary policies that cause animals to die needlessly even in the face of lifesaving alternatives. This is the status quo in many communities throughout the
United States and it begs the question of why—despite overwhelming evidence to the contrary—anyone would continue to believe that collaboration is the key to No Kill success.

Furthermore, in a movement of conscience, promoting unity above
spirited debate can lead to stagnation, and may even allow animals to continue to suffer. If achieving movement unity is the primary goal that
trumps all others, there would be no TNR, nor would there be a No Kill
movement, because these efforts were begun largely in opposition to and
disagreement with the views of traditional shelters. Disagreement in the
advancement of saving lives is absolutely crucial to the vitality of No Kill
and is our great hope for the future of this movement. In the end, success
will only be guaranteed when all shelters and animal welfare groups fully
embrace—or are forced to embrace—the No Kill paradigm, not when we
cease demanding that they do.

Instead, in the *Accords* we have a "vision" for the future which allows

---

* There are many different animal welfare "stakeholders" in a particular community, including municipal animal control shelters, private shelters, rescue groups, advocacy organizations, feral cat TNR groups, and individual animal rescuers.

feral cats to be killed without recrimination, cats and dogs to be killed under draconian animal ordinances, and shelters to continue to oppose the very programs that brought No Kill success to other communities. Its signatories contend that we must all work together, even when they refuse to do what is necessary to stop the killing.

With the *Accords* and the "can't we just all get along" model being promoted to the detriment of shelter animals, the national non-profit No Kill Advocacy Center, in conjunction with Alley Cat Allies, responded with an alternative—"*The Declaration of the No Kill Movement in the United States.*" It calls upon communities to implement the programs and services of the No Kill Equation, and for shelters to open their doors to public scrutiny. It provides guiding principles, a statement of demands, and a roadmap to saving lives. In the end, it calls for shelters to bring about an end to the killing without delay. (The *Declaration* appears in appendix I.)

The *Declaration* proves the irreconcilability between the No Kill philosophy on the one hand and, on the other, the archaic voices of tradition. Unlike the *Asilomar Accords*, which allow shelters to ignore the programs of the No Kill Equation (leaving these pivotal programs to "local decision-making"), the No Kill *Declaration* calls for comprehensive and rigorous adoption of all of them. Sadly, not one of the signatories of the *Accords* has endorsed the *Declaration*.

Within a day of its publication in September of 2005, however, thousands of individuals and animal groups did pledge their support, and thousands more have signed it since. Its popularity, compared with the scarcity of support the *Accords* have garnered, is due to one simple fact about which Avanzino was right: Americans are tired of the killing. The *Declaration* embodies the fully idealized version of the lifesaving philosophy of No Kill, and the public supports it wholeheartedly.

If we are to reach the goal of a No Kill nation, we must move past the notion that animals are being killed because of pet overpopulation, because we don't have enough laws, or because the public is irresponsible. We must no longer accept criticisms of programs that are successful, and we must insist on their immediate implementation. Finally, we must stop pretending that the animal lover saving feral cats in the neighborhood, the rescuer who finds homes for wayward dogs, and the No Kill shelter which believes and practices the maxim that all life is precious are all a part of the same movement as the animal control director who is content to pass the blame to others and who kills animals in the face of alternatives. All of these are the great myths at the core of shelter killing. And they have, as their genesis, the entirely false belief that we are a nation of "too many animals and not enough homes." This is a claim that is unassailably false for many reasons, not the least of which is something that can be found in shelters every single day.

The Myth of Pet Overpopulation

"Custom will reconcile people to any atrocity."

—William Shakespeare (circa 1600)

SOMETIMES THE OBVIOUS eludes us. We are told something so often that we accept it *a priori*. We ignore evidence to the contrary, even overwhelming evidence. It is so because we believe it is so. And we believe it is so because we have been told it is so for as long as we can remember. Each time we say, read, or write it, we reconfirm it. It is so. It is so. It is so. But pet overpop- ulation is *not* so.

There is little reason why most people, your average animal lovers in the United States, would know pet overpopulation is a myth. The one fact that would dispel the myth is something they almost never see consistent- ly because they do not go to shelters everyday. But animal rescuers see it. Animal activists see it. And others in sheltering do also. They see it daily, but still believe in pet overpopulation. What do they see every time they go into animal shelters? They see empty cages. Shelters kill dogs and cats every single day, despite empty cages.

The City of Los Angeles Animal Services Department kills every day despite empty cages. A veterinarian who tried to keep more animals alive by keeping the cages full was fired in 2005, in part, due to staff complaints of "too much work." In September of 2006, the Department killed twenty-five kittens because they had a cold, despite empty cages. In Eugene, Oregon, activists noted a high percentage of empty cages at their local shelter in the summer of 2006 due to killing that shelter management blamed on pet overpopulation and a lack of a cat licensing law. The Lane County Animal Regulation Authority kept all but a half dozen cat cages empty at the height of the busy season, even though it killed approximately 70 percent of cats during the last year, many of them ostensibly for "lack of space." According to local activists, doing so makes it easier for staff to clean. In Philadelphia before a new leadership team took over later that year, I counted over seventy empty cat cages in February of 2005 on a day they were killing "for space." These are not isolated examples. They are epidemic—and endemic—to animal control.

Empty cages mean less cleaning, less feeding, less work. Some shelter directors simply don't care and do it for that reason. Others do it because they falsely believe that no one will adopt the animals anyway. Still others kill because they believe the cages will get full. And others—such as Tompkins County before my arrival—require a certain number of animals to be killed in the morning to make room for the new animals they expect that day—animals who might or might not come, animals who might come after those animals killed could have been adopted, lost animals who might be reclaimed, thereby opening up space without the need to kill, animals who instead could have been transferred to rescue groups or placed into foster care.

There are many reasons why shelters kill animals at this point in time, but pet overpopulation is not one of them. In the case of a small percentage of animals, the animals may be hopelessly sick or injured, or the dogs are so vicious that placing them would put adoptive families at risk.* Aside from this relatively small number of cases (only seven percent of the animals in Tompkins County), shelters also kill for less merciful reasons.

They kill because they make the animals sick through sloppy cleaning and poor handling. They kill because they do not want to care for sick animals. They kill because they do not effectively use the Internet and the media to promote their pets. They kill because they think volunteers are more trouble than they are worth, even though those volunteers would help to eliminate the "need" for killing. They kill because they don't want a foster care program. They kill because they are only open for adoption when people are at work and families have their children in school. They

---

* This killing is also being challenged by sanctuaries and hospice care groups, a movement that is also growing in scale and scope and which all compassionate people must embrace.

kill because they discourage visitors with their poor customer service. They kill because they do not help people overcome problems that can reduce impounds. They kill because they refuse to work with rescue groups. They kill because they haven't embraced TNR for feral cats. They kill because they won't socialize feral kittens. They kill because they don't walk the dogs, which makes the dogs so highly stressed that they become "cage crazy." They then kill them for being "cage crazy." They kill because their shoddy tests allow them to claim the animals are "unadoptable." They kill because their draconian laws empower them to kill.

Some kill because they are steeped in a culture of defeatism, or because they are under the thumb of regressive health or police department oversight. But they still kill. They never say, "we kill because we have accepted killing in lieu of having to put in place foster care, pet retention, volunteer, TNR, public relations, and other programs." In short, they kill because they have failed to do what is necessary to stop killing.

What allows them to continue killing without total condemnation for doing so is the religion of pet overpopulation. It is the political cover that prevents even the animal rescuers and advocates from demanding an immediate end to the whole bloody mess. And, at its core, it is an unsupportable myth. The syllogism goes as follows: shelters kill a lot of animals; shelters adopt out few of them; therefore, there are more animals than homes. Hence, there is pet overpopulation. It is as faulty a syllogism and as untrue a proposition as exists in sheltering today. But people believe it, and because they do, local governments under-fund their shelters, appoint and retain incompetent employees in animal control, and give shelter directors the *carte blanche* they need to kill because the problem is portrayed as insurmountable.*

* This also begs the question of why pet stores and commercial breeding operations (sometimes referred to as "puppy mills" or "kitten mills") are still in business. Hobby breed enthusiasts notwithstanding (since these groups often support No Kill and assist in animal rescue), pet stores and puppy/kitten mills are motivated by profit, and they would not go into the business if homes weren't available. In addition, the more animals dying in a given community (which traditionalists claim means lack of homes), the greater number of pet stores that sell dogs and cats (which shows homes readily available). Generally, pet stores succeed when a shelter is not meeting market demand or competing effectively, and because animal lovers do not want to go into a shelter that kills the vast majority of the animals as this is usually accompanied with under-performing staff, poor customer service, and dirty and unwelcoming facilities.

In 2005, Best Friends Animal Society, the nation's largest sanctuary for animals, retold on its website the story of a dog named Lorenzo as follows:

Black dogs are a dime a dozen. Big dogs are hard to find homes for. Poor Lorenzo was both. He had been at St. Joseph's Animal Control and Rescue in Missouri for over 15 days and was taking up precious space in the municipal shelter world. It was time.

There are three misstatements in this paragraph. The first is that "black dogs are a dime a dozen." As we shall see below, there are twice as many homes for dogs available each year in the United States than the number of dogs entering shelters. The second error is that "big dogs are hard to find homes for." Lorenzo would prove the faultiness of this statement himself, and it is also borne out by the experiences of San Francisco, Tompkins County, and as we shall see, other cities. The third, and most important, misstatement is the notion that "it was time." Time for what? If Best Friends agreed with St. Joseph Animal Control staff that it was time to kill Lorenzo because he was big and black or because he had been at the shelter for two weeks, they could not have been more wrong. In fact, the story has a positive ending for Lorenzo, because he was not killed. Best Friends explains that the "rescue groups couldn't take him, but one put his story on the web. [The shelter] started getting phone calls and he pretty much sold himself!"

Had Lorenzo been killed, another sacrifice would have been chalked up to the great myth of pet overpopulation. Instead, Lorenzo's story shows the power of public relations and marketing to successfully promote and adopt out animals. The millions of dogs and cats being killed in shelters every year are dying for the same reason Lorenzo was almost killed—because these shelters have failed to put in place the programs and services that make up the No Kill Equation, including proactive marketing and public relations.

When Southern Hope Humane Society took over Fulton County Animal Services in 2003, the change was dramatic, to say the least. According to its director, they

took over the horribly mismanaged Fulton County Animal Control from Atlanta Humane Society (AHS) in 2003. This Fulton shelter which impounded 13,500 animals a year under AHS was the one that didn't allow adoptions, that killed every animal not reclaimed within 3 days (about a 90 percent [kill] rate), that didn't disinfect properly, had no vaccination protocol, had employees with horrible customer service, didn't work with rescue groups, it was a given that all puppies would contract parvovirus, had employees stealing animals, killing animals in horrific ways, etc. And wildlife was killed on intake, which meant that many reptiles and bats were stuck alive in a freezer to do so. We could go on and on with what we found when we arrived.

We have reduced the kill rate at the shelter from killing 11,500 animals a year to killing half that amount within the first year and now about 4,500 a year under our management. [And] we were able to accomplish all of this in an old, cramped, small animal shelter that was built in 1978 and is about [one-fourth] the size that we need for the volume of animals that we handle.

She further states that "since we started on March 21, 2003—we have never, I repeat never, killed a healthy young puppy or kitten."

Despite Southern Hope's tremendous success using the No Kill Equation, many people still proclaim that overpopulation and what more than one director has called the "Bubba Factor"—a pejorative term that intimates that people from the South are simple minded and have antiquated attitudes—are responsible for high rates of shelter killing in the South.* They have gone so far as to say that successes in San Francisco, Upstate New York, and even places like Philadelphia (as we shall see in the next chapter) are "nirvana" compared to the South.

This view misses the boat entirely. Each community that has experienced some measure of success was as bad as Atlanta before embracing the No Kill paradigm. Not only were San Francisco shelters described as a "blood bath," but it was San Francisco's Pit Bull fighting rings that helped lead to the establishment of a felony dog fighting law in California. In New York State it took decades to get a law passed that required dogs to have a doghouse. Before 2002, it was legal in Tompkins County to chain a dog to

---

* Although Fulton County Animal Services in Atlanta is not No Kill yet, that has less to do with a perceived overpopulation of pets or an irresponsible public than with a need to build capacity and an infrastructure to save those lives. Providing high volume, low-cost spay/neuter will also help because a reduction in intakes means less pressure is put on existing resources, especially in the case of Atlanta, where the allocation of resources by local government has been abysmally inadequate.

a tree, with no shelter of any kind despite temperatures that dropped to twenty-five degrees below zero.

In Philadelphia, two thirds of the population make under 20,000 dollars per year, the city's largest employer is in fact the city, there is no manufacturing to speak of, there is a crumbling infrastructure, no garbage pick up in parts of North Philadelphia, entire city blocks have only one or two legally occupied houses (the remainder are condemned or inhabited by squatters living with no electricity or running water), and the shelter is built near an ash dump in one of the city's most dangerous neighborhoods.

Yet these cities have either achieved No Kill, are a whisper away from doing so, or have begun moving aggressively in that direction by implementing the programs and services of the No Kill Equation. Building the capacity to save lives, after years of failing to do so, may take time, but that does not obviate the fact that shelter killing is a result of shelter practices, not "pet overpopulation." Furthermore, the argument that success in the South is precluded by the "Bubba Factor" is not only wrong, elitist and mean-spirited, it is simply another example of excuse making. It ignores success in *rural* Tompkins County. It ignores tremendous success being experienced in Charlottesville, Virginia, a community in the South. It goes against a study by a South Mississippi humane society that found 69 percent of people with unsterilized pets would get them spayed/neutered if it were free, a fact which is not surprising for a state with some of the lowest per capita income levels in the United States.

PLENTY OF HOMES FOR SHELTER ANIMALS

In theory, we could be a No Kill nation tomorrow. Based on the number of existing households with pets who have a pet die or run away, more homes potentially become available each year for cats than the number of cats who enter shelters, while more than twice as many homes potentially become available each year for dogs than the number of dogs who enter shelters. Based on the average lifespan of existing pet dogs and cats, every year more families are potentially looking to bring a new dog or cat into their home than currently enter shelters. According to one commentator, "since the inventory of pet-owning homes is growing, not just holding even, adoption could in theory replace all population control killing right now— if the animals and potential adopters were better introduced." In other words, if shelters did a better job at adoptions, they could eliminate all population control killing today. This does not include the fact that the market of homes (the number of homes which do not currently have a dog or cat but will acquire one) is expanding rapidly. If shelters increased market share by just a few percentage points, we could be a No Kill nation right now. But we are far from it.

As a movement, the humane community has accepted the idea that the best shelters can do for homeless animals is to adopt out some and kill the rest, summarized in the nineteenth-century policy of the Animal Rescue League of Boston. That we are living in the twenty-first century and this is still the status quo is a profound and dismal failure. To try to avoid criticism for this, to justify a paltry number of adoptions, these groups have perpetuated the myth that the only way to increase the number of adoptions is to decrease the quality of the homes to which a shelter is willing to adopt. They claim that doing so would only put the animals in the hands of abusers and animal hoarders, or relegate them to neglect. The notion that one needs to reduce the quality of homes in order to increase quantity is one more example of the anachronisms of old-guard, reactionary shelters who needed—and still need—a way to justify a paradigm of high impounds, high kill rates, and low adoptions.

During the early 1990s, the progressive North Shore Animal League (NSAL) was adopting out over 20,000 animals each year, even while rejecting a third of all applications. According to NSAL:

> The best adoption programs are designed to ensure that each animal is placed with a responsible person, one prepared to make a lifelong commitment, and to avoid the kinds of problems that may have caused the animal to be brought to the shelter. An important part of the process is to match the lifestyle and needs of the adopter with the individual dog or cat. If the screening process occasionally seems overly strict, try to remember that the shelter's first priority is to protect the animal's best interests. After selecting a pet, each potential adopter is thoroughly screened, including identity verification and reference checks. Because placing our pets in proper homes is so important to us, only two out of three applicants are ultimately approved. But for the more than 800,000 new pet owners who have met our high standards, the joy of providing a good home for a loving pet is well worth the extra trouble.

No Kill's focus on high volume adoptions has nothing to do with lowering the quality of those adoptions. Increasing the number of adoptions has to do with keeping the shelter open when working people and families with children can visit. It means taking animals offsite to where people work, live, and play. It includes adoption incentives, foster care programs, and working with rescue groups. Increasing adoptions means greater visibility in the community, competing with pet stores and puppy/kitten mills, good customer service, thoughtful but not overly bureaucratic screening, making the shelter a fun and exciting place to visit, and—as Lorenzo himself proved—proactive marketing.

By contrast, people only get their pets from shelters fifteen percent of the time because shelters have historically done a poor job of getting good homes to adopt animals. Some shelters undermine lifesaving because of arbitrary rules that prevent adoption, such as not adopting out animals to homes with very young children or not adopting dogs to homes without fenced yards. Other shelters limit lifesaving because they make it difficult to adopt, still others because they just don't care. An animal lover explained it best:

> I tried to adopt from my local shelter, but they weren't open on the weekend, it was almost impossible to reach them on the telephone and when I did, I was treated rudely. Nonetheless, I raced down there one day after work, and the place was so dirty. It made me cry to look into the faces of all those animals I knew would be killed. But I found this scared, skinny cat hiding in the back of his cage and I filled out an application. I was turned down because I didn't turn in the paperwork on time, which meant a half hour before closing, but I couldn't get there from work in time to do that. I tried to leave work early the next day, but I called and found out they had already killed the poor cat. I will never go back.

The bottom line is that there are plenty of homes out there, and it is up to shelters to promote their pets effectively so they find their way into those homes. In other words, if shelters better promoted their animals, they could increase the number of homes available and replace all population control killing with adoptions. Adopting an animal means a shelter does not kill that animal. Instead of adopting their way to No Kill, however, too many shelters continue to make excuses for their own failures and rely on meaningless platitudes to justify their refusal to change, a practice the fifth largest city in the United States took to the extreme.

In 2004, it took only nine minutes for staff at the Philadelphia Animal Care and Control Association to kill a lost, cherished family pet, before the family searching for her had time to come to the shelter to find her. It was

easier to kill than not to kill because a belief in pet overpopulation protected not only the shelter staff, but the bureaucrats in the health department
who were supposed to be holding them accountable and did not. Nine
minutes would shatter the myth that shelter killing was anything but the
shelter's fault, and finally bring an end to what one journalist accurately described as an "understaffed, mismanaged house of horrors that abuses and
neglects some animals in its care."

Part III

TOWARD A NO KILL NATION

The Power of One

"There are a thousand hacking at the branches of evil to one who is striking at the roots."

—Henry David Thoreau (1854)

To GET A COMMUNITY on track requires a spark—sometimes borne of anger, other times of compassion, most of the time from a combination of the two—which can ignite the fire of change. In Philadelphia, it was a little dog named Sheea, who was lost, found, and then taken to the Philadelphia Animal Care and Control Association (PACCA) where her family came looking for her. By the time they arrived, it was too late: Sheea was dead. Although health department officials pulled out the tired old arguments about pet overpopulation, no amount of bureaucratic spin or talk of public irresponsibility could erase the truth. Sheea's death is essential to understanding why we are not a No Kill nation today and how we can be, even in a shelter that was under-funded by millions, took in some 25,000 animals each year, had a staff rife with nepotism and favoritism, an inadequate building in a bad part of town, and that was labeled a"house of horrors" in a cover story by the local daily newspaper. Put simply by one of PACCA's chief critics:

If there ever was a shelter where the No Kill philosophy just wouldn't work, it was Philadelphia Animal Care and Control Association. With a [kill] rate near 80 percent, and an administration mired in the attitudes of the past, things did not

167

look promising. But for those of us with a commitment to save lives, PACCA was exactly where we needed to start to make a change in our community.

The Tip of the Iceberg

On August 11, 2004, a stray dog was taken to PACCA, the animal control agency for the fifth largest city in the United States. Under Pennsylvania State law, PACCA was required to hold the dog for forty-eight hours before making her available for adoption or killing her. The law is designed to provide people a "reasonable" opportunity to find and reclaim their lost pets. Sheea, however, was killed within nine minutes of arriving.

According to an undisputed court filing, Sheea's family was given neither an explanation nor an apology. They were misled, stonewalled, and lied to. Shelter workers ignored their pleas for answers and health department bureaucrats provided conflicting answers to protect those employees. As if borrowing a page from a shelter excuses playbook, responses ranged from blaming the public for overpopulation, to claiming the dog was "unpredictable," to claiming she was "surrendered by her owner." In the end, the family was simply asked to leave the shelter.

Health department officials and the then-shelter manager promised an investigation, which never materialized. This was an agency that had never fired an employee despite rampant under-performance, non-performance, theft and animal cruelty. It was also an agency that was overseen by officials in the health department who did not provide necessary leadership. Not surprisingly, Sheea's death was not an isolated instance.

In 2004, a series of exposés in the Philadelphia Daily News by reporter Stu Bykofsky found more allegations of abuse. According to one such report:

> *Martin Thomas' 1-year-old American bulldog named Sage got out of his yard on August 6. Martin searched for the dog, which wore a collar with a rabies tag and his owner's cell phone number... Thomas, 31, put up fliers in the neighborhood and went to PACCA, told them of his missing dog and was allowed to walk in to the kennel to look for her.*

> *A few days later, he learned that the dog had been picked up by police and brought to PACCA on the same day he got out. Thomas got the police report and went to PACCA to get his dog.*

A PACCA staff member claimed Sage was never brought in. Thomas produced the police report. After hemming and hawing, he said, the staffer said Sage was put down. 'The police report says the dog was brought in at 9:05, the death certificate was for 9:06'...

Sage lasted one minute. "My reporting was the tip of the iceberg," Bykofsky would tell city council members. "For every horror story I reported, there are 25 more." These included dogs being hosed down with high-pressure hoses and caustic chemicals, cats roughly and abusively handled, animals underfed, a culture of killing, and retaliation against employees who went public.

Despite killing over 22,000 of the animals received, Bykofsky reports that it is "still within 'norms' outlined [to him] by the ASPCA and the Humane Society of the United States." What he calls "animal slaughter-houses," the nation's largest and wealthiest animal protection groups call "norms." It is no wonder shelter leadership and health department officials appeared unswayed by the reports.

It was the political cover of "norms" that allowed bureaucrats within the health department to boldly proclaim that PACCA was doing a good job. It also allowed them to dismiss Sheea's killing with the irrelevant point that "a lot of [people who surrender animals to PACCA] are owners that don't like that the dog doesn't match the new rug, or for whatever reason." The point that Sheea was a stray and was killed in violation of laws protecting lost pets was a fact they chose to ignore.

The state of PACCA, however, should not have been a surprise. PACCA was created, like many animal control agencies around the country, for one reason and one reason only: to warehouse and kill animals at the lowest possible cost. While the health department was assuring Philadelphians that PACCA was committed to the highest level of lifesaving for animals, this assertion was directly contradicted not only by the practices of its employees, but also by the mission of PACCA, as articulated in the agency's own business plan it wrote and adopted. The mission of PACCA was identified as protecting the health of people from injury and disease "caused or transmitted by domestic or feral animals within the city's boundaries." A list of seventeen duties was outlined to meet the mission. None of them speak to services such as adoption, spay/neuter, education, or helping responsible people retain their pets.

Adoption programs were not identified in the expected list of services to be provided by the agency (although a perfunctory sentence about "preferring" adoption is mentioned in a contract for services). To save money, the city placed PACCA deep in North Philadelphia, next to an ash dump, in an area of the city that several officials noted for "high rates of poverty, crime and violence." Many people in the city had no idea of the shelter's physical location, and many potential adopters, in the prime retail areas of Philadelphia's Center City and/or its outlying suburbs, will not travel to this area of the city.

PACCA was to provide minimal services at the lowest possible cost. Giving the agency sufficient resources to do high-quality work or to save lives was not reflected in its mission. The emphasis was on reducing costs and staff to a bare minimum. The poor quality and location of the shelter and lack of competent managers and effective programs are testament to that emphasis. Some public officials, however, were aware of the problems and wanted more to be done. Jack Kelly, a city councilman, asked for public hearings to determine the extent of the problem and what would be necessary to fix it. It was during these hearings that it was determined that an outside expert was needed to do a top-to-bottom review of PACCA operations.

I was brought in as that expert. I arrived on February 3, 2005, as part of a fourteen-day onsite assessment of PACCA operations. I went straight from the airport to the facility. I was not expected at that hour of the evening, although my visit was anticipated by management and staff, and I was told by one official that they are "getting PACCA ready for my arrival." I should have found PACCA and the staff at their personal and professional best. Sadly, I did not.

For most of my fourteen-day visit, there was trash everywhere outside of the shelter: old newspapers, magazines, food wrappers, cigarette butts, and piles of dog excrement. The only time during my visit that the front area of the shelter and the parking lot were not littered with trash was on February 11, eight days after my arrival, on a day with strong gusts of wind: the area was clean only because high winds were blowing trash away. I watched trash get blown toward the far corner of the yard and then down the street.

Inside, where the wind could not reach, cabinets in the medical/surgery room, which should have been the cleanest and most sterile room in the facility, were filled with old food wrappers, used drink cups, and other trash. Vaccines were left un-refrigerated and, nearly 150 years after the advancement of germ theory, clinic staff did not wash their hands between handling individual sick animals.

Cat cages and crates were routinely reused without cleaning and crammed on top of one another, leading to urination and defecation passing from the cats in top crates to the cats in bottom crates. Water bowls in dog kennels were not cleaned while I was there, with several bowls containing algae spores, dog hair, and dirt even after the kennels were supposedly "cleaned" and empty. It was not uncommon to see food and fecal matter in cages even though staff claimed they had just been cleaned, and there was no periodic "spot" cleaning throughout the day. As a result, once the kennels were "cleaned," the dogs were allowed to languish in urine and fecal matter all day and throughout the night with no re-cleaning, even though supervisors and managers periodically walked by.

During my visit, there was an outbreak of "kennel cough" in the shelter, a relatively benign condition that is easily treated and, with good sanitation practices, can be avoided, or at least contained. Unfortunately, kennel cough was a death sentence at PACCA, and yet staff continued the practice of not washing bowls and poorly cleaning kennels, all of which would contribute to its spread. During any outbreak, the shelter manager should have clamped down on "cutting corners" and increased oversight to help contain any illnesses and protect the animals from cross-contamination (which in this case meant a death sentence). This did not occur.

The cats and animals in other rooms fared little better. Cat food bowls and litter boxes were not cleaned daily, and rags used to clean cat cages were reused, spreading disease. Most cat room cleaners did a poor job, taking no time to scrape away caked-on fecal matter and bodily fluids. On one occasion, I witnessed the floor being mopped with water from a dirty bucket without first being swept and a cage being cleaned and then lined with newspaper that was obviously soaked in urine. I also observed that food or water was not provided to the cats after cleaning on several occasions.

PACCA's problems, however, ran deeper than poor cleaning. It was common for the rabbits and other small animals, for example, to have no care whatsoever. Rabbits were often dehydrated because no one took care to ensure that they were cleaned, fed and provided fresh water daily. According to one of the veterinary technicians, the "bunnies can go two to three days without water."

At one point, I counted approximately seventy empty cages, which could have been used to hold cats at a time when PACCA was killing cats "for space." At the same time, staff also intentionally kept every other set of dog kennels empty for ease of cleaning, while dogs were being killed "for

space." And despite being strapped for funds, some employees were walking away with what little income the shelter made; up to hundreds of dollars a day were missing from the cash receipts.

If the old adage that "actions speak louder than words" is true, no action
was more telling about PACCA and the health department's lack of interest in lifesaving than a comparison between its adoption hours and the
hours available to surrender an animal. PACCA was open twenty-four
hours a day/seven days a week for surrendering animals, yet it was only
open Wednesday through Friday from 10:00 a.m. until 3:00 p.m. for adoptions, and on weekends until 2:30 p.m. The adoption application had to be
turned in thirty minutes prior to closing, making adoptions actually end at
2:30 p.m. on weekdays and 2:00 p.m. on weekends. Given that the most
sought-after adopters are working people and families, PACCA's adoption
hours effectively eliminated these two demographics from adopting every
day except Saturday and Sunday. Since most adoption staff took weekend
days off, moreover, there was often only one adoption counselor available
on weekends, whose availability was further limited when he or she was on
breaks. In other words, one could surrender an animal 168 hours per week
but only adopt an animal twenty-one hours. In this environment, it should
have surprised no one that adoptions were few and intakes were many.

Furthermore, a University of Pennsylvania Veterinary College staff
member, speaking on condition of anonymity, described witnessing
heightened levels of stress in the animals at PACCA due to "poor and hostile treatment by staff." Based on the claimed observations of un-trained
and under-performing staff, animals were dragged by the neck, mishandled, and worse, scheduled for destruction. On one occasion, an eyewitness
reported that:

> An adopter brought his cat in a carrier. The cat was adopted from PACCA
> and brought back for neuter. Because the cat was fractious during examination,
> the veterinarian on duty apparently asked that no one handle the cat. One staff
> member attempted to handle the cat by using a control stick but did so in an
> inept manner. The cat's teeth were knocked out.

When an opportunity existed to save an animal's life, that opportunity
was wasted. I witnessed kennel staff arguing over who would respond to
requests to assist a potential adopter. One asked the other, and the other
argued back: "you go," "no, you go." At one point, staff was called four times

to assist an adopter over the intercom, while the staff assigned was wasting time, having a personal conversation in the lunch room with other staff members.

Staff routinely ignored telephone calls, socialized, and carried on personal conversations while people waited for service. Much of this was the result of lax oversight by mid-level managers who shared the indifference of staff and/or were related to staff by marriage or other familial ties. As a result, there appeared to be an arrogance by staff that poor performance would go unpunished. For example, a staff member finally disciplined during my visit received a five-day suspension for failure to report to work, his first disciplinary action despite a history of being late, calling in sick, or not reporting to work thirty-four times in a seven month period—from August 2004 to February 2005.

Even the animals outside the shelter suffered. When a citizen calls and complains about improper care of animals (a neighbor who isn't taking care of a dog or someone moving out and abandoning his cat), a case record is generated. That case remains open until it is investigated and action taken. When the case is complete (e.g., an animal is rescued or a citation is issued), the case is "closed." So long as the case is open, the situation has not been fully remedied.

My review of animal control cases found 384 such open cases, many with no action or follow-up, providing no audit trail to gauge the performance of field services staff. These cases ranged in severity, but all of them potentially allowed animals to endure prolonged suffering needlessly, including the following open case: "Dog left out in cold all day chained up. Numerous complaints from different people. Dog looks like it's not being fed properly. Very thin."

A fair number of cases showed that no action was taken whatsoever, that officers never even went out to look at the situation. These cases included:

+ Three dogs abandoned with no food or water in an empty apartment;
+ A dog with no shelter;
+ A skinny dog;
+ Malnourished dogs; and,
+ A mother cat with four kittens abandoned on a porch.

Add to this the health department's "circle the wagons" approach of either flatly denying that problems existed or failing to investigate complaints before making sweeping statements about "a professional, hard working, well trained staff in a state of the art facility" who were "doing their very best," and the picture becomes clear: the situation in Philadelphia appeared hopeless.

THE NO KILL EQUATION COMES TO PHILADELPHIA

But the situation was not hopeless. As part of my review of PACCA, I was also asked to help write the job description for its new executive director, review resumes, and to recommend a candidate for the position. The person I recommended to be put in charge of animal control for the fifth largest city in the United States was an animal lover with absolutely no experience running shelters, and one of PACCA's chief critics. Choosing someone with lack of sheltering experience was intentional.

To get the right person, Philadelphia needed to broaden the field of candidates and remove the requirement of animal sheltering experience, in order to make the job description as inclusive as possible. While many shelters insist on multi-year experience running shelters or animal control facilities, this often brings set methods and short-sightedness that prevent innovation in lifesaving. In other words, it brings an over-reliance on killing.

Since experienced shelter directors have uniformly failed to create No Kill in their current communities and presided over the killing of the majority of shelter animals in their care, there was no reason to believe they would succeed in Philadelphia. I did not want to reward failure.

Nor did I want to reward shelter directors who may have run private No Kill shelters, but who were not meeting that shelter's potential to save more animals if other shelters in their communities were still killing at alarming rates. America's love of dogs and cats has resulted in no shortage of private shelters and animal advocacy organizations with vast resources at their disposal, yet not enough of these groups are leveraging those resources to end the killing of companion animals in the communities where they reside. Though they themselves are not doing the killing, they are not working hard enough to end it.

There are private shelters and national groups with tens of millions of dollars sitting in bank accounts. Many of these shelters are adopting out 500 animals a year when they have the potential to save ten times that number, but lack commitment to put forth that degree of effort. When a shelter is under-performing because it does not invest in lifesaving, or is spending time watching its investments grow rather than investing in the infrastructure necessary to build a No Kill nation, a great tragedy and betrayal is taking place. That does not mean private shelters should accept animals who will be killed; the era when private shelters kill animals on behalf of government should be over.

But to the extent that private shelters are not using the full force of their ability to save lives and continue to divert resources to "pet" projects such as daycare for children and kids camps while homeless animals continue to die in appalling numbers at the animal control facility in the same community, they are wasting their potential to increase lifesaving. All shelters in a community owe a duty to one thing: *the homeless animals being killed.* If animal control is willing, these shelters must work with them to reduce and ultimately end killing "for space" in their community. If animal control is unwilling, they must fight the animal control bureaucracy that continues to needlessly administer the gas or lethal injections.

To avoid recycling failure, I succeeded in convincing the City of Philadelphia to remove the job requirement for the director of specific *shelter experience*, seeking instead specific *skills* (accountability, working in a team environment, leadership, financial responsibility, management, bottom line results), which can be transferred to the shelter environment. I argued that doing so would increase the base of qualified candidates, many of whom would bring a fresh perspective and innovation to shelter operations. I learned firsthand from my own experience that it did not take long to learn the basics of running an animal shelter. The quality that was needed most for reforming PACCA was not knowledge of parvocides or zoonotic diseases; it was a passion for saving lives.

At the same time, I put together a 135-page assessment and list of recommendations for the future of PACCA—a playbook for success. There was no talk of passing laws and no talk of blaming the public. The focus was on eliminating under-performing staff, building the programs and services of the No Kill Equation, embracing the public, and involving them in the lifesaving enterprise.

Thankfully, my recommendation was accepted and a newcomer to sheltering was hired. The first order of business was to fire the long list of incompetents who passed for the shelter's mid-level managers and core staff. Tara Derby, the new director described it best: "When a manager accepts sloppiness, mediocrity, and incompetence as the standard... you get more sloppiness and more failure and more incompetence."

A short seven months after the new director was hired, PACCA's new leadership team doubled the number of animals saved and reported the following in an e-mail addressed to the rescue community and the public:

> *We reached a tremendous milestone of saving more than half of the entire number of animals that entered our facility. In all of its history, PACCA has never achieved that level of life saving and we could not have reached it without your help. You have accepted the healthy, the ill, the old, the injured and the newborn, truly lives that were saved because you were there. Even more amazing than this, in a facility that accepted 756 cats in the month of January, we did not kill a single cat simply because there was no space. Once again that is a milestone that had never before been achieved...*

Success did not stop there. PACCA closed the dreaded "e-room" (the euthanasia room where animals were once killed in shifts virtually around the clock, seven days per week). It is now used primarily for medical care and treatment. The positions of full time "euthanasia technicians," whose job it was to kill animals, were eliminated. Instead, veterinary technicians primarily care for sick and injured animals.

How did this happen in less than one year at an agency depicted as a "house of horrors," with arguably one of the worst records of lifesaving in the United States? The answer is simple. PACCA began to implement the programs and services of the No Kill Equation: comprehensive adoption efforts including taking animals to offsite locations, working with rescue groups, sterilizing all animals before adoption, promoting the agency, and more.

There is still a long way to go, some of the programs are not being comprehensively put into place, and there are still far too many Philadelphia animals facing death. It is my belief that if PACCA more fully embraces the No Kill Equation, if it develops a comprehensive foster care network and a fully integrated offsite adoption program, it can much more quickly improve rates of lifesaving than it is unfortunately currently doing.

It will also take continued leadership and commitment to make No Kill a reality in Philadelphia and to overcome the real but not insurmountable roadblocks PACCA faces. The prognosis for that success remains guarded at best due to a poor infrastructure, hostility to reform from the health department that oversees PACCA, lack of support for the No Kill initiative by the two other community shelters, and its unfavorable location relative to retail and residential sectors of the city. But, at the very least, the days are gone when animals were not fed, the place was filthy while staff socialized, lost animals were killed within minutes of arrival before their families could find them, when Pit Bulls faced certain death, and when rescue groups were driven out of the facility while the animals they were trying to rescue were discarded in body bags at the local landfill.

This is also true in another city, also staffed with a newcomer to animal sheltering. And this city, perhaps more than any other place, provides a glimpse of the promise that the future can hold.

THE SOUTH RISES AGAIN

In April 2005, a new director, with no prior experience running an animal shelter, took over as head of the Charlottesville-Albemarle SPCA, an agency which contracts for animal control sheltering in Charlottesville, Virginia. Historically, the Charlottesville SPCA was the subject of relentless public criticism for what many in the rescue community saw as poor customer service, inadequate care of animals, and unnecessary killing. By hiring a new director who embraced the No Kill paradigm, they finished the year saving nearly nine out of ten dogs and almost seven out of ten cats. In an exciting public announcement, director Susanne Kogut explains,

> In 2005, we doubled the number of animals placed in foster care from the previous year. This gave life to many underage kittens and puppies who just needed temporary care until they were ready for adoption. We also treated and found homes for many sick and injured dogs and cats, as well as older, blind, deaf, or other "special needs." We are excited about 2006, as we know that these life-saving programs work.

In a little over one year, under new leadership committed to change, the Charlottesville SPCA saved over 90 percent of all dogs and cats in 2006, achieving a level of success equivalent to Tompkins County and unmatched in the vast majority of other communities. This was accomplished under a director with no prior experience running a shelter. There is a larger lesson here from the experiences of San Francisco, Tompkins County, Fulton County, Philadelphia, Charlottesville, and a few other notable exceptions to the status quo. And it can be described as one more element of the No

Kill Equation, perhaps the most important one: a hard-working animal control director who is not content to hide behind the myth of pet overpopulation, blame the public, and regurgitate tired clichés about too many animals and too few homes.

In the end, there may be an overpopulation problem in the United States, but it is not the one we traditionally define. What we are actually suffering from, what is actually killing a high number of animals, is an overpopulation of shelter directors mired in the failed philosophies of the past and complacent with the status quo. As a result, a culture of lifesaving is not possible without wholesale regime change in shelters and national animal protection groups. Consequently, the most important single act— and the crucial first step—in achieving a No Kill nation is firing the current leadership of shelters across the country.

In the final analysis, animals in shelters are not being killed because there are too many of them, because there are too few homes, or because the public is irresponsible. Animals in shelters are dying for primarily one reason—because people in shelters are killing them.

Afterword

"No army can withstand the strength of an idea whose time has come."

—Victor Hugo (circa 1850)

IF HISTORY IS ANY INDICATION, insiders in the animal sheltering industry, particularly some activists and those who run national organizations, will be critical of this book. They will fall into one of four camps. The first group will agree with the message, be sympathetic to the cause, and want the same goal. Nonetheless, they will claim it ignores the success of others and focuses too much attention on San Francisco and later Tompkins County, communities in which I played a significant role. However, this is not an exercise in self-promotion. To begin with, the hero of San Francisco is not me. It is Richard Avanzino, the president of the San Francisco SPCA from 1976 to 1998, and the father of the modern No Kill movement.

In addition, it is true that others implemented many of the programs of the No Kill Equation and consequently saved a significant number of lives over the past three decades. New York City's North Shore Animal League, for example, advocated high volume adoptions through advertising, public relations, offsite adoptions, and a customer service-oriented staff at a time when most shelters were not doing so. Alley Cat Allies promoted an innovative, humane, non-lethal program to save feral cats, when most shelters advocated mass killing. Spay USA advocated high volume, low-cost spay/neuter including pediatric surgeries* as a way to reduce shelter impounds, at a time when most shelters were adopting unsterilized animals to the public, and then failing to provide them with low-cost alternatives to the prohibitively high prices charged by some private-practice veterinarians. According to *Animal People*, these groups:

> *pioneered virtually all the techniques that have dramatically increased neutering, adoptions, and public financial support, reduced pet abandonment, and cut shelter killing from 17.8 million in 1987 to barely four million in 1996. In between, the North Shore Animal League popularized high-volume adoption as a specialty and showed the value of radio and TV advertising; …Spay/USA took low-cost neutering to all parts of the country; PetSmart sold the concept of pet store as adoption outlet; the San Francisco SPCA reintroduced the idea that humane societies should do humane work instead of animal control; Alley Cat Allies taught neuter/release…*

While I do not wish to downplay their success and role, the reality is that until 2001, only San Francisco implemented all of these programs as a comprehensive total package. In fact, organizations like North Shore Animal League and Alley Cat Allies may have been the most vocal proponents of these programs, but mass adoptions—and holiday promotions— were pioneered by the San Francisco SPCA, a citywide non-lethal feral cat initiative was integrated most effectively by the San Francisco SPCA, and mass spay/neuter was implemented with the most zeal by the San Francisco SPCA.

The heads of these other organizations have advocated the right message, and deserve our praise and gratitude, but it was a message of follow-the-leader—and the leader was clearly Avanzino. More importantly, the San Francisco SPCA was able to show what the other groups, whose efforts were widely dispersed across the country, could not: that an entire community can end the killing of each and every healthy homeless dog and cat. And until Tompkins County took all of these programs to their logical conclusion, No Kill success remained an elusive dream. In fact, until Tompkins County became the nation's first No Kill community (saving 100 percent of healthy and treatable animals, and 100 percent of feral cats),

---

* Historically, veterinarians waited until dogs and cats were sexually mature before spaying or neutering. However, advances in veterinary medicine proved that spay/neuter as young as six weeks old was not only safe, but actually better for the animals.

even ardent advocates of this new paradigm were resigned to the fact that success was still years, perhaps even decades, away. This fact turned out to be based on false assumptions when the Tompkins County SPCA proved that No Kill could be achieved virtually overnight.

Finally, it was the success of San Francisco and Tompkins County that fully electrified the No Kill movement. As a result, the public's desire for No Kill is spreading like wildfire across this nation. Unfortunately, however, No Kill success is not. The achievements of communities like San Francisco, Tompkins County, Charlottesville, and a few others remain a small minority. The reason is that while activists and animal lovers are sincere in their advocacy for No Kill, their efforts are being squandered, because ultimately they are attacking the wrong problem. In order to achieve No Kill, these animal advocates believe they must attack the problem of pet overpopulation. To them, that means addressing the issue of public irresponsibility through a series of punitive laws like cat licensing, pet limits, and mandatory spay/neuter which, as their logic goes, will force people with pets to be more responsible. This approach has never worked, and never will. As a result, the positive results they seek have not been forthcoming.

Unfortunately, they will never be forthcoming, because pet overpopulation is a myth and public irresponsibility is not why animals are being killed in shelters. The *real* problem, the real reason we are not closer to a No Kill nation today, even though San Francisco and Tompkins County have shown us how to achieve it, the reason why people's desire for a No Kill nation is continuously being thwarted, is because those in power—the directors who run the shelters, the health department bureaucrats who often oversee them, the local governments which fund them (often inadequately), and the large, national non-profit animal welfare agencies which provide them political cover, are failing. They are failing to learn from the past. They are failing to implement the programs and services with a demonstrated track record of saving lives and/or to demand that shelters do. They are failing because they lack the vision to see the possibilities.*

---

*To their credit, the American Humane Association co-hosted a No Kill conference (although it was very careful to say they were "exploring" No Kill and not "endorsing" it). The ASPCA has also pledged five million dollars to help New York City rescue groups save dogs and cats and has begun speaking positively about No Kill. Unfortunately neither agency has completely rejected killing nor put the blame where it belongs: on the shelters themselves. And as signatories to the *Asilomar Accords*, they continue to embrace old philosophies that legitimize killing.

In short, it is easier for them to kill than do what is necessary to stop it, even though stopping it requires no more money or staff than the status quo. In some cases, for example, it is actually less expensive to save lives, than it is to end them.

The second group that will take issue with this book are the animal activists who are intent on doing what they have always done, regardless of the facts. They will continue to blame the public and fight for more and tougher laws—once again buying into the false paradigm of pet overpopulation and public irresponsibility. As stated earlier, they will argue that their community is different and that citizens in their community are particularly irresponsible. The evidence clearly shows that none of this is true.

What is true is that shelters are filled with animals, in no small part because of a small segment of the public's throwaway attitudes about their pets. But that is why shelters exist in the first place. They are supposed to be the safety net for animals the same way orphanages and child protective services are the safety net for parentless and abused children. While people surrender animals to shelters it is the shelters that kill them, and one does not necessarily follow or excuse the other.

The third group of critics of this book will be the shelter directors themselves—those who are involved in the killing of five million dogs and cats a year and who erroneously claim that doing so is both necessary and proper. They will see this book as nothing more than a personal attack. They will argue that we should all get along, not fight each other, and focus on our common enemy—the irresponsible public which fills shelters with discarded animals. This point of view is nothing more than a smokescreen and is contradicted by the facts.

First and foremost, this is a history book. Writing that the Humane Society of the United States called mass extermination of feral cats the only "practical and humane" solution in 1992 or that volunteers were fired from a Virginia shelter in 2002 because they tried to save the lives of underaged kittens is retelling the history of animal sheltering. Imagine a history book on the civil rights movement that did not discuss racist governors, Jim Crow laws, and segregation. Simply stating the truth is not "bashing."

Second, in a movement of conscience, promoting unity and a "get along" philosophy above spirited debate can lead to stagnation, and would allow animals to continue to suffer. American history is littered with examples of progress that began with conscientious individuals taking initially unpopular positions. Success will only be guaranteed when all shelters and animal welfare groups fully embrace the No Kill paradigm, not when we "respect" opposing views that legitimize the killing. To the extent that these shelter bureaucrats oppose the No Kill philosophy, animals will continue to die needlessly. To the extent that animals continue to die needlessly, we are morally bound to speak. Now that we know the key to ending the killing, the time has come when silence is betrayal.

Third, it is often the shelter's very own policies that result in animals entering shelters—from draconian animal control laws to bans that condemn dogs to death for no other reason that they were born a particular breed.

Fourth, what shelters mired in killing mean when they say "we should all get along" is that people who disagree with them should not say so publicly. We are also told that we must wait for change, that we must be patient as we try to build consensus. But how can we remain silent in the face of such injustice? It has been over twelve years since San Francisco showed us how to end the killing. How many more millions of animals must be killed before No Kill programs are implemented? I am reminded of Dr. Martin Luther King's letter from a Birmingham jail. It is just as apt today for the rights of sheltered animals as it is was—and is—for civil rights:

> We know through painful experience that freedom is never voluntarily given by the oppressor; it must be demanded by the oppressed. Frankly, I have yet to engage in a direct-action campaign that was "well timed" in the view of those who have not suffered unduly... For years now I have heard the word "Wait!" ... This "Wait" has almost always meant "Never." We must come to see... that "justice too long delayed is justice denied."

Fifth, it is our duty as advocates for the animals to point out that there is a better way, to unmask the hypocrisy of shelters that argue the public should not treat animals as disposable, when they in fact treat animals that way by killing them. Again I turn to Dr. King:

> We merely bring to the surface the hidden tension that is already alive. We bring it out in the open, where it can be seen and dealt with. Like a boil that can never be cured so long as it is covered up but must be opened with its ugliness exposed to the natural medicines of air and light, injustice must be exposed, with all the tension its exposure creates, to the light of human conscience and the air of national opinion before it can be cured.

Lastly, the truth is we are not a unified movement, nor are we even the same movement. We were not part of the same movement when Henry Bergh, the founder of the nation's first SPCA, fought the dogcatchers of New York City. We were not part of the same movement when Richard Avanzino fought an entrenched animal control bureaucracy in San Francisco. We were not the same movement when the Humane Society of the United States argued that caring for feral cats through TNR was tantamount to animal abandonment in North Carolina. And we are not part of the same movement today. No Kill advocates, on the one hand, and kill-oriented traditionalists, on the other, are on a collision course.

It is my hope that No Kill will be fully embraced by everyone because the animals deserve it and the public wants it. Achieving it, however, is not likely to happen while the current leaders of most shelters and national organizations continue to hold the positions or promote the views that they do. In the end, a No Kill nation will require replacement of the old guard with committed animal advocates passionate about saving lives and deeply committed to the No Kill enterprise.

If it makes me a divisive force to say so, I tender a guilty plea. But I trust that you—the reader—will agree that killing is never an act of kindness toward an animal when he or she is not suffering. And putting an end to that systematic practice is the ultimate goal of this book.

The fourth and final group of people who will criticize this book are a group I collectively call the "naysayers." The naysayers are those who have a predetermined agenda of support for animal control, regardless of how many animals the local shelter kills or how otherwise dysfunctional the agency is. They cannot be swayed by logic, facts, or alternative points of view. They seek out that which fits their beliefs and reject everything else to the point of taking facts out of context—and in some cases, making up "facts"—to fit the story. The naysayers have pointed to the fact that San Francisco no longer uses the term No Kill in its literature and has shifted its focus to other endeavors. That is certainly true and definitely tragic. They further argue that if San Francisco is proof of anything, it is that No Kill is not sustainable. Nothing could be further from the truth. San Francisco's demise as the reigning leader of the No Kill movement does indeed have important lessons for the future, and in depth discussion is certainly warranted to answer any lingering questions as to what this means for the movement it spawned to end the shelter killing of dogs and cats.

When Avanzino left the San Francisco SPCA, he handed his successor one of the best-funded, most successful humane societies in the country. With an infrastructure that included a state-of-the-art pet adoption center and spay/neuter clinic, an animal hospital, a fundraising program that included a bequest stream of over three million dollars per year, a car donation program that was inching its way toward revenues of one million dollars annually, property values in excess of fifty million dollars and over forty million dollars in the endowment, the San Francisco SPCA was at the peak of its success. It not only had achieved a level of financial success which was the envy of SPCAs nationwide, it was saving homeless animals at two and three times the national average, resulting in the lowest death rate of any major urban city and the only one which guaranteed to save all healthy dogs and cats.

The new president, however, was not interested in day-to-day operations, and had different priorities than his predecessor. Moving away from the programs that had made it so successful, the San Francisco SPCA replaced nuts-and-bolts programs that were the underpinning of the SPCA's lifesaving efforts at an astonishing clip. In their place, partnerships with the University of California at Davis for fee-for-service behavior counseling, as well as architectural plans for a twenty million dollar fee-for-service specialty veterinary hospital were drawn up. And esoteric conferences on animal spirituality and telepathically communicating with animals, which catered to a more affluent, "new age" San Francisco crowd, were held at great expense—in luxury hotels or in posh vacation places like Jackson Hole, Wyoming.

Within a few short years, the SPCA's feral cat program was virtually abolished. The spay/neuter clinic, the core of San Francisco's No Kill accomplishments, restricted its hours, significantly raised fees and, at one point, even closed its doors. On a day that came to be called "Black Monday," the legions of feral cat caretakers who made their regular pilgrimage to use the services of the spay/neuter clinic were turned away. Many of the cats brought in that day were likely re-released unspayed or unneutered into parks and alleyways. Plans to phase out programs in the animal hospital for indigent clients and homeless animals were in full swing. Entire departments, including those which protected the city's wildlife, worked to find apartments for renters with pets, and advocated for stronger protections of animals, were eliminated. The crown jewel of the No Kill movement quietly passed into obscurity.

The lesson is sobering and speaks volumes about the importance of leadership. No Kill is only succeeding in some communities because of the commitment by individual shelter leaders, who are few and far between. Traditional sheltering, by contrast, is institutionalized. In a shelter reliant on killing, directors can come and go and the shelter keeps killing, local government keeps ignoring that failure, and the public keeps believing "there is no other way." By contrast, the success of an organization's No Kill policies depends on the commitment and vision of its leader. When that leader leaves the organization, the vision can quickly be doomed. It is why an SPCA can be progressive one day, and moving in the opposite direction the next.

For No Kill to succeed in the long term, organizations must build a culture of accountability and lifesaving that allows agencies to continue on their path to No Kill even when their visionary leaders move on to other pursuits. To do that, shelters need to create a No Kill-oriented Board of Directors, staff, and volunteer corps, and to share their success publicly until the community "owns" it. This will provide a wedge against backsliding later, by creating a lifesaving expectation among a shelter's Board, volunteers, and the community at large.

The more successful this effort is, the more No Kill will shift from being personality based (a result of the efforts of individual leaders) to becoming institutionalized (the doctrine of the shelter and the expectation of the community). In addition, when more communities become successful, the less relevant the backsliding of shelters like the San Francisco SPCA will be. In the end, if such regression occurs, it should have no impact on the widening success of the No Kill revolution nor be seen as a negative reflection of No Kill's long-term viability. Anyone with a deep and abiding love for animals and a "can do" attitude can take on positions of leadership at SPCAs, humane societies, and animal control shelters across the nation, and quickly achieve the kind of lifesaving results that were once dismissed as nothing more than "hoaxes" or "smoke and mirrors" by the leaders of the past.

With no allegiance to the status quo or faith in conventional "wisdom," new leaders can cause dog and cat deaths to plummet in cities and counties by rejecting the "adopt some and kill the rest" inertia of the past one hundred years. Instead of San Francisco, there can be renewed hope for the future in other places. It is time for the humane movement to develop a new definition of "leadership," a definition not based on who has the biggest budget or the loudest voice, but rather on success relating to the most important job a shelter has—saving lives.

In the late nineteenth century, Henry Bergh was the subject of relentless criticism for his desire to bring compassion to the streets of New York City through his ASPCA. Wrote his biographer:

It was commonly thought that he was callous to ridicule but few were more sensitive to the criticism of friends and enemies. His wife, who was his loyal supporter and gave him moral encouragement when things looked black, said that he often cried over the vexatious difficulties that were heaped his way. In spite of this sensitiveness, he did not let it interfere with his crusade. He once said: "Two or three years of ridicule and abuse have thickened the epidermis of my sensibilities, and I have acquired the habit of doing the thing I think right, regardless of public clamor."

The shelters, rescue groups, feral cat caretakers and No Kill proponents who have tried to restore Bergh's vision through the No Kill revolution became the subject of this same type of ridicule and abuse at the hands of those who squandered his legacy, led in part by the very ASPCA he founded. It would have hurt Bergh very deeply.

For far too many years, the ASPCA and its progeny have routinely killed millions of dogs and cats. Many of these animals were healthy and friendly, and would have made excellent companions had they been afforded a little bit of space and time—space and time enough to find a loving home. But with holding periods ranging from zero to ten days, most did not, under the outdated belief that solutions were impossible, no one would adopt them, and the best we can do for homeless animals is provide a quick death behind closed doors.

When Bergh and his colleagues set down the first bricks in a foundation dedicated to building a humane nation, the challenges they faced were different than the ones we face today. But, as Avanzino once said,

Their mission remains our mission, and we strive to carry it out with the same values taught by their example: believe in your dreams, hold on to your principles, and never doubt that through perseverance and hard work you can succeed.

We have the power to build a new consensus, which rejects killing as a method for achieving results. And we can look forward to a time when the wholesale slaughter of animals in shelters is viewed as a cruel aberration of the past. To get to that point, we must learn from history and reject our failures.

Whether we realize, appreciate, or believe it, as history marches toward greater compassion toward non-human animals, No Kill's conquest of the status quo is inevitable. If we remain silent at this moment, however, an opportunity will be lost to speed that process along. Our silence, therefore, has a body count. The price to be paid for our refusal to seize this opportunity will be the lives of millions of dogs and cats needlessly killed in shelters next year. And the year after that.

We have a choice. We can fully, completely, and without reservation embrace No Kill as our future. Or we can continue to legitimize the two-pronged strategy of failure: adopt a few and kill the rest. It is a choice which history has thrown upon us. We are the generation that questioned the killing. We are the generation that has discovered how to stop it. Will we be the generation that does?

> "Sometimes it falls upon a generation to be great.
> You can be that great generation."
>
> —Nelson Mandela (2005)

Appendix I

The Declaration of the No Kill Movement in the United States— September 2005

I. Preamble

One hundred and fifty years ago, societies for the prevention of cruelty to animals and other humane organizations were founded to establish standards for humane treatment of animals, to promote their rights, and to protect them from harm. This marked the formal beginning of the humane movement in the United States.

The scope and influence of these early humane organizations were testament to the public's concern for animals. It did not take long for them to set their sights on the abuse of homeless animals and cruel methods of killing by public pounds. It was common practice at the time for city and town dogcatchers to beat, drown, or shoot homeless animals.

Many humane agencies responded by entering into animal control contracts with towns and cities to ensure that the killing was done more humanely. But in taking on municipal animal control duties, these agencies abandoned their lifesaving and life-enhancing platforms when those beliefs conflicted with their contractual responsibilities. In the current era, where laws require killing by even more "humane" methods, these contradictions have become starker.

Increasingly, the practices of both humane societies and municipal animal control agencies are out of step with public sentiment. Today, most Americans hold the humane treatment of animals as a personal value, which is reflected in our laws, cultural practices, the proliferation of organizations founded for animal protection, increased per capita spending on animal care, and great advancements in veterinary medicine. But the agencies that the public expects to protect animals are instead killing more than five million animals annually.

Lifesaving alternatives to the mass killing of animals in shelters have existed for decades. These lifesaving methods are based on innovative, humane, nonlethal programs and services that have proven that the killing can be brought to an end. Too many of these agencies, however, remain mired in the kill philosophies of the past, unwilling to or hampered from exploring and adopting methods that save lives. This is a breach of their public trust, a gross deviation from their responsibility to protect animals, and a point of view that we, as caring people and a humane community, can no longer accept or tolerate.

We assert that a No Kill nation is within our reach—that the killing can and must be brought to an end. It is up to each of us working individually and together to implement sheltering models that have already saved tens of thousands of animals in progressive communities. If we work together—with certainty of purpose, assured of our own success, with the commitment that "what must be done, will be done"—the attainment of our goals will not be far off.

II. No Kill Resolution

Whereas, the right to live is every animal's most basic and fundamental right;

Whereas, societies for the prevention of cruelty to animals and other humane organizations were founded to establish standards for humane treatment of animals, to promote their rights, and to protect them from harm;

Whereas, traditional sheltering practices allow the mass killing of sheltered animals;

Whereas, every year shelters in the United States are killing millions of healthy and treatable animals who could be placed in homes, and are also killing millions of feral cats who do not belong in shelters;

Whereas, life always takes precedence over expediency;

Whereas, the No Kill movement in the United States has successfully implemented new and innovative programs that provide alternatives to mass killing;

Whereas, lifesaving change will come about only if No Kill programs are embraced and further developed;

Whereas, failure to implement No Kill programs constitutes a breach of the public's trust in the sheltering community;

Now, therefore, be it resolved that No Kill policies and procedures are the only legitimate foundation for animal sheltering; and,

It is incumbent upon all shelters and animal groups to embrace the philosophy of No Kill, to immediately begin implementing programs and services that will end the mass killing of sheltered animals, and to reject the failed kill-oriented practices of the past.

III. STATEMENT OF RIGHTS

We acknowledge the following:
+ Sheltered animals have a right to live;
+ Feral cats have a right to their lives and their habitats;
+ Animals, rescuers, and the public have a right to expect animal protection organizations and animal shelters to do everything in their power to promote, protect, and advocate for the lives of animals;
+ Animal protection groups, rescue groups, and No Kill shelters have a right to take into their custody animals who would otherwise be killed by animal shelters;
+ Taxpayers and community members have a right to have their government spend tax monies on programs and services whose purpose is to save and enhance the lives of all animals;
+ Taxpayers and community members have a right to full and complete disclosure about how animal shelters operate.

IV. Guiding Principles

No Kill is achieved only by guaranteeing the following:

+ Life to all healthy animals, and to all sick, injured, or vicious animals where medical or behavioral intervention would alter a poor or grave prognosis;
+ The right of feral cats to live in their habitats.

These conditions can be achieved only through adherence to the following:

+ Shelters and humane groups end the killing of healthy and treatable animals, including feral cats;
+ Every animal in a shelter receives individual consideration, regardless of how many animals a shelter takes in, or whether such animals are healthy, underaged, elderly, sick, injured, traumatized, or feral;
+ Shelters and humane organizations discontinue the use of language that misleads the public and glosses over the nature of their actions, such as "euthanasia," "unadoptable," "fractious," "putting them to sleep," and other euphemisms that downplay the gravity of ending life and make the task of killing easier;
+ Shelters are open to the public during hours that permit working people to reclaim or adopt animals during nonworking hours;
+ Shelters and other government agencies promote spay/neuter programs and mandate that animals be spayed or neutered before adoption;
+ Public shelters work with humane animal adoption organizations to the fullest extent to promote the adoption of animals and to reduce the rate of killing;
+ Shelters provide care and treatment for all animals in shelters to the extent necessary, including prompt veterinary care, adequate nutrition, shelter, exercise, and socialization;
+ Shelters are held accountable for and make information publicly available about all the animals in their care.

V. No Kill Standards

The implementation of these lifesaving procedures, policies, and programs must be the immediate goal of every shelter, and animal control and animal welfare agency:

- Formal, active commitment by shelter directors, management, and staff to lifesaving programs and policies, and dedication to promptly ending mass killing of shelter animals;
- Immediate implementation of the following programs by all publicly funded or subsidized animal shelters:
    - High-volume, low- and no-cost spay/neuter services;
    - A foster care network for underaged, traumatized, sick, injured, or other animals needing refuge before any sheltered animal is killed, unless the prognosis for rehabilitation of that individual animal is poor or grave;
    - Comprehensive adoption programs that operate during weekend and evening hours and include offsite adoption venues;
    - Medical and behavioral rehabilitation programs;
    - Pet retention programs to solve medical, environmental, or behavioral problems and keep animals with their caring and responsible caregivers;
    - Trap-Neuter-Return or Release (TNR) programs;
    - Rescue group access to shelter animals;
    - Volunteer programs to socialize animals, promote adoptions, and help in the operations of the shelter;
    - Documentation before any animal is killed that all efforts to save the animal have been considered, including medical and behavioral rehabilitation, foster care, rescue groups, neuter and release, and adoption.
- An end to the policy of accepting trapped feral cats to be destroyed as unadoptable, and implementation of TNR as the accepted method of feral cat control by educating the public about TNR and offering TNR program services;
- An end to the use of temperament testing that results in killing animals who are not truly vicious (e.g., shy/timid cats and frightened dogs) but who can be placed in homes, or are feral cats who can be returned or released;
- Abolishment of trapping, lending traps to the public to capture animals, and support of trapping by shelters, governments, and pest control companies for the purposes of removing animals to be killed;

* An end to owner-requested killing of animals unless the shelter has made an independent determination that the animal is irremediably suffering or cannot be rehabilitated;
* The repeal of unenforceable and counter-productive animal control ordinances such as cat licensing and leash laws, pet limit laws, bans on feeding stray animals, and bans on specific breeds.

Appendix II

A No Kill Blueprint for Shelters

In 1994, San Francisco became the first community in the nation to end the killing of healthy dogs and cats in its animal shelter system. An agreement between the city's Animal Care and Control Department and the private San Francisco SPCA ensured a home not only to each and every healthy dog and cat, but to thousands who were sick or injured but treatable. In addition, a focus on neutering over killing also reduced the death rate for feral cats by 73 percent and for underaged kittens by 81 percent.

By the year 2000, roughly 74 percent of all dogs and cats (nearly three out of four) were being released alive, either back to their caretakers or to new homes. This achievement was over twice that of any other major urban city and approximately three times the national average.

Unfortunately, most people misunderstand the San Francisco model, or offer various excuses for their inability to replicate its success. While many shelters unnecessarily continue to kill large numbers of animals in the face of lifesaving alternatives for no other reason than it is convenient to do so, the primary reason for the failure to replicate the San Francisco model of those who want to is a fundamental misinterpretation of what actually allowed San Francisco to succeed in its efforts. It was not—as many people have been led to believe—a collaboration between the San Francisco SPCA and the San Francisco Animal Care and Control Department.

Most agencies mistakenly assume that No Kill is not possible without a large private shelter subsidizing the work of a municipal animal control agency. This view has even been adopted by former administrators of the San Francisco SPCA. They focus on the "partnership" aspect between the private SPCA and the public pound. Consequently, they tend to emphasize collaboration at the expense of programs, though it is actually the latter that accounted for San Francisco's success. These programs and services include Trap-Neuter-Return for feral cats, foster care for sick, injured, unweaned or traumatized animals, and working with rescue groups.

COLLABORATION IS NOT ALWAYS KEY

A focus on collaboration at the expense of programs is a recipe for failure, as the fiasco of the *Asilomar Accords* aptly demonstrates. These *Accords* are an agreement endorsed by many national organizations, including the Humane Society of the United States. While the *Accords* focus on building collaborations, they allow shelters to work actively against No Kill by killing rather than sterilizing feral cats, keeping volunteers out of the shelter, and using temperament testing to label dogs unfairly as "unadoptable." None of the programs that made San Francisco successful are endorsed by the *Accords*. In some cases—like TNR for feral cats—these programs were actually voted down. All programs are left to "local decision-making," which can and often does mean opposition and continued killing.

While the job is certainly made easier if all parties are willing to work together, collaboration only succeeds when animal control or private shelters are dedicated to the No Kill endeavor. If they are not, a focus on collaboration can actually delay lifesaving efforts or even doom them altogether. In such cases, the effort at coalition building detracts from the real impediment to saving lives: reforming the animal shelter or forcing regime change within those agencies that continue to cling to outdated models of sheltering.

To call what occurred in San Francisco a partnership is to elevate form above substance. The San Francisco city shelter was hardly a willing participant, and had to be brought to the table by threats of public initiative and external pressure. In the end, it never fully embraced the paradigm, choosing to expend its energy on efforts to downplay the success of San Francisco and belittle No Kill achievements.

The focus on collaboration at the expense of reforming animal control agencies that are not implementing the programs that accounted for San Francisco's success is a recipe for continued killing. The success of San Francisco was a two-part strategy, which has been largely ignored and is not reliant on a private SPCA or humane society or willing collaboration.

The first part of the No Kill strategy is to reduce the intake of homeless dogs and cats through various programs, but most notably through spaying and neutering initiatives. The second is to implement a series of programmatic initiatives for animals already impounded.

Reducing Intakes

The first part of the model involves responsibly reducing impounds so that more resources can be used to provide care for individual animals. Fewer animals impounded also means less strain on foster homes, cage and kennel space, volunteer and staff attention, and other overall efforts to save lives.

This was accomplished, in part, through a series of pet retention programs that helped people overcome behavioral, medical, and environmental obstacles to keeping their pets–programs including subsidized medical care and a behavior problem help-line. In the final analysis, the primary mechanism for reducing impounds involved subsidizing the cost of spay/neuter for the pets of the community's low-income population, for targeted human demographics (e.g., the homeless, the elderly), and for targeted pet populations (e.g., feral cats and Pit Bulls). The success of this approach cannot be overstated: in the 1980s, San Francisco impounded over 20,000 dogs and cats per year; by 2005, that number was just over 7,000, despite community population growth to 800,000 human residents. In comparative terms, that is less than one dog or cat for every 1,000 human residents. The national average is about fifteen dogs and cats for every 1,000 human residents, and many communities have intake rates more than two times that average. In short, a commitment to high-volume, low-cost public spay/neuter has resulted in an intake rate over thirty times lower per capita in San Francisco than in many communities. This strategy does not depend on whether the agency is public or private.

Increasing Lifesaving

The second part of the No Kill strategy involved shifting from a reactive
and traditional public health orientation to a proactive and community
based adoption and rescue agency: animal control must place much more
emphasis on its animal "care" functions and balance them with its animal
"control" duties. By asserting a unique identity, having autonomy in its operations distinct from those of a health department or police agency, and
by putting itself on more equal footing in scope and service with private
animal welfare organizations, animal control can save more lives. In San
Francisco, this involved putting in place programs and services that had a
measurable lifesaving impact, rather than basing shelter responses on tradition or longstanding practices.

Exporting the Model

In 2001, this model was exported to Tompkins County, New York, where
it was implemented at a shelter that served as the animal control authority for the county. The agency took in all dogs and cats (including vicious
and feral animals), and was staffed with New York State humane officers
charged with enforcing local animal control ordinances and state anti-cruelty laws.

The combination of subsidized spay/neuter for pets of low-income
households, feral cat, and Pit Bull populations, combined with proactive
community based programs also allowed Tompkins County to realize reduced impounds of key populations, as well as a corresponding increase in
lifesaving rates. These efforts resulted in a dramatic 75 percent decline in
the shelter death rate in a period of two years.

In 2005, the animal control authority for the City of Philadelphia endorsed and took measures consistent with the "San Francisco Model" and
also realized their benefits. After an implementation and transition phase,
this has resulted in doubling the percentage of animals saved in only eight
months. Prior to implementation, the shelter was killing over 80 percent of
all impounded animals. In Charlottesville, the local SPCA and animal
control authority saved 92 percent of all cats and dogs in 2006 using the
same model.

A focus on programs trumps a need for collaboration, although the latter
can reduce the time frame of success if all agencies are committed to No

Kill. Nonetheless, any model which reverses the order, which elevates collaboration over programs, as the *Asilomar Accords* do, will fail, as aptly demonstrated in the last few years by several nationwide No Kill attempts and coalitions which were long on promise and short on results. (This should not apply to rescue groups and feral cat organizations: working with these groups is key to lifesaving success.)

The success of San Francisco and Tompkins County, and the growing success of other communities, shows the efficacy of the programs approach. The model works. If implemented with rigor, any community can and will achieve No Kill, regardless of outside funding or the existence of a broad-based coalition. To the extent a shelter isn't implementing this model, animals are needlessly being killed. For No Kill advocates to represent the interests of the animals, they must first demand these programs, and then fight for them. The first step to success is often the hardest one of all: finding a hard working, compassionate animal control or shelter director not content to regurgitate tired clichés or hide behind the myth of "too many animals, not enough homes." Unfortunately, this individual is often the hardest to demand and find, but find him or her we must. The public wants No Kill, the animals deserve it, and if it requires regime change to get it, we must fight for that, too.

Closely following a commitment to No Kill is the need for accountability. Accountability means having clear definitions, a lifesaving plan, and charting successes and failures. Clear protocols should be established, and staff should be properly trained to ensure that each and every animal is given a fair evaluation and a chance for placement or treatment. Accountability also allows, indeed requires, flexibility. Too many shelters lose sight of this principle, rigidly retaining shelter protocols, believing these are engraved in stone. Protocols are important because they ensure accountability from staff, but protocols without flexibility can have the opposite effect: stifling innovation, causing lives to be lost needlessly, and allowing shelter employees who fail to hide behind a paper trail. The decision to end an animal's life is an extremely serious one, and should always be treated as such. No matter how many animals a shelter kills, each and every animal is an individual, and each deserves individual consideration.

Finally, to meet the challenge that No Kill entails, shelter leadership needs to get the community excited, to energize people for the task at hand. By working with people, implementing lifesaving programs, and treating each life as precious, a shelter can transform a community.

The mandatory programs and services include:

I. Feral Cat TNR Program

Many animal control agencies in communities throughout the United States are embracing Trap, Neuter, Return programs (TNR) to improve animal welfare, reduce death rates, and meet obligations to public welfare and neighborhood tranquility demanded by governments. In San Francisco, for example, the program was very successful, resulting in fewer impounds and a 73 percent decline in the cat killing rate in less than a decade. In Tompkins County, an agreement with county officials and the rabies control division of the health department provided for TNR as an acceptable complaint, nuisance, and rabies abatement procedure. In specific cases, the health department paid the Tompkins County SPCA to perform TNR.

II. High-Volume, Low-Cost Spay/Neuter

Spay/neuter is the cornerstone of a successful lifesaving effort. Low-cost, high-volume spay/neuter will quickly lead to fewer animals entering the shelter system, allowing more resources to be allocated toward saving lives.

In the 1970s, the City of Los Angeles was the first in the country to provide municipally funded spaying and neutering for low-income people with pets. A city study found that for every dollar invested in the program, Los Angeles taxpayers were saving ten dollars in animal control costs due to reductions in animal intakes and fewer field calls. Los Angeles shelters were taking in half the number of animals after just the first decade of the program, and killing rates in the city dropped to the lowest third per capita in the United States. This result is consistent with outcomes in San Francisco and elsewhere.

Research shows that investment in programs balancing animal "care" and "control" can provide not only immediate public health and public relations benefits but also long-term financial savings to a jurisdiction. According to the International City/County Management Association:

> An effective animal control program not only saves cities and counties on present costs—by protecting citizens from dangerous dogs, for example—but also helps reduce the costs of animal control in the future. A city that impounds and euthanizes 4,000 animals in 2001... but does not promote spaying and neutering will probably still euthanize at least 4,000 animals a year in 2010.
> A city that... [institutes a subsidized spay/neuter program] will likely euthanize significantly fewer animals in 2010 and save on a host of other animal-related costs as well.

III. Rescue Groups

An adoption or transfer to a rescue group frees scarce cage and kennel space, reduces expenses for feeding, cleaning, and killing, as well as improving a community's rate of lifesaving. Getting an animal out of the shelter and into an appropriate placement is important and rescue groups, as a general rule, can screen adopters as well or better than many shelters. In an environment of five million dogs and cats killed in shelters annually, rare is the circumstance in which a rescue group should be denied the opportunity to take care and custody of an animal.

IV. Foster Care

At some point in time, nearly every animal shelter feels the pinch of not having enough space. A volunteer foster program can be an ideal way to greatly increase the number of lives a shelter can save, while at the same time providing an opportunity for community members to volunteer.

Not only does a foster program maximize the number of animals rescued, it allows an organization to care for animals who would be difficult to care for in a shelter environment—orphaned or feral kittens, sick or injured animals, or dogs needing one-on-one behavior rehabilitation. For animals who may need a break from the shelter environment, foster care provides a comfortable home setting that keeps animals happy and healthy.

During the busy summer months, the Tompkins County SPCA routinely took in over three times the number of animals than there was space in the shelter to care for them, but did not kill a single one for lack "of space." A foster program provided these animals with the care they needed before they could be made available for adoption.

V. Comprehensive Adoption Programs

Adoptions are vital to an agency's lifesaving mission. The quantity and quality of shelter adoptions is in shelter management's hands, making lifesaving a direct function of shelter policies and practice.

Studies, however, show people get their dogs from shelters only 15 percent of the time overall, and less than 10 percent of the time for cats. If shelters better promoted their animals and had adoption programs responsive to the needs of the community such as weekend and evening hours and offsite events, they could increase the number of homes available and replace population control killing with adoptions. Shelter killing is more a function of market share than "public irresponsibility." Contrary to conventional wisdom, shelters can adopt their way out of killing.

VI. *Pet Retention*

While some of the reasons animals are surrendered to shelters are un-avoidable, others can be prevented—but only if shelters are willing to work with people to help them solve their problems. Saving shelter animals requires communities to develop innovative strategies for keeping people and their companion animals together. The more a community sees its shelter as a place to turn for advice and assistance, the easier this job will be.

Animal control agencies can maintain "libraries" of pet care and behav-ior fact sheets in the shelter and on a website. Articles in local newspapers and radio and television spots all provide opportunities to feature topics like solving litter box avoidance and excessive barking. Other pet retention programs include free in-home dog behavior problem solving by volun-teers, low-cost dog training, pet friendly rental programs, dog walker refer-rals, and pet behavior classes.

VII. *Medical and Behavior Rehabilitation*

A shelter begins helping treatable animals by closely analyzing statistics. How many animals entering a shelter are treatable? What types of injuries and illnesses are most common? The answers to these questions will deter-mine what types of rehabilitation programs are needed and how to allocate resources effectively. For example, one community may have many under-age kittens in its shelters. Another may have substantial numbers of cats with upper respiratory infections, or dogs with kennel cough. Yet another may find that a large portion of treatables are dogs with behavior prob-lems. Each will need a different lifesaving program.

These programs can include creating a fund dedicated solely to med-ical and behavioral rehabilitation. Such a fund lets the public direct its do-nations and allows a shelter to demonstrate what they are doing to help treatables. In addition, the shelter can establish relationships to have local veterinarians come to the shelter to do rotations. These veterinarians can supplement the work of a staff veterinarian and veterinary technicians and help diagnose animals, give vaccinations, and administer medication and treatment.

A relationship with a veterinary college can allow veterinary students to volunteer at the shelter on a regular basis, providing the students with real life on-the-job training, while shelter animals receive high-quality care under the direction of the veterinary college faculty.

VIII. *Public Relations/Community Involvement*

Rebuilding a relationship with the community starts with redefining one-self as a "pet rescue" agency. The community must see improvement at the shelter, and improvements in the area of lifesaving. Public contact with the agency must include good customer service, more adoptions, and tangible commitments to give the shelter the tools it needs to do the job humanely. Public contact, however, is not necessarily a face-to-face encounter. The public has contact with an agency by reading about it in the newspaper, seeing volunteers adopting animals at a local shopping mall, or hearing shelter leadership promoting spay/neuter on the radio. It means public relations and community education.

The importance of good public relations cannot be overstated. Good, consistent public relations are the key to getting more money, volunteers, adoptions, and community good will. If lifesaving is the destination, public relations is the vehicle that will get a shelter there. Without it, the shelter will always be struggling with animals, finances, and community recognition. To do all these things well, the shelter must be in the public eye.

A survey of more than 200 animal control agencies conducted by a graduate student at the University of Pennsylvania College of Veterinary Medicine, for example, found that "community engagement" was one of the key factors in those agencies who have managed to reduce killing and increase lifesaving. One agency noted that "public buy-in is crucial for long-term improvements" placing primary importance on "the need to view community outreach and public engagement as integral to the agency's overall purpose and programs rather than simply as an add-on accomplished with a few public service announcements..."

IX. *Volunteers*

Volunteers are a dedicated "army of compassion" and the backbone of a successful No Kill effort. There is never enough staff, never enough dollars to hire more staff, and always more needs than paid human resources. That is where volunteers come in and make the difference between success and failure and, for the animals, life and death.

In San Francisco, a community of approximately 800,000 people, volunteers spent over 110,000 hours at the shelter each year. Assuming the prevailing hourly wage, payroll taxes and benefits, it would cost the San

Francisco SPCA over one million dollars annually to provide those services. In Tompkins County, a community of about 100,000 people, volunteers spend over 12,500 hours walking dogs, grooming cats, helping with adoptions, and doing routine but necessary office work, at a cost savings of approximately $85,000 dollars if the SPCA were to pay for those services at the entry level hourly rate.

The purpose of a volunteer program is to help a shelter help the animals. It is crucial to have procedures and goals in mind as part of the program. In Tompkins County, for example, the agency required all dogs available for adoption to get out of kennel socialization four times per day. Staff alone could not accomplish this; therefore, volunteers were recruited, trained, and scheduled for specific shifts that would allow the agency to meet those goals. It became apparent quickly that having volunteers come in whenever they wanted did not serve those goals and so all volunteers were given instructions and a specific schedule.

X. A Compassionate Director

The final element of the No Kill Equation is the most important of all, without which all other elements are thwarted—a hard working, compassionate animal control or shelter director not content to regurgitate tired clichés or hide behind the myth of "too many animals, not enough homes." Unfortunately, this individual is also often the hardest one to demand and find.

But it is clear—as better than a decade of success in San Francisco, Tompkins County, and now elsewhere demonstrates—that No Kill is simply not achievable without rigorous implementation of each and every one of these programs and services. It is up to us in the humane movement to demand them of our local shelters, and no longer to settle for the illusory excuses and smokescreens shelters often put up in order to avoid implementing them.

COMPREHENSIVE IMPLEMENTATION

To succeed fully, however, shelters should not implement the programs piecemeal or in a limited manner. If they are sincere in their desire to stop the killing, animal shelters will implement and expand programs to the point that they replace killing entirely. Combining rigorous, comprehensive implementation of the No Kill Equation with best practices and accountability of staff in cleaning, handling, and care of animals, must be the standard.

In 2004, for example, the Pennsylvania SPCA conducted fewer than 200 free spay/neuter surgeries for the pets of the community's low-income population. Shelter leaders can boast of a low-cost and free spay/neuter program, but 200 surgeries in a city of nearly 1.5 million people, with one in four of them below the federal poverty line, will not impact the numbers of animals entering Philadelphia shelters. By contrast, the San Francisco SPCA, in a city with roughly half the population of Philadelphia, performed approximately 9,000 surgeries a year throughout the late 1990s. Eight out of ten of them were free.

Similarly, animal control in Austin, Texas allows only employees to participate in its foster care program. The shelter can say it is implementing the programs and services of the No Kill Equation, but it is excluding thousands of animal lovers from participating in the lifesaving effort, seriously limiting how many lives they save.

A shelter committed to No Kill does not send neonatal orphaned kittens into foster care "sometimes," but rather every time. A shelter committed to No Kill does not merely allow rescue groups access to animals "some of the time," but every time a legitimate rescue group is willing to take over care and custody of the animal. Indeed, a No Kill shelter actively seeks these groups out and contacts a particular rescue organization whenever an animal meets its criteria.

Shelters must also put forth more effort to reunite lost animals with their families. Traditional shelters do little more than have people fill out lost pet reports. As a result, in a typical shelter, less than 2 percent of cats and roughly 20 percent of dogs are reclaimed by their families. This is unfortunate because being more proactive and comprehensive would have a significant impact on lifesaving.

Those rare communities who have systematized their approach and become more proactive have more than doubled this rate of redemption. Washoe County Animal Services in Nevada, for example, returned 7 percent of lost cats and 60 percent of lost dogs to their homes in 2008. The agency accomplished this while community shelters took in about 39 dogs and cats for every 1,000 human residents. That is over two times the national average, over four times that of San Francisco and over three times that of the City of Los Angeles. Given the high per capita intake of animals (which some suggest would evidence high rates of "public irresponsibility") one would expect Washoe County to have a very low redemption rate.

Instead, it is very near the top in the nation. Why? The shelter is proactive in finding the people who have lost the pets.

Before impounding stray dogs, Washoe County animal control officers check for identification, scan for microchips, knock on doors in the neighborhood where the animal was found, and talk to area residents. They also carry mobile telephones so that they can immediately call the missing animal's family and facilitate a quick reunion. While this may seem an obvious course of action, it is, unfortunately, uncommon–often with tragic outcomes. The more traditional approach is simply to impound any animals found wandering the streets and to transport them immediately to the pound. Once there they can get lost in the system, compete for kennel space with other animals, and are often put to death.

In Washoe County, impound is a last resort. But if animals are impounded, shelter staff is equally as proactive as field officers are in facilitating redemptions. They immediately post to the Internet photographs, identifying information, and the location of where the animal was found. People can search for the animals from their computers at home or at work.

These efforts in Washoe County, combined with an over 50% increase in the adoption rate in the community thanks to the Nevada Humane Society, has resulted in a 90 percent communitywide rate of shelter lifesaving in 2007 and 2008. The difference between the average community and Washoe County is striking, but even more so because this latter community is still only scratching the surface of what can be accomplished in terms of redemption rates. Some communities in the United States have achieved a nearly 65 percent reclaim rate for stray dogs; even higher rates have been achieved in other countries. The reclaim rate for cats can—and should—match these, rather than remain at deplorably low national averages.

This not only shows how the achievement of a No Kill community is well within our reach—indeed, it is low hanging fruit—it demonstrates how modernization of shelter practices by bringing them in line with the No Kill Equation can yield dramatic declines in killing virtually overnight.

In short, shelters must take killing off the table for savable animals, and utilize the programs and services of the No Kill Equation not sometimes, not merely when it is convenient or politically expedient to do so, but for every single animal, every single time. A half-hearted effort isn't enough. It is primarily the shift from a reactive to proactive orientation and from a casual, ad-hoc, limited implementation to a comprehensive one, which will lead to the greatest declines in killing, and fix our broken animal shelter system.

Appendix III

Companion Animal
Protection Act

To ACHIEVE A NO KILL NATION, we must move beyond a system in which the lives of animals are subject to the discretion and whims of shelter leaders or health department bureaucrats. In a shelter reliant on killing, directors can come and go, the shelter continues killing, local government ignores the ongoing failure, and the public is led to believe that "there is no other way."

Meanwhile, No Kill is succeeding in communities where individual shelter leaders are committed to it by establishing the programs and services that make it possible. Unfortunately, such leaders are few and far between. When that leader leaves the organization, moreover, the vision can quickly be doomed. For No Kill success to be widespread and long lasting, we must move past the personalities and give shelter animals the rights and protections afforded by law.

Every successful social movement results in legal protections that codify expected policies and provide consequences for future conduct that violates normative values. We need to regulate shelters in the same way we regulate hospitals and other agencies which hold the power over life and death.

The answer lies in passing and enforcing shelter reform legislation that mandates how all shelters must operate. The ideal animal control law would ban the killing of dogs and cats, and would prohibit the impounding of feral cats except for purposes of spay/neuter and release. At this time in history, it is unlikely that local governments would pass such sweeping laws. The Companion Animal Protection Act (CAPA), therefore, was written as interim "model" legislation to provide animals with maximum opportunities for lifesaving. No law can anticipate every contingency, and CAPA is no exception. It is not intended to be complete or to eliminate the need for other animal protection laws. Nor is it intended to reduce stronger protections that animals may have in a particular jurisdiction. The legislation can and should be modified in such circumstances. As such, it is considered a work in progress.

But it is clear that too many shelters are not voluntarily implementing the programs and services that make No Kill possible. As a result, animals continue to be needlessly killed. In response, CAPA mandates these programs and services, follows the only model that has actually created No Kill communities, and focuses its efforts on the very shelters that are doing the killing. In this way, shelter leadership is forced to embrace No Kill and operate their shelters in a progressive, life-affirming way—removing the discretion which allows shelter leaders to ignore the best interests of the animals.

Companion Animal Protection Act Highlights

+ Establishes the shelter's primary role as saving the lives of animals
+ Declares that saving lives and protecting public safety are compatible
+ Establishes a definition of No Kill that includes all savable animals including feral cats
+ Protects rabbits, birds, and other animals, as well as dogs and cats
+ Requires shelters to spay/neuter animals before adoption
+ Makes it illegal for a shelter to kill an animal if a rescue group or No Kill shelter is willing to save that animal
+ Requires shelters to provide animals with fresh food, fresh water, environmental enrichment, exercise, veterinary care, and cleanliness
+ Requires shelters to have fully functioning adoption programs including offsite adoptions and the use of the Internet to promote their

animals, and further mandates that animal control be open seven days per week for adoption

+ Prohibits shelters from killing animals based on arbitrary criteria such as breed bans or when alternatives to killing exist
+ Requires animal control to allow volunteers to help with fostering, socializing, and assisting with adoptions
+ Bans the use of gas chambers and other cruel methods of killing
+ Requires shelters to be truthful about how many animals they kill and adopt and to report those statistics regularly
+ Allows citizens to sue the shelter and compel compliance if shelters fail to do so

CAPA Text

Part 1. Purpose and Intent

SECTION 1

(a) It is the intent of the City Council to end the killing of savable animals in the city. In order to accomplish this, the City Council finds and declares:

  (1) protecting animals is a legitimate and compelling public interest;

  (2) the killing of savable animals in city shelters is a needless tragedy that must be brought to an end;

  (3) no animal should be killed if the animal can be placed in a suitable home, if a private sheltering agency or rescue group is willing to take care and custody of the animal for purposes of adoption, or, in the case of feral cats, if they can be sterilized and released to their habitats;

  (4) animals held in shelters deserve proper care and humane treatment including prompt veterinary care, adequate nutrition, shelter, exercise, environmental enrichment, and water;

  (5) shelters have a duty to make all savable animals available for adoption for a reasonable period of time;

  (6) owners of lost animals should have a reasonable period of time within which to redeem their animals;

(7) shelters should not kill savable animals at the request of their owners;

(8) all efforts should be made to encourage the voluntary spaying and neutering of animals;

(9) government is obligated to taxpayers and community members to spend tax monies on programs and services whose purpose is to save and enhance the lives of animals;

(10) when animals are killed, it should be done as humanely and compassionately as possible;

(11) taxpayers and community members deserve full and complete disclosure about how animal shelters operate;

(12) citizens have a right to ensure that agencies follow the law;

(13) saving the lives of animals, identifying and eliminating animal neglect and abuse, and protecting public safety are compatible interests; and,

(14) policies that undermine the public's trust in animal shelters should be eliminated.

(b) The City Council further finds and declares that all public and private sheltering agencies that operate within the city shall:

(1) commit themselves to ending the killing of savable animals in their care and custody;

(2) work with other animal adoption organizations to the fullest extent to promote the adoption of animals and to reduce the rate of killing;

(3) provide every animal in their custody with individual consideration and care, regardless of how many animals they take in, or whether such animals are healthy, unweaned, elderly, sick, injured, traumatized, feral, aggressive, or of a particular breed;

(4) not ban, bar, limit or otherwise obstruct the adoption of any animal based on arbitrary criteria, such as breed, age, color, or any other criteria unrelated to the individual animal's medical condition or temperament.

(c) The City Council further finds and declares that all public sheltering agencies that operate within the city shall:

(1) be open to the public for adoption seven days per week;

(2) implement programs to save lives, including free and low-cost spay/neuter services for animals, including feral cats; a foster-care network for animals needing special care, including unweaned, traumatized, sick and injured animals; comprehensive adoption programs that operate during weekend and evening hours and include adoption venues other than the shelter; medical and behavioral rehabilitation programs; pet-retention programs to solve medical, environmental, and behavioral problems and keep animals with their caring and responsible owners; and, volunteer programs to help socialize animals, promote adoptions, and assist in the operations of the shelter.

(d) The City Council further finds and declares that ending the killing of savable animals will occur when all public and private sheltering agencies and rescue groups work together to achieve this goal, and therefore expects private sheltering agencies and rescue groups to:

(1) be open to the public during hours that permit working people to adopt animals during non-working hours;

(2) implement programs to save lives, including free and low-cost spay/neuter services for animals, including feral cats; a foster-care network for animals needing special care, including unweaned, traumatized, sick and injured animals; comprehensive adoption programs that operate during weekend and evening hours and include adoption venues other than the shelter; medical and behavioral rehabilitation programs; pet-retention programs to solve medical, environmental, and behavioral problems and keep animals with their caring and responsible owners; and, volunteer programs to help socialize animals, promote adoptions, and assist in the operations of the shelter.

Part II. Definitions

SECTION 2

(a) For purposes of this Act, the following definitions shall apply:

(1) a *Public Sheltering Agency* is a public animal control shelter or private shelter, society for the prevention of cruelty to animals, humane society, or animal adoption group that receives city

funding and/or has a contract with the city under which it accepts stray or owner-relinquished animals.

(2) a *Private Sheltering Agency* is a shelter, society for the prevention of cruelty to animals, humane society, or animal adoption group, which is designated as a non-profit under Section 501(c)(3) of the Internal Revenue Code, and: (a) which does not receive city funding or have a contract with the city under which it accepts stray or owner-relinquished animals; (b) accepts animals into a physical facility other than a private residence; and, (c) places into new homes stray and/or owner-relinquished animals and/or animals who have been removed from a public or private sheltering agency.

(3) a *Rescue Group* is a collaboration of individuals not operated for a profit, whose primary stated purpose is animal protection, which places into new homes stray and/or owner-relinquished animals and/or animals who have been removed from a public or private sheltering agency. Individual rescuers who keep animals in their own homes but are not part of a larger collaboration are not a rescue group for purposes of this Act.

(4) an *Animal* is any domestic non-human living creature normally kept as a pet, or a feral cat.

(5) an *Impounded* animal is any animal who enters a public or private sheltering agency or rescue group regardless of whether the animal is a stray, owner-relinquished, seized, taken into protective custody, transferred from another private or public sheltering agency, or is an animal whose owner requests that the animal be killed, except for any animal presented to a medical clinic associated with such agencies for purposes of preventative or rehabilitative medical care, or sterilization.

(6) a *Stray* animal is any animal who is impounded without a known owner present at impound who is voluntarily relinquishing custody.

(7) a *Savable* animal is any animal who is either healthy or treatable, and is not a vicious or dangerous dog.

(8) a *Healthy* animal is any animal who is not sick or injured.

(9) a *Treatable* animal is any animal who is sick or injured, whose prognosis for rehabilitation of that illness and/or injury is excellent, good, fair, or guarded as determined by a veterinarian licensed to practice in this state.

(10) a *Non-rehabilitatable* animal is any animal with severe illness or injury whose prognosis for rehabilitation is either poor or grave as determined by a veterinarian licensed to practice in this state.

(11) an *Irremediably Suffering* animal is any animal with a medical condition who has a poor or grave prognosis for being able to live without severe, unremitting pain, as determined by a veterinarian licensed to practice in this state.

(12) a *Feral Cat* is a cat who is free-roaming, unsocialized to humans, and unowned.

(13) a *Feral Cat Caregiver* is someone who cares for feral cats and has an interest in protecting the cats, but is not the owner of those cats.

(14) an *Unweaned* animal is any neonatal animal who, in the absence of his/her mother, requires supplemental bottle feeding by humans in order to survive. In the case of puppies and kittens, unweaned animals are animals who fit the above description and are from 0 to 4 weeks of age.

(15) a *Litter* of animals includes two or more animals who are under twelve weeks of age as determined by a veterinarian licensed to practice medicine in this state, or by a veterinary technician or veterinary assistant working under the direction of a veterinarian licensed to practice medicine in this state.

(16) a *Vicious Dog* is a dog who exhibits aggression to people even when the dog is not hungry, in pain, or frightened, and whose prognosis for rehabilitation of that aggression is poor or grave as determined by a trained behaviorist who is an expert on canine behavior.

(17) a *Dangerous Dog* is a dog adjudicated to be vicious by a court of competent jurisdiction and where all appeals of that judicial determination have been unsuccessful.

Part III. Sterilization Requirements

SECTION 3

(a) Except as otherwise provided in this section, no public or private sheltering agency or rescue group shall sell, adopt, or give away to a new owner any dog, cat, rabbit, or other animal who has not been spayed or neutered, except as follows:

(1) This section shall not apply to reptiles, amphibians, birds, fish, and small animals such as mice and hamsters, where the anesthesia or sterilization procedure is likely to result in the animal's death.

(b) If a veterinarian licensed to practice veterinary medicine in this state certifies that an animal is too sick or injured to be spayed or neutered, or that it would otherwise be detrimental to the health of the animal to be spayed or neutered, the adopter or purchaser shall pay the public or private sheltering agency or rescue group a deposit of not less than fifty dollars ($50), and not more than one hundred dollars ($100). This deposit shall be returned if the adopter or purchaser presents the entity from which the animal was obtained with proof that the animal has been spayed or neutered within 60 days of receiving the animal, or presents a signed letter from a veterinarian licensed to practice medicine in this state, certifying that the animal has died, including a description of the animal and most likely cause of death. This deposit shall also be returned upon the expiration of the 60-day period if the adopter or purchaser presents a signed letter from a veterinarian licensed to practice medicine in this state, certifying that upon the expiration of the 60-day period, the animal remains too sick or injured, or that it would otherwise be detrimental to the health of the animal, to be spayed or neutered.

(c) The adopter or purchaser of an animal must spay or neuter that animal within 60 days of adoption, purchase, or receipt from a public or private sheltering agency, or rescue group, except as follows:

(1) If a veterinarian licensed to practice medicine in this state certifies that an animal is too sick or injured or that it would otherwise be detrimental to the health of the animal to be spayed or neutered within the time period, such animal shall be spayed or neutered within 30 days of the veterinarian certifying that the animal may safely be spayed or neutered.

(d) Notwithstanding subsection (b), if a veterinarian licensed to practice medicine in this state certifies that an animal is too sick or injured to be spayed or neutered, or that it would otherwise be detrimental to the health of the animal to be spayed or neutered, and that the animal is not likely to ever be healthy enough to be spayed or neutered, no deposit shall be required.

(e) For purposes of this section, a determination that a dog or cat is too sick or injured to be spayed or neutered, or that it would otherwise be detrimental to his or her health, may not be made based solely on the youth of the dog or cat, so long as the dog or cat is at least eight weeks of age.

(f) Notwithstanding the other requirements of this section, animals may be transferred to organizations listed on the registry required under Section 9 before they have been spayed or neutered and without a spay/neuter deposit, as long as the receiving organization represents that it will spay or neuter all animals before placing them into homes.

(g) Any funds from unclaimed deposits made pursuant to this section shall be expended only for programs to spay or neuter animals.

(h) A licensed veterinarian shall perform spay/neuter operations under this Act.

SECTION 4

(a) A person is subject to civil penalties of not less than two hundred dollars ($200) or more than five hundred dollars ($500) if that person does any of the following:
   (1) falsifies any proof of spaying or neutering submitted for the purpose of compliance with this Act;
   (2) intentionally issues a check for insufficient funds for any spaying or neutering deposit required under this Act;
   (3) falsifies a signed letter from a veterinarian submitted for the purpose of compliance with this Act, certifying that an animal is too sick or injured to be spayed or neutered;
   (4) fails to sterilize the animal as required.

(b) An action for a penalty proposed under this section may be commenced in a court of competent jurisdiction by the administrator of the public or private animal sheltering agency or rescue group from which the recipient obtained the animal who is the subject of the violation.

(c) All penalties collected under this section shall be retained by the agency bringing the action under subsection (b) to be used solely for programs to spay or neuter animals.

Part IV. Feral Cats

SECTION 5

(a) Caretakers of feral cats shall be exempted from any provision of law proscribing the feeding of stray animals, requiring permits for the feeding of animals, requiring the confinement of cats, or limiting the number of animals a person can own, harbor, or have custody of, except as follows:

   (1) Nothing in this section shall be construed to limit the enforcement of a statute having as its effect the prevention or punishment of animal neglect or cruelty, so long as such enforcement is based on the conditions of animals, and not based on the mere fact that a person is feeding feral cats in a public or private location.

(b) In order to encourage spay/neuter of feral cats and to protect cats, public or private sheltering agencies or rescue groups shall not lend, rent, or otherwise provide traps to the public to capture cats, except to a person for the purpose of catching and reclaiming that person's wayward cat(s), to capture injured or sick cats or cats otherwise in danger, to capture feral kittens for purposes of taming and adoption, or, in the case of feral cats, for purposes of spay/neuter and subsequent re-release;

   (1) For purposes of this subsection, the location of the cats, without more, does not constitute "otherwise in danger";

   (2) A person is subject to civil penalties of not less than two hundred dollars ($200) or more than five hundred dollars ($500) if that person uses a trap from a public or private sheltering agency or rescue group for purposes other than those enumerated above.

(c) An action for a penalty proposed under this section may be commenced in a court of competent jurisdiction by the administrator of the public or private animal sheltering agency or rescue group from which the recipient obtained the trap that is the subject of the violation.

(d) All penalties collected under this section shall be retained by the agency bringing the action under subsection (c) to be used solely for programs to spay or neuter animals.

Part V. Holding Periods

SECTION 6

(a) The required holding period for a stray animal impounded by any public or private sheltering agency shall be five business days, not including the day of impoundment, unless otherwise provided in this section:

   (1) Stray animals without any form of identification and without a known owner shall be held for owner redemption during the first two days of the holding period, not including the day of impoundment, and shall be available for owner redemption, transfer, and adoption for the remainder of the holding period;

   (2) Stray animals may be adopted into new homes or transferred to a rescue group or private sheltering agency for the purpose of adoption after the first two days of the holding period, not including the day of impoundment, except as provided in subsections (a)(3) to (9);

   (3) If a stray animal is impounded with a license tag, microchip, or other form of identification, or belongs to a known owner, the animal shall be held for owner redemption during the first three days of the holding period, not including the day of impoundment, and shall be available for owner redemption, transfer, and adoption for the remainder of the holding period;

   (4) Litters of animals or individual members of a litter of animals, including the nursing mother, and unweaned animals may be transferred to a private sheltering agency or rescue group for the purpose of adoption immediately after impound;

   (5) Individual members of litters of animals who are at least six weeks of age, including the mother, may be adopted immediately upon impound;

(6) A feral cat caregiver has the same right of redemption for feral cats as an owner of a pet cat, without conferring ownership of the cat(s) on the caregiver;

(7) Irremediably suffering animals shall be euthanized without delay, upon a determination made in writing and signed by a veterinarian licensed to practice medicine in this state. That certification shall be made available for free public inspection for no less than three years;

(8) Dogs and cats with confirmed cases of parvovirus or cats with confirmed cases of panleukopenia may be euthanized without delay, upon a certification made in writing and signed by a veterinarian licensed to practice medicine in this state. That certification shall be made available for free public inspection for no less than three years;

(9) Unweaned animals impounded without their mother may be killed so long as the shelter has exhausted all efforts to place the animals in foster care, made an emergency appeal under the requirements of Section 9, and certified that it is unable to provide the needed care and feeding in its facility. That certification shall also state in clear and definitive terms why the agency is unable to place the animals in foster care, which private sheltering agencies and rescue groups it made an appeal to, and what would be required in the future in order to provide the needed care and feeding in foster care or its facility, and what steps are being taken to do so. This certification shall be made in writing, signed by the director of the agency or by a veterinarian, and be made available for free public inspection for no less than three years.

SECTION 7

(a) The required holding period for an owner relinquished animal impounded by public or private sheltering agencies shall be the same as that for stray animals and applies to all owner relinquished animals, except as follows:

(1) Any owner-relinquished animal that is impounded shall be held for adoption or for transfer to a private sheltering agency or rescue group for the purpose of adoption for the entirety of the holding period;

(2) Owner-relinquished animals may be adopted into new homes or transferred to a private sheltering agency or rescue group for the purpose of adoption at any time after impoundment.

(b) When an animal is surrendered or brought to a shelter to be killed at the owner's request, the animal shall be subject to the same holding periods and the same requirements of all owner relinquished animals notwithstanding the request.

(c) An animal seized by an officer of a public or private sheltering agency under the provisions of a state statute having as its effect the prevention or punishment of animal neglect or cruelty, or seized under the provision of state dangerous dog laws or under state quarantine or disease control regulations, shall be impounded and held as consistent with the requirements of those laws, except as follows:

(1) Where any statute under the provisions of those laws permits a holding period, care, or disposition which affords an animal less protection than the mandates of this Act, this Act shall supersede those specific provisions regarding holding, care, and disposition.

Part VI. Animal Care Standards

SECTION 8

(a) Except as otherwise provided in this section, public and private sheltering agencies shall provide all animals during the entirety of their shelter stay with fresh food; fresh water; environmental enrichment to promote their psychological well-being such as socialization, toys and treats; and exercise as needed; however, never less than once daily, except as follows:

(1) dogs who are vicious to people or dangerous dogs may but are not required to be exercised during the holding period.

(b) Notwithstanding subsection (a), public and private sheltering agencies shall work with a veterinarian licensed to practice medicine in this state to develop and follow a care protocol, which is consistent with the goals of this Act as defined in Part I, for animals with special needs such as, but not limited to, nursing mothers, unweaned animals, sick or injured animals, geriatric animals, or animals needing therapeutic exercise. This care protocol shall specify any deviation from the standard requirements of subsection (a) and the reasons for the deviation(s).

(c) During the entirety of their shelter stay, animals shall be provided prompt and necessary cleaning of their cages, kennels, or other living environments no less than two times per day, to ensure environments that are welcoming to the public, hygienic for both the public and animals, and to prevent disease. This cleaning shall be conducted in accordance with a protocol developed in coordination with a veterinarian licensed to practice medicine in this state, provided as follows:

(1) animals shall be temporarily removed from their cages, kennels, or other living environments during the process of cleaning, to prevent them from being exposed to water from hoses or sprays, cleaning solutions, detergents, solvents, and/or chemicals.

(d) During the entirety of their shelter stay, all animals shall be provided with prompt and necessary veterinary care, including but not limited to preventative vaccinations, cage rest, fluid therapy, pain management, and/or antibiotics, sufficient to alleviate any pain caused by disease or injury, to prevent a condition from worsening, and to allow them to leave the shelter in reasonable condition, even if the animals are not candidates for redemption, transfer, or adoption.

(e) Public and private sheltering agencies shall work with a veterinarian licensed to practice medicine in this state to develop and follow a protocol to prevent the spread of disease, including, but not limited to, appropriate evaluation and testing of newly impounded animals, administration of vaccines, proper isolation and handling of sick animals, and measures to protect those animals most vulnerable to infection.

Part VII. Additional Programs and Duties

SECTION 9

(a) All public and private sheltering agencies that kill animals shall maintain a registry of organizations willing to accept animals for the purposes of adoption, as follows:

(1) All public or private sheltering agencies, and rescue groups designated as non-profits by Section 501(c)(3) of the Internal Revenue Code, shall be immediately placed on this registry upon their request, regardless of the organizations' geographical location or any other factor except as described under subsection (a)(5);

(2) The public or private sheltering agency may, but is not required to, include on the registry any rescue groups that are not designated as non-profits under Section 501(c)(3) of the Internal Revenue Code;

(3) The registry shall include the following information as provided by the registered organization: organization name, mailing address, and telephone number; website and e-mail address, if any; emergency contact information for the organization; the types of animals about whom the organization wishes to be contacted, including species-type and breed; and whether or not the organization is willing and able to care for unweaned animals, sick or injured animals, and/or feral or aggressive animals;

(4) All public and private sheltering agencies shall seek organizations to include on the registry;

(5) A public or private sheltering agency may refuse to include an organization on the registry, or delete it from the registry, until such time as this is no longer the case, if any of the organization's current directors and/or officers have been convicted in a court of competent jurisdiction of a crime consisting of cruelty to animals or neglect of animals; or if such charges are pending against any of the organization's current directors or officers; or if that organization or its current directors or officers are constrained by a court order or legally binding agreement that prevents the organization from taking in or keeping animals. An agency may require an organization to disclose any or all convictions, charges, and legal impediments described in this subsection;

(6) A public or private sheltering agency may require that registered organizations provide the following summary information on no more than a monthly basis: the total number of animals the organization has taken from the agency who have been adopted, died, were transferred, were killed, and are still under

the organization's care. This information may be provided in an informal format, such as via electronic mail;

(7) A public or private sheltering agency shall not demand additional information, other than that described in this section, as a prerequisite for including an organization on the registry or for continuing to maintain that organization on the registry.

(b) No public or private sheltering agency may kill an animal unless and until the agency has notified, or made a reasonable attempt to notify, all organizations on the registry described in subsection (a) that have indicated a willingness to take an animal of that type.

(1) Such notification must take place at least two business days prior to the killing of the animal;

(2) At a minimum, such notification shall include calling the organization's regular and emergency contact numbers, and sending an email to its email address, if any. Notification is considered complete as to each individual group when this has been accomplished;

(3) No animal may be killed if an organization on the registry is willing and able to take the animal within two business days after being notified;

(4) No fee may be assessed for animals released to organizations listed on the registry.

(c) No public or private sheltering agency may kill an animal unless and until the agency has notified, or made a reasonable attempt to notify, individual rescuers, rescue groups who are not designated as a nonprofit under Section 501(c)(3) of the Internal Revenue Service, and the public at large so that they may consider adopting or rescuing the animal consistent with the agency's normal adoption or transfer protocols.

(1) Such notification must take place at least two business days prior to the killing of the animal;

(2) Such notification can be accomplished in any manner reasonably likely to lead to lifesaving, but must, at a minimum, include posting a notice in the shelter on the particular animal's cage or kennel, and on the agency's website that states: "This animal is to be killed on [date] and [time]."

(d) The following exceptions shall apply to the requirements of subsections (b) and (c):

(1) All irremediably suffering animals shall be euthanized without delay. The determination that an animal is irremediably suffering shall be made in writing, signed by a veterinarian licensed to practice medicine in this state, and made available for free public inspection for no less than three years;

(2) Dogs and cats with confirmed cases of parvovirus or cats with confirmed cases of panleukopenia may be euthanized without delay, upon a certification made in writing and signed by a veterinarian licensed to practice medicine in this state. Such certification shall be made available for free public inspection for no less than three years;

(3) Dangerous dogs may, but are not required to be, released to organizations listed on the registry;

(4) Upon the impoundment of unweaned animals without their mother, all public and private sheltering agencies which have not placed the animals into foster care or have not committed to provide supplemental feeding shall immediately make an emergency appeal to organizations on the registry that have indicated that they are willing and able to care for unweaned animals, and give such organizations a reasonable amount of time to respond to the appeal. Unweaned animals impounded without their mother may then be killed before the expiration of the two business days notification period if the requirements of Section 6(a)(9) are met.

(e) All public and private sheltering agencies shall require organizations taking animals under this section to sign a contract providing:

(1) That the animals are being taken for the purposes of adoption;

(2) That all animals taken from the agency will be spayed or neutered before adoption, unless a licensed veterinarian certifies that an animal is too sick to be spayed or neutered or that it would otherwise be detrimental to the health of the animal to be spayed or neutered as required under Section 3 of this Act.

SECTION 10

(a) All public and private sheltering agencies shall take appropriate action to ensure that all animals are checked for all currently acceptable methods of identification, including microchips, identification tags, and licenses. All public and private sheltering agencies shall maintain continuously updated lists of animals reported lost, and attempt to match these lost reports with animals reported found and animals in the shelter, and shall also post all stray animals on the Internet with sufficient detail to allow them to be recognized and claimed by their owners. If a possible owner is identified, the agencies shall undertake reasonable efforts to notify the owner or caretaker of the whereabouts of the animal and any procedures available for the lawful recovery of the animal. These efforts shall include, but are not limited to, notifying the possible owner by telephone, mail, and personal service to the last known address. Upon the owner's or caretaker's initiation of recovery procedures, the agencies shall retain custody of the animal for a reasonable period of time to allow for completion of the recovery process. Efforts to locate or contact an owner or caretaker, and communications with persons claiming to be owners or caretakers, shall be recorded and be made available for free public inspection for no less than three years.

SECTION 11

(a) Every public or private sheltering agency shall have adoption programs which include adoption programs to place animals into homes and to transfer animals to other private sheltering agencies or rescue groups for adoption; promotion of animals to the community through means such as the local media and the Internet; evening and weekend adoption hours; and, community-based adoption events or venues at locations other than the shelter.

   (1) In addition to the requirements of subsection (a), all public sheltering agencies shall be open for public adoption seven days per week for a minimum of six hours per day, except on the following federally recognized holidays, when the shelter may, but is not required to, be open for adoptions: New Years Day, Independence Day, Thanksgiving Day, Christmas Day.

SECTION 12

(a) No public or private sheltering agency shall ban, bar, limit or otherwise obstruct the adoption of any animal based on arbitrary criteria, such as breed, age, color, or any other criteria unrelated to the individual animal's medical condition and temperament.

SECTION 13

(a) Every public sheltering agency shall provide the following public services:

(1) low-cost spay/neuter services for animals;

(2) volunteer opportunities for people to assist the shelter, including fostering animals, socializing animals, assisting with adoptions, and otherwise helping in the operations of the shelter;

(3) programs to assist people in overcoming situations that may cause them to relinquish or abandon their animals, including, but not limited to, programs that address animal behavior problems, medical conditions, and environmental conditions.

(b) Nothing in this section shall prohibit an agency from enacting reasonable rules to facilitate the orderly operation of these programs, so long as the rules are designed to meet the goals of this Act, as defined in Part I.

SECTION 14

(a) No person shall procure or use any living animal from a public or private sheltering agency or rescue group for medical or biological teaching, research or study. No hospital, educational or commercial institution, laboratory, or animal dealer, whether or not such dealer is licensed by the United States Department of Agriculture, shall purchase or accept any living animal from a public or private sheltering agency, rescue group, commercial kennel, kennel, peace officer, or animal control officer.

(b) No public or private sheltering agency, rescue group, commercial kennel, kennel, peace officer, or animal control officer shall sell, adopt, transfer, or give away any living animal to a person, hospital, educational or commercial institution, laboratory, or dealer in animals,

whether or not such dealer is licensed by the United States
Department of Agriculture, for purposes of medical or biological
teaching, research or study.

SECTION 15

(a) No savable animal in a public or private sheltering agency shall be
killed simply because the holding period has expired. Before an
animal is killed, all of the following conditions must be met:

  (1) there are no empty cages, kennels, or other living environments
  in the shelter;

  (2) the animal cannot share a cage or kennel with another animal;

  (3) a foster home is not available;

  (4) organizations listed on the registry described in Section 9 are
  not willing to accept the animal;

  (5) the animal is not a feral cat subject to sterilization and release;

  (6) all mandates, programs and services of the Act have been met; and

  (7) the director of the agency certifies he or she has no other
  alternative.

(b) The determination that all conditions of subsection (a) have been met
shall be made in writing, signed by the director of the agency, and be
made available for free public inspection for no less than three years.

SECTION 16

  (a) All animals impounded by a public or private sheltering agency or
  rescue group shall be killed, only when necessary and consistent
  with the requirements of this Act, by lethal intravenous injection of
  sodium pentobarbital, except as follows:

    (1) intraperitoneal injections may be used only under the direction
    of a licensed veterinarian, and only when intravenous injection is
    not possible for infant animals, companion animals other than
    cats and dogs, feral cats, or in comatose animals with depressed
    vascular function.

    (2) intracardiac injections may be used only when intravenous
    injection is not possible for animals who are completely

unconscious or comatose, and then only under the direction of a veterinarian.

(b) No animal shall be allowed to witness any other animal being killed or being tranquilized/sedated for the purpose of being killed.

(c) Animals shall be sedated/tranquilized as necessary to minimize their stress or discomfort, or in the case of vicious animals, to ensure staff safety, except as follows:

    (1) neuromuscular blocking agents shall not be used.

(d) Following their injection, animals shall be lowered to the surface on which they are being held and shall not be permitted to drop or otherwise collapse without support.

(e) An animal may not be left unattended between the time procedures to kill the animal are commenced and the time death occurs, nor may the body be disposed of until death is verified.

(f) Verification of death shall be confirmed for each animal in all of the following ways:

    (1) by lack of heartbeat, verified by a stethoscope;

    (2) by lack of respiration, verified by observation;

    (3) by pale, bluish gums and tongue, verified by observation; and

    (4) by lack of eye response, verified if lid does not blink when eye is touched and pupil remains dilated when a light is shined on it.

(g) The room in which animals are killed shall be cleaned and regularly disinfected as necessary, but no less than once per day on days the room is used, except as follows:

    (1) The area where the procedure is performed shall be cleaned and disinfected between each procedure.

(h) The room in which animals are killed shall have adequate ventilation that prevents the accumulation of odors.

(i) A veterinarian licensed to practice medicine in this state or a euthanasia technician certified by the state euthanasia certification
program shall perform these procedures, except as follows:
(1) If a state certification program does not exist, the procedure
may be performed by a trained euthanasia technician working
under the direction of a veterinarian.

Part VIII. Public Accountability

SECTION 17

(a) All public and private sheltering agencies must post, in a conspicuous
place where animals are being relinquished by owners, a sign which
is clearly visible and readable from any vantage point in the area, and
at least 17 inches by 22 inches, which has all of the following information identified by species-type:
(1) the number of animals impounded for the prior calendar year;
(2) the number of animals impounded for the prior calendar year
who were adopted;
(3) the number of animals impounded for the prior calendar year
who were transferred to other agencies for adoption;
(4) the number of animals impounded for the prior calendar year
who were reclaimed by their owners;
(5) the number of animals impounded for the prior calendar year
who died, were lost, and/or were stolen while under the direct
or constructive care of the agency; and
(6) the number of animals impounded for the prior calendar year
who were killed by the agency, at the agency's direction, with the
agency's permission, and/or by a representative of the agency.
(b) All public or private sheltering agencies must provide all owners who
are relinquishing an animal with accurate information, in writing,
about the likely disposition of their animal which includes, but is not
limited to: (1) if the animal is the breed or type who is normally
killed, (2) if the animal is likely to be killed because of some current,
usual, or unusual circumstances, and (3) the information provided
in Section 17(a)(1)-(6).

(c) Any owner surrendering an animal to a public or private sheltering agency must sign a statement on a form provided by the agency which includes the specific language: "I understand that the shelter may kill my pet." If such statements are provided on a form which has additional information, the owner must initial the statement where these words appear. If the person refuses to sign such statement, the shelter, or its agents, must recite the statement aloud to the owner and then write: "Refused to sign." Such statements must be kept on file for a period of no less than three years.

(d) All public and private sheltering agencies must make available for free public inspection the care protocol required under Section 8(b), the cleaning protocol required under Section 8 (c), and the disease-prevention protocol required under Section 8 (e).

(e) All public and private sheltering agencies shall include on their websites and post, in a conspicuous place near the entrance of the shelter, a list of organizations included on the registry described in Section 9, as well as an invitation for all public or private sheltering agencies and rescue groups to inquire about being listed on the registry, so that they may be notified before any animal is killed. Such lists shall not include any contact information the registered organizations do not wish to make public.

SECTION 18

(a) All public or private sheltering agencies shall provide to the City Council and, upon request, for free public inspection, a monthly summary by the tenth day of the month that includes the following information by species-type:

    (1) the number of animals impounded during the previous month;

    (2) the number of impounded animals sterilized and/or sterilized by contract with participating outside private veterinarians during the previous month;

    (3) the number of animals who were killed by the agency, at the agency's direction, with the agency's permission, and/or by a representative of the agency during the previous month;

(4) the number of animals who died, were lost, and/or were stolen while in the direct or constructive care of such agency during the previous month;

(5) the number of animals who were returned to their owners during the previous month;

(6) the number of animals who were adopted during the previous month;

(7) the number of animals who were transferred to other organizations for adoption during the previous month; and

(8) the number of animals impounded into the reporting agency from outside the city during the previous month.

(b) Every public or private sheltering agency shall provide an annual summary by January 31 to the City Council and, upon request, for free public inspection, which includes the following information by species-type:

(1) the number of animals impounded during the previous calendar year;

(2) the number of impounded animals sterilized and/or sterilized by contract with participating outside private veterinarians during the previous calendar year;

(3) the number of animals who were killed by the agency, at the agency's direction, with the agency's permission, and/or by a representative of the agency during the previous calendar year;

(4) the number of animals who died, were lost, and/or were stolen while in the direct or constructive care of such agency during the previous calendar year;

(5) the number of animals who were returned to their owners during the previous calendar year;

(6) the number of animals who were adopted during the previous calendar year;

(7) the number of animals who were transferred to other organizations for adoption during the previous calendar year; and

(8) the number of animals impounded into the reporting agency from outside the city during the previous calendar year.

SECTION 19

(a) Revenues from dog licenses, as required under any existing state or local laws, shall be deposited into an account for use by the public animal control agency as follows:

    (1) 60 percent shall be used exclusively for free and low-cost spay/neuter of feral cats and owned animals under the provision of subsection (b);

    (2) 40 percent shall be used exclusively for free and low-cost medical assistance, including vaccinations, of feral cats and owned animals under the provision of subsection (b).

(b) These funds shall be used to provide low-cost spay/neuter and medical care for animals if the owner or feral cat caretaker meets income guidelines set by the shelter or city except as follows:

    (1) These funds shall be used to provide free spay/neuter for animals if the owner is on public assistance or is eligible for any type of city, county, state, or federal aid of the kind that is normally given to individuals based on lack of sufficient income;

    (2) These funds shall be used to provide low-cost medical care, including vaccinations, for animals if the owner is on public assistance or is eligible for any type of city, county, state, or federal aid of the kind that is normally given to individuals based on lack of sufficient income;

    (3) These funds shall be used to provide free spay/neuter and vaccinations against rabies for feral cats regardless of the feral cat caretaker's income.

(c) These services shall be performed under the direction of a licensed veterinarian.

(d) These funds shall not be deducted from the public animal control agency's overall city budget.

SECTION 20

(a) Any resident of the City may compel a public or private sheltering agency or rescue group to follow the mandates of this Act through a lawsuit asking a court of competent jurisdiction to grant declaratory and injunctive relief including, but not limited to: restraining orders, preliminary injunctions, injunctions, writs of mandamus and prohibition, and other appropriate remedies at law which will compel compliance with this Act.

(b) Any public or private sheltering agency or rescue group may compel a public or private sheltering agency to follow the mandates of this Act through a lawsuit asking a court of competent jurisdiction to grant declaratory and injunctive relief including, but not limited to: restraining orders, preliminary injunctions, injunctions, writs of mandamus and prohibition, and other appropriate remedies at law which will compel compliance with this Act.

SECTION 21

(a) Any law, ordinance, or policy which requires the licensing of cats, the confinement of cats, limits the number of animals a household can own or care for, prohibits or requires permits for the feeding of stray domestic animals, or prohibits the adoption of specific breeds of dogs is hereby repealed as contrary to the public interest except as follows:

(1) Nothing in this section shall be construed to limit the enforcement of a statute having as its effect the prevention or punishment of animal neglect or cruelty, so long as such enforcement is based on the conditions of animals or the environment, and not based on the mere fact that a household has a certain number of animals, a person is feeding stray domestic animals, and/or a dog is of a particular breed.

SECTION 22

(a) If the provisions of any article, section, subsection, paragraph, subdivision or clause of this Act shall be adjudged invalid by a court or other tribunal of competent jurisdiction, such determination, order, or judgment shall not affect or invalidate the remainder of any article, section, subsection, paragraph, subdivision or clause of this Act. Any such invalidity shall be confined in its operation to the clause, sentence, paragraph, section or article thereof directly involved in the controversy in which such determination, order, or judgment shall have been rendered.

Glossary

Adoptable. See Unadoptable.

American Humane Association. A large national organization founded in 1879, which tries to influence shelter policies.

Animal Control. An open-admission sheltering agency that may also enforce laws relating to companion animals. Also known as a city pound. See Open Admission.

Animal Hoarder. A mentally ill person who acquires more animals than they can adequately care for, which often results in neglect, cruelty, and animal deaths.

Asilomar Accords. An agreement signed in 2004 by large national groups and local shelters that fails to endorse No Kill and allows groups to continue failed policies which result in unnecessary killing of dogs and cats in shelters.

ASPCA. Founded in 1866 by Henry Bergh, the American Society for the Prevention of Cruelty to Animals was the first SPCA in North America and is completely independent of any other shelter.

Dogcatcher. The term used for a humane or animal control officer who rounds up stray animals and enforces laws relating to them. See Stray.

Euthanasia. Webster's dictionary defines euthanasia as "the act or practice of killing or permitting the death of hopelessly sick or injured individuals in a relatively painless way for reasons of mercy." Using the term "euthanasia" when a shelter is killing for population control, because it has run out of cages, or because the shelter is opposed to TNR or other progressive programs is misleading.

Feral Cat. Also known as barn cats, alley cats, or wild cats, feral cats are not socialized to people.

Foster Care. A program in which volunteer and temporary private homes are used to care for animals, such as unweaned puppies and kittens, sick and injured animals, animals needing a break from the shelter, or when space is at a premium in the shelter environment.

Fractious Cat. Often used to describe a cat who is difficult to handle in a shelter environment, the "category" is often misused to kill shy and scared cats, or cowering cats who have been mishandled by shelter staff.

Humane Society. See SPCA.

Humane Society of the United States. Founded in 1954, HSUS is the largest and wealthiest animal protection agency in the world. Although it does not run a shelter, it exerts great influence over local shelter policies by virtue of its size, training conferences, industry magazine, and other direct and indirect means.

Licensing. A method for localities to raise revenues, demand compliance with local laws, and keep track of dogs or cats.

Limited Admission. A private shelter that does not take in more animals than it can humanely care for by killing the excess.

National Animal Control Association. Founded in 1978, NACA provides training for animal control officers throughout the country.

No Kill. An industry term used to define a shelter or community that does not kill animals for lack of space, or lack of necessary treatment. It is a community where healthy dogs and cats, sick and injured but treatable dogs and cats, behaviorally challenged or traumatized dogs and cats, and healthy and treatable feral cats are saved. The only dogs and cats being killed by shelters in a No Kill community are those who are either too sick or too injured to be rehabilitated, or, in the case of dogs, are vicious with a poor prognosis for rehabilitation and, as such, cannot be adopted into homes.

No Kill Community. A jurisdiction where all shelters in the community are No Kill. While some argue that the term in misleading because irremediably suffering animals and those with a poor prognosis for rehabilitation are killed, this is largely a smokescreen used by shelters to deflect blame for their own failures to save even healthy or treatable animals. That we may never be able to reach zero euthanasia (there will always be terminally injured and suffering animals) does not mean we should not embrace the No Kill philosophy.

No Kill Declaration of the United States. The statement of grievances and listing of rights that provide the roadmap for the future of animal sheltering in the United States. (See Appendix I.)

No Kill Equation. The programs and services that are necessary to achieve No Kill. These include comprehensive adoption programs, behavior and medical rehabilitation, use of volunteers, foster care, working with rescue groups, TNR for feral cats, and more. (See Appendix II.)

No Kill Shelter. A shelter that does not kill healthy dogs and cats, treatable dogs and cats, or healthy and treatable feral cats. A No Kill shelter can be private or public, limited or open admission.

Open Admission. A shelter, usually animal control, that takes in all dogs and cats in a particular jurisdiction. Also known as a pound.

Panleukopenia. Also known as feline distemper, this is a highly virulent and contagious disease in cats and can quickly spread in a shelter that is plagued by under-performing staff with poor cleaning and handling protocols.

Parvovirus. This is a highly virulent and contagious disease in dogs and can quickly spread in a shelter that is plagued by under-performing staff with poor cleaning and handling protocols.

PETA. People for the Ethical Treatment of Animals, an animal rights organization that argues against exploiting animals for food, entertainment, research and hunting.

Pit Bull. The three breeds that are commonly referred to as "Pit Bulls" are the American Pit Bull Terrier, the American Staffordshire Terrier, and the Staffordshire Bull Terrier.

Poundmaster. The person or agency in a jurisdiction who runs the pound or animal control shelter. See Animal Control.

Redemption. When a person finds his stray dog or cat in the shelter, he pays a fine and fees and can take his animal home. This is called a reclaim or redemption.

San Francisco SPCA. A private, independent non-profit humane society in San Francisco, California which was founded in 1868.

Spay/Neuter. Surgery resulting in the sterilization of dogs and cats by removing their reproductive capacity. A female animal is "spayed." A male animal is "neutered."

SPCA. SPCA is an acronym for "Society for the Prevention of Cruelty to Animals." Contrary to popular opinion, each SPCA or humane society is a unique entity with its own funding, leadership, staff, set of rules, policies, and governing structure. Some organizations call themselves "SPCA" and others "humane society."

Stray. An animal without a known human address. When a stray dog or cat enters a shelter, shelters typically must hold that animal for a period ranging between 48 hours to ten days depending on state law, so that people have a reasonable opportunity to find them. By contrast, many states allow shelters to kill animals who are no longer wanted by people (known as "owner relinquishments") within minutes of arriving, since presumably no one is out looking for them.

Temperament Test. Temperament testing is a series of exercises designed to evaluate whether a dog is aggressive. The goal of the test is to simulate the experiences the dog might encounter in the home and evaluate whether the dog responds aggressively.

TNR. Trap-Neuter-Return is a humane, effective, non-lethal program to trap, sterilize, and release feral cats back into their habitats. For jurisdictions that want to reduce the number of feral cats and reduce killing in shelters, it is the only effective and humane program that exists, beyond leaving the cats alone.

Treatable. An animal who is sick, injured, or traumatized, but whose prognosis for rehabilitation is either good, fair, or guarded. Examples of treatable conditions include eye injuries, broken bones, respiratory infections, food guarding, and many others regardless of time, costs, and other external factors.

Tompkins County SPCA. An independent humane society in Tompkins County, New York, founded in 1902. Though private, the Tompkins County SPCA has animal control contracts making it an open admission "public" facility with all the same requirements as a municipal animal control facility.

Unadoptable. The term "unadoptable" is supposed to mean an animal whose prognosis for rehabilitation is poor to grave, or in the case of dogs, vicious with a poor prognosis for rehabilitation. In reality, the term is misused to provide political cover for population control killing. As a result, the term has become virtually meaningless.

Bibliography

The bulk of this book was drawn from the research and experience of the author. The notes below include citations for quotations and other facts that illuminate the themes of the book. Other material from this book comes from unpublished material or interviews by the author.

Alley Cat Allies, Rabies Control and Feral Cats in the U.S., www.alleycat.org, 2003. (Last visited November 11, 2004.)

American Association of Wildlife Veterinarians, Draft Resolution on Feral Cats, Newsletter, January 1996.

American Bird Conservancy, American Humane Association, Humane Society of the United States, Keeping Cats Indoors Isn't Just For The Birds, brochure, undated.

American Humane Association, A Critical Evaluation of Free-Roaming/Unowned/Feral Cats in the United States, 1997.

American Pet Products Manufacturers Association, Industry Statistics and Trends, www.appma.org, 2006. (Last visited September 27, 2006.)

Animal Farm Foundation, American Temperament Test Results, 2004.

Animal's Agenda, The Role of Animal Shelters, March/April 1997.

Armstrong, Martha, Good Work, Humane Society of the United States, HSUS News, Fall 1996.

Armstrong, Martha, Susan Tomasello and Christyna Hunter, From Pets to Companion Animals, A Brief History of Shelters and Pounds, Humane Society of the United States, The State of the Animals, 2001.

Arnold, Christine, Open-Door Versus No-Kill Shelters: The Facts, The Humane Society of Santa Clara Valley News, Spring 1995.

Asher, Susan, KIND Community, Pet Folio, April/May 1998.

Asilomar Accords, www.asilomaraccords.org, 2004. (Last visited August 7, 2006.)

Associated Press, Two PETA Employees Arrested for Animal Cruelty, June 17, 2005.

Avanzino, Richard, President, The San Francisco SPCA, Letter to Dr. Larry
    Barrett, California Department of Health Services, dated July 30, 1993.

Avanzino, Richard, President, The San Francisco SPCA, Letter to Robert Rohde,
    President, Society of Animal Welfare Administrators, dated October 31, 1995.

Avanzino, Richard, President, San Francisco SPCA, Letter to Roger Caras,
    President, American Society for the Prevention of Cruelty to Animals, dated
    June 26, 1997.

Avanzino, Richard, President, San Francisco SPCA, Letter to Paul Irwin, President,
    Humane Society of the United States, dated November 21, 1997.

Avanzino, Richard, President, San Francisco SPCA, Letter to Wellesley Dombek,
    Editor, Pet Folio, dated June 8, 1998.

Avanzino, Richard, The San Francisco SPCA Path to No Kill, Maddie's Fund,
    www.maddiesfund.org, 2002.

Avanzino, Richard, Maddie's Fund, Personal Communication, October 3, 2006.

Barakat, Matthew, PETA Euthanized More than 1,000 Animals Last Year,
    Associated Press, July 30, 2000.

Barker, Malcolm E., Ed., More San Francisco Memoirs, 1852-1899, San Francisco:
    Londonborn Publications, 1996.

Barker, Malcolm E., Bummer & Lazarus, San Francisco's Famous Dogs, San
    Francisco: Londonborn Publications, 2001.

Barry, John M., The Great Influenza, New York: Penguin Books, 2004.

Barrett, Larry, Chief, Veterinary Public Health Section, Feline Rabies Immunization
    and Licensing: A Public Health Review, California Department of Health
    Services, 1993.

Baus, Michael, Various Personal Communications, 1999-2006.

Bennett, Kyla, Mismanaging Endangered and Exotic Species in the National Parks,
    Northwestern School of Law of Lewis & Clark College, Environmental Law,
    Comment, 1990.

Berg, Robert, Statement on Decline of California Quail, Animal Welfare
    Commission, March 12, 1993.

Berkeley, Ellen Perry, Maverick Cats: Encounters with Feral Cats, Vermont: The
    New England Press, 1982.

Berkeley, Ellen Perry, TNR Past, Present and Future: A History of the Trap-
    Neuter-Return Movement, Washington D.C.: Alley Cat Allies, 2004.

Berkeley, Ellen Perry, Personal Communication, July 5, 2005.

Best Friends Animal Sanctuary, The First Kittens to Leave Alive, No More
    Homeless Pets Weekly News, www.bestfriends.org, March 28, 2003.

Best Friends Animal Sanctuary, Shelter Dog Asks for his Life, No More Homeless Pets Weekly News, www.bestfriends.org, June 3, 2005.

Best Friends Animal Society, Yea for L.A.!, No More Homeless Pets News, www.bestfriends.org, May 13, 2006.

Bialik, Carl, Trying to Herd a Cat Stat, Wall Street Journal Online, www.wsj.com, October 12, 2006.

Blohm, Marilyn, New York City Center for Animal Care & Control, Using Objective Criteria to Determine Adoptability, in American Humane Association, Leadership Forum Proceedings, National Humane Conference, September 19-22, 2002.

Bowlin, Cynthia L., The American Cat at Midlife: Overfed, Under-exercised, and on Prozac, American Association of Feline Practitioners, Toronto, Canada, October, 2006.

Brestrup, Craig, Unintended Consequences, Best Friends Animal Society, www.bestfriends.org, 1997. (Last visited May 25, 2006.)

Brown, Bonney, Personal Communications, various, 2005-2006.

Browne, Malcolm, Rabies, Rampant in U.S., Yields to Vaccine in Europe, New York Times, July 5, 1994.

Bryant, Cal, Dumping Cases are Similar, Roanoke-Chowan News Herald, June 30, 2005.

Bryant, Taimie L., J.D., Ph.D., Personal Communication, March 9, 2004.

Bryant, Taimie L., J.D., Ph.D., Hayden Law: An Analysis, www.maddiesfund.org, 2004. (Last visited August 8, 2006.)

Bryant, Taimie L., J.D., Ph.D., Personal Communication, October 20, 2006.

Buel, C.C., Henry Bergh and His Work, Scribner's Monthly, Vol. XVII, November 1878 to April 1879.

Burdick, Alan, The Truth about Invasive Species, Discover, May 2005.

Bykofsky, Stu, 9 Minutes to Doom, Philadelphia Daily News, October 13, 2004.

Bykofsky, Stu, The Cruel Cages, Philadelphia Daily News, October 28, 2004.

Bykofsky, Stu, Boarded Up, Philadelphia Daily News, November 2, 2004.

Bykofsky, Stu, Advocates Want No Kill Shelter, Philadelphia Daily News, November 9, 2004.

Bykofsky, Stu, Car of city aide who beefed about PACCA is vandalized, Philadelphia Daily News, November 11, 2004.

Bykofsky, Stu, Pet Owners Bark Over PACCA Killings, Philadelphia Daily News, November 16, 2004.

Bykofsky, Stu, 'Tara the Terrible' is Terrific, Philadelphia Daily News, November 17, 2005.

Caler, Judi, The No Kill Shelter, Golden Empire Humane Society, www.animal-save.org/nokill2.htm, undated. (Last visited May 23, 2006.)

Caras, Roger, President, American Society for the Prevention of Cruelty to
    Animals, The Way it Seems to Me, Animal Watch, Summer 1997.
Caras, Roger, President, American Society for the Prevention of Cruelty to
    Animals, Letter to Val Beatty and Bonney Brown, dated August 21, 1997.
Cassidy, Barbara, Director of Animal Sheltering and Control, Humane Society
    of the United States, Letter to Charles R. Kemmer, Clark County Department
    of Public Works, dated July 13, 1990.
Cervantes, Niki, Ontario Woman Heads to Court Over Law Against Taking in,
    Feeding Strays, Buffalo News, January 8, 1996.
Chagrin, Teresa Lynn, People for the Ethical Treatment of Animals, Letter to
    Charlottesville-Albemarle SPCA Board of Directors, December 28, 2005.
Cistaro, Penny, Euthanasia Workshop, Anaheim, CA, Humane Society of the
    United States Expo, March, 2006.
Clifton, Merritt, Editor, Can We Outlaw Pet Overpopulation?, Animal People,
    May 1993.
Clifton, Merritt, HSUS: Prosecute Cat Rescuers because Feral Dogs are
    Dangerous, Animal People, September 1994.
Clifton, Merritt, Letter to Roger Caras, President, American Society for the
    Prevention of Cruelty to Animals, dated August 29, 1997.
Clifton, Merritt, Editor, Self-Defeat in Los Angeles, Animal People, May 2000.
Clifton, Merritt and Dan Knapp, Personal Communication, May 3, 2000.
Clifton, Merritt, Editor, The Editor Responds, Animal People, December, 2000.
Clifton, Merritt, Editor, 20th Century Leaders Squandered 19th Century Humane
    Movement Legacy, Animal People, July/August 2002.
Clifton, Merritt, Personal Communication, July 4, 2002.
Clifton, Merritt, Personal Communication, July 13, 2002.
Clifton, Merritt, Editor, HSUS Rep Samantha Mullen is Sued in N.Y. for
    Knocking No Kill,, Animal People, September 2003.
Clifton, Merritt, Editor, Channel Islands National Park Ex-Chief Hits Cruelty
    of Killing 'Invasive Species,' Animal People, April 2005.
Cline, Mariah, Personal Communication, October 9, 2006.
CNN.com, North Carolina Sheriff Puts Dog's Euthanasia on TV,
    www.cnn.com/US/9808/07/televised.euthanasia/, August 7, 1998.
Coleman, John and Stanley Temple, On the Prowl, Wisconsin Natural Resources,
    1996.
Coleman, John and Stanley Temple, Cats and Wildlife: A Conservation Dilemma,
    www.wisc.edu, 1997.
Coleman, Sydney H., Humane Society Leaders in America, 1924.
Cochrane, Laura, DVM, personal communications, 2005-2006.
Commings, Karen, American Society for the Prevention of Cruelty to Animals,
    TNR: The Humane Alternative, Animal Watch, Fall 2003.

Cosby, Susan, Chief Operating Officer, Philadelphia Animal Care and Control Association, E-Mail, February 2, 2006.

Curtin, Kevin, Request for Life for Stray Animals Shelter, The Macomb Daily, December 27, 2005.

Cuzdey, Jo-Anne, Cruelty Caseworker, People for the Ethical Treatment of Animals, Letter to Seymour Gelber, Mayor of Miami Beach, dated July 12, 1995.

Derby, Tara, Chief Executive Officer, Philadelphia Animal Care and Control Association, Personal Communication, April 12, 2006.

Derby, Tara, Chief Executive Officer, Philadelphia Animal Care and Control Association, How to Go No Kill, February 25, 2006, www.bestfriends.org. (Last visited May 25, 2006.)

DiGiacomo, Natalie, I Used to Work at a "No-Kill" Shelter, Humane Society of the United States, Animal Sheltering, September-October 1997.

Donald, Rhonda, Should Feral Cats be Euthanized?, Humane Society of the United States, Shelter Sense, May 1992.

Donaldson, Jean, Director, Department of Dog Behavior and Training, San Francisco SPCA, Personal Communication, June 20, 2005.

Dowling, Julie Miller, Putting Your Behavior Evaluation Program to the Test, Humane Society of the United States, Animal Sheltering, September-October 2003.

Dowling, Julie Miller & Cynthia Stitely, Killing Ourselves Over the Euthanasia Debate, Humane Society of the United States, Animal Sheltering, October 1997.

Dracker, Pune, Regarding Henry, ASPCA, American Society for the Prevention of Cruelty to Animals, http://www.aspca.org/site/PageServer?pagename=bergh, undated. (Last Visited July 25, 2001.)

Duvin, Edward, Speciesism Alive and Well, 1992.

Eigenhauser, George, AVMA's New Position on Free-Roaming, Abandoned, and Feral Cats: A Concern for Cat Lovers?, Cat Fanciers' Association, Franc-E-Mews, Volume 6, May 2005.

Elliott, Jeff, Of Cats and Birds and Science: A Criticism of the Churcher Study, 1994.

Ells, Natalie, Foreman, Grand Jury Indictments, Justice Court of Hartford County, State of North Carolina vs. Cook/Hinkle, October 30, 2005.

Feingold, Susan, Director, Southern Hope Humane Society, Personal Communication, May 24, 2006.

Fish, Ronnie, Parting Thoughts on No-Kill Delusion, National Animal Control Association, NACA News November/December 2004.

Foro, Lynda, Foro For Animals, E-Mail, December 4, 2006.

Foster, J. Todd, Are There Animal Shelters Truly Humane?, Reader's Digest, July, 2000.

Freeman, Darren, Animal Cruelty Trial Delayed for a Month, Virginian-Pilot, September 14, 2005.

Friedman, Carl, Taking a Hard Look at the No Kill Label, Woofer Times, August 2005.

Friedman, Carl, Kill vs. No Kill Controversy, Tails of the City, San Francisco Department of Animal Care and Control, Winter 1990.

Frommer, Stephanie S. and Arnold Arluke, Loving Them to Death: Blame-Displacing Strategies of Animal Shelter Workers and Surrenderers, Tufts University School of Veterinary Medicine, 1999.

Fund For Animals, Hidden Holocaust: The Overpopulation Crisis, undated.

Garrett, Bill, Update Your Gang of Fellow Rogues, E-mail, January 11, 2002.

Guinn, Rebecca, Personal Communication with Bonney Brown, October 3, 2006.

Guthrie, Julian, Shelter Sued by Animals' Friends, San Francisco Chronicle, March 25, 2004.

Hankins, Michelle, Personal Communication with Becky Robinson, March 25, 2003.

Hess, Elizabeth, Lost & Found: Dogs, Cats, and Everyday Heroes at a Country Animal Shelter, New York: Harcourt, Inc., 1998.

Higgins, Dan, Tompkins SPCA Boasts Lowest Kill Rate in U.S., Ithaca Journal, January 3, 2003.

Holton, Louise, Update on Riverside National Park Campaign, Alley Cat Action, Autumn 1994.

Holton, Louise and Becky Robinson, Alley Cat Allies, Personal Communications, 1994.

Humane Society of the United States, Responsible Animal Regulation, 1986.

Humane Society of the United States, Seven Basic Policies for Every Animal Shelter, Animal Sheltering, January/February 1996.

Humane Society of the United States, HSUS Statement on Free-Roaming Cats, Animal Sheltering, September/October 1998.

Humane Society of the United States, New Law Leaves Little Leeway in California, Animal Sheltering, November/December 1999.

Humane Society of the United States, Cat Licensing, Fact Sheet, August 2002.

Humane Society of the United States, Guide to Cat Law, 2002.

Humane Society of the United States, Cat Care Basics, 2002.

Humane Society of the United States, A Safe Cat is a Happy Cat, 2003.

Humane Society of the United States, Tallahassee Leon Community Animal Service Center, July 2005.

Humane Society of the United States, There Ought to be a Law, Animal Sheltering, July/August 2005.

Humane Society of the United States, HSUS Position Statement: Trap-Neuter-Return (TNR), March 20, 2006.

Humane Society of the United States, HSUS Pet Overpopulation Estimates, www.hsus.org, undated. (Last visited September 1, 2006.)

Humane Society of the United States, About Us, www.hsus.org, undated. (Last visited October 6, 2006.)

Hutchinson, Sue, Pet Executions Shocking Tactic, Houston Chronicle, October 28, 1990.

Johnson, Bill, Pit-Bull Ban May Reveal Unwarranted Prejudices, Rocky Mountain News, May 11, 2005.

Kandel, Jason, Jammed Shelters Imperil Dogs, Workers, December 3, 2000, from www.acofunstop.com/jammed%20Shelters.htm. (Last visited February 27, 2001.)

Keyes, Dolores, California Animal Control Directors' Association, Adoptable Animals in the State of California, in American Humane Association, Leadership Forum Proceedings, National Humane Conference, September 19-22, 2002.

King, Dr. Martin Luther, Letter from a Birmingham Jail, April 16, 1963.

Kindler, Roger, General Counsel, Humane Society of the United States, Letter to H.P. Williams, Jr., District Attorney, Elizabeth City, North Carolina, May 11, 1994.

King County Animal Services, Statistics, www.metrokc.gov/animals/, 2006. (Last visited August 18, 2006.)

Kirkwood, Scott, Free-Roaming Cats: In Search of New Approaches, Humane Society of the United States, Animal Sheltering, September/October 1998.

Kuhn, Thomas, The Structure of Scientific Revolutions, www.des.emory.edu, undated. (Last visited April 7, 2006.)

Kogut, Susanne, Executive Director, Charlottesville-Albemarle SPCA, Personal Communications, various, 2006.

KSAT-TV, San Antonio, Cat-Trapping Policy Angers Activist, October 20, 2006, www.ksat.com/news (Last visited November 3, 2006.)

LaBruna, Danielle, Domestic Cat (Felis Catus), Introduced Species Summary Project, www.columbia.edu, January 29, 2001. (Last visited September 1, 2006.)

La Ganaga, Maria, 'No-Kill' Shelters Divide Animal Advocates, Los Angeles Times, August 31, 1997.

Lapham, Ron, Director, Sequoia Humane Society, Chain Mail: The No Kill Conference Controversy, Spring 1996.

Launer, Alan, Wendy Fox and Lindsay Stallcup, Feral Cats at Stanford, Center for
    Conservation Biology, July 27, 1998.
Lawson, Nancy and Carrie Allan, Humane Society of the United States, Navigating
    the Road Between Dreams and Reality, Animal Sheltering, March/April 2002.
LeBlanc, Karen, Outer Banks Spay/Neuter Fund, Personal Communication,
    August 1, 1994.
Lewis, Belinda, Director, Animal Care & Control 2003 Annual Report, City of Fort
    Wayne, Indiana.
Line, Les, Silence of the Songbirds, National Geographic, June 1993.
Longfellow, Henry Wadsworth, Selected Poems, 1807-1882.
Lord, Linda K., Et. Al., Demographic Trends for Animal Care and Control
    Agencies in Ohio from 1996 to 2004, Journal of the American Veterinary
    Association, July 1, 2006.
Los Angeles Times, Editorial: Misguided Animal Aid Law, November 24, 1998.
Lucich, Jennifer, Thou Shall Not Kill, Emagazine, www.emagazine.com, 2006.
    (Last visited August 18, 2006.)
Lydon, Jeff, The Disturbing Facts About PETA, No Kill Sheltering, May/June
    2006.

MacInnes, Alexander, Stray-Cat Feeders to Face Stiff Fine, Herald News, May 18,
    2006.
Maddie's Fund, No More Homeless Pets in Utah, Completed Project,
    www.maddiesfund.org, 2005. (Last visited May 26, 2006.)
Maggitti, Phil, The Stray Cat: Whose Life is it Anyway?, Animal's Agenda,
    Volume 14, No. 6, 1994.
Mandeville, John, Vice President, The American Kennel Club, Letter to John
    Hamil, DVM, dated August 20, 1993.
Marin Humane Society, Feral Cats, Board Policy No. C-4, Adopted July 18, 1991.
Marinelli, Janet, Native or Not?: Debating the Link between Fascism and Native-
    plant Gardening, www.bbg.org, undated. (Last visited September 7, 2000.)
Mayor, Tim, Officials: New State Law is Killing Animals, North County Times,
    August 6, 1999.
Mazor, William, Riverside Cats Scooped up by Park Service, Mount Vernon
    Gazette, May 12, 1994.
McCall, Jane, Dubuque Humane Society, Adoptable: What Does That Mean?, in
    American Humane Association, Leadership Forum Proceedings, National
    Humane Conference, September 19-22, 2002.
McDonald, Susan, Personal Communication, September 30, 2006.
McHugh-Smith, Jan, Humane Society of Boulder Colorado, 100% Placement of
    Adoptable Animals, in American Humane Association, Leadership Forum
    Proceedings, National Humane Conference, September 19-22, 2002.
McCloskey, Megan, Man's Best Friend Becomes Foe in Denver, Orange County
    Register, July 21, 2005.

Miller, Julie, Animal Shelters Debate the Role of Euthanasia, Humane Society of the United States, Animal Sheltering, Winter 1998.

Miller, Lila and Stephen Zawistowski, Ed., Shelter Medicine for Veterinarians and Staff, Iowa: Blackwell Publishing, 2004.

Miller, Lila, DVM, Dog and Cat Care in the Animal Shelter, Shelter Medicine for Veterinarians and Staff, Iowa: Blackwell Publishing, 2004.

Miller, Pat, President, California Animal Control Director's Association, Chain Mail: The No Kill Conference Controversy, Spring 1996.

Mooney, Joe, Animal Activists Here May Copy Grim Ad Campaign, Seattle Post-Intelligencer, February 7, 1991.

Morris, Desmond, Catwatching, New York: Random House, 1986.

Mullen, Samantha, Program Coordinator, Humane Society of the United States, Letter to Rockland County Executive C. Scott Vanderhoef, February 19, 2003.

Mussey, Henry Raymond & William L. Ransom, Ed., Proceedings of the Academy of Political Science in the City of New York, Volume VI, 1915-1916.

National Animal Control Association, HBO Documentary Shelter Dogs, NACA News, November/December 2003.

National Humane Education Society, Euthanasia: The Killing of Healthy Animals, 2002, www.nhes.org. (Last visited May 15, 2006.)

Nethaway, Rowland, 'No-Kill' Policy is a Threat to Animal Shelters, Waco Tribune Herald, 1997.

New York Times, High-Tech Medicine is Keeping Pets Fit, New York Times, September 17, 1990.

New York Times, Styles, New York Times, June 14, 1992.

New York Times, Influence of Pets Reaches New High, New York Times, August 17, 1988.

Newkirk, Ingrid, Deadly, Abused, Doomed, San Francisco Examiner, undated (circa 2000).

Newkirk, Ingrid, Personal Communication, November 21, 1994.

Newkirk, Ingrid, Personal Communication, December 12, 1994.

Newkirk, Ingrid, E-mail from info@abolitionist-online.com, March 31, 2006.

Nieves, Evelyn, A Campaign for a No Kill Policy For the Nation's Animal Shelters, New York Times, January 18, 1999.

Outer Banks SPCA, Statement of Disassociation, 1994.

Pacelle, Wayne, President and Chief Executive Officer, Humane Society of the United States, Personal Communication, August 10, 2005.

Pacelle, Wayne, President and Chief Executive Officer, Humane Society of the United States, Personal Communication to Activists, August 10, 2005.

Palo Alto Humane Society, Non-Lethal & Non-Punitive Control of Feral Cat Populations at a Glance, April 1995.

Patronek, Gary, Free-Roaming and Feral Cats: Their Impact on Wildlife and
    Human Beings, Journal of American Veterinary Association, January 15, 1998.
Paulhus, Marc, Vice-President for Companion Animals, Tough Choices About
    Feral Cats, Humane Society of the United States, Shelter Sense, May 1992.
Pender, Terry, Dog's Life on the Line, The Record, February 9, 2006.
Peninsula Humane Society, Dog and Cat Shelter Population Summary, 2004.
People for the Ethical Treatment of Animals, Euthanasia: The Compassionate
    Option, PETA Fact sheet, Companion Animals, Number 9, 1995.
People for the Ethical Treatment of Animals, Trapping Feral Cats: The Animal
    Comes First, PETA Fact sheet, www.petaeurope.org, undated.
    (Last visited July 11, 2002.)
People for the Ethical Treatment of Animals, Feral Cats: How You Can Help
    Them, 2004.
People for the Ethical Treatment of Animals, Mission Statement, www.peta.org.
    (Last visited November 20, 2004).
People for the Ethical Treatment of Animals, The Disturbing Facts about 'No-Kill'
    Shelters, Animal Times, Fall 2005.
People for the Ethical Treatment of Animals, Ask Carla, www.askcarla.com/an-
    swers.asp?QuestionandanswerID=241, undated. (Last visited May 10, 2006.)
Peretti, Jonah, Nativism and Nature: Rethinking Biological Invasion, Environmental
    Values 7, 1998.
Philadelphia Department of Public Health, Vector Control Services, Keep the Lid
    On! E-Rat-I-Cate Rats, undated.
Philadelphia Department of Public Health, The Enemy: The Norway Rat, undated.
Pollan, Michael, Against Nativism, New York Times Magazine, May 15, 1994.
Presenza, Louis, Presiding Judge and Patricia R. McDermott, Deputy Court
    Administrator, Philadelphia Municipal Court, Notice of Judgment, Susan Troy
    v. Philadelphia Animal Care and Control Association, May 1, 2006.
Proceedings of the San Francisco City and County Animal Welfare Commission,
    October 1993.
Proceedings of the National Conference on Dog and Cat Control, February 3-5,
    1976.
Proceedings of the National Conference on the Ecology of the Surplus Dog and
    Cat Problem, May 21-23, 1974.
Progressive Animal Welfare Society, Cats & Wildlife: Wildlife Protection Begins
    at Home, brochure, September 1993.

Raghunathan, Abhi, Kitten Saving Raises Hackles at Va. Shelter, Washington Post,
    June 22, 2002.
Reick, Don, National Animal Control Association, NACA News,
    November/December 2004.
Rindy, Kate and Rhonda Lucas Donald, Just One Litter, HSUS News, Fall 1990.
Robertson, Diana, Personal Communication, September 28, 2006.

Rogers, Elizabeth, SPCA Ready to Launch Own Shelter Operation, Ithaca Journal, July 13, 1962.

Rubinstein, Dana, On the Prowl with Brooklyn's Cat Lady, The Brooklyn Papers, Vol. 29, October 2006.

San Antonio Express-News, Editorial, Absurd Law Plagues Cat Lover, September 13, 2006, www.mysanantonio.com. (Last visited September 15, 2006.)

San Diego County Animal Control Advisory Committee Subcommittee on Cat Licensing, Report to the San Diego County Board of Supervisors, November 22, 1993.

San Mateo Times, World's Bird Population in Worrisome Decline, January 24, 1994.

Seligman, Del, Seligman and Seligman, Attorneys, Friends of Rockland Shelter Animals, Inc. vs. Samantha Mullen and Humane Society of the United States, Complaint, June 20, 2003.

Shelter Reform Action Committee, Response to the 1998 Humane Society of the United States evaluation of the Center for Animal Care and Control, www.shelterreform.org, undated. (Last visited March 13, 2006.)

Shultz, William J., The Humane Movement in the United States 1910-1922, 1924.

Slack, Gordy, The Rights (and Wrongs) of Cats, California Wild, Summer 1998.

Smith, Kathryn, Why We Do What We Do, National Animal Control Association, NACA News, May/June 2000.

South L.A. Dogs, The Truth About Overpopulation, www.southladogs.fateback.com/page5.html, undated. (Last Visited May 18, 2006.)

Spencer, Buffy, Unwanted Cats Flood MSPCA, Massachusetts Live, January 23, 2006.

Spivak, Lynn, Personal Communication, July 15, 2002.

Steele, Zulma, Angel in Top Hat, New York: Harper & Brothers, 1942.

Stephen, Annelisa, War of the Weeds, Southern Sierran, Angeles Chapter of the Sierra Club, July 2005.Sternberg, Sue, The Controversial Pit Bull, www.greatdogproductions.com (videotaped lecture), 2000.

Stevenson, Adlai E., Governor, Veto Message, Senate Bill Number 93, State of Illinois, 1949.

Stinson, Patrice, Personal Communication, October 9, 2006.

Stuart, Courtney, Bless the Beasts: Kogut Takes SPCA to No Kill, The Hook, October 12, 2006.

Sturla, Kim, Ed., Spay/Neuter Legislative Bulletin, The Fund For Animals, June 1994.

Swallow, William Alan, Quality of Mercy: History of the Humane Movement in the United States, Boston: Mary Mitchell Humane Fund, 1963.

Tabor, Roger, Cats: The Rise of the Cat, 1991.

Tantillo, James, Killing Cats and Killing Birds: Philosophical Issues Pertaining to Feral Cats, Draft Manuscript, July 31, 2004.

Tedford, Jim, Regional Director, Humane Society of the United States, Letter to Renee Welch, Outer Banks SPCA, dated March 3, 1994.

Tenant, Diane, PETA and Meower Power Clash over Care of Norfolk's Feral Cats, Pilot Online, December 20, 1996.

Terpstra, Karen and Ricky Whitman, Know When to Hold 'Em, Pasadena Humane Society and SPCA, HSUS Expo 2001.

Thoreau, William David, Walden, 1854.

Trogg, Ceily, Supervisor of Animal Control, St. Bernard Parish, New Orleans, Personal Communication, June 25-26, 2005.

University of Texas Feral Cat Group, http://orgs.unt.edu/feralcat/adoption/policies.htm, undated. (Last Visited October 4, 2004.)

USA Today, Thousand of Songbirds Have Died of Salmonellosis, July 28, 1994.

Vassilatos, Ken, Personal Communication, October 9, 2006.

Walsh, Sheila, Phyllis Wright: The Woman Who Gave Shelters and Their Animals More Dignity, Humane Society of the United States, www.hsus.org/ace/20506. (Last Visited February 27, 2004.)

Washington, April, Pit-Bull Aficionados Criticize Denver Ban, Rocky Mountain News, April 22, 2005.

Weldon, Luci, Were Local Animal Rescue Efforts in Vain?, The Warren Record, July 13, 2005.

Weir, Kirsten, Shelter Under Siege, New York Resident, July 15, 2002/

White, Debra J., Can No-Kill be Cruel?, National Animal Control Association, NACA News, May/June 2004.

White, Kenneth, 'No-Kill' Shelters Not Necessarily Best, Arizona Republic. February 20, 1999.

Wilford, Christine, DVM, Seattle Feral Cat Spay/Neuter Project, Personal Communication, June 25-26, 2006.

Williams, Phil and Amber Keyser, Fewer Songbirds may be Result of Forest Fragmentation Across the American South, New Study Suggests, University of Georgia, October 13, 1998.

Wilson, Leslie, Various Personal Communications, 1998-2005.

Winograd, Nathan, Against Mandatory Cat Licensing, 1994.

Winograd, Nathan, Cats and Wildlife at Stanford University, September 7, 1998.

Winograd, Nathan, Feral Cats on the Firing Line, San Francisco SPCA, 2000.

Winograd, Nathan, Evaluation and Program Plan for Philadelphia, No Kill Solutions, May 2005.

Wright, Phyllis, Why We Must Euthanize, Humane Society of the United States, HSUS News, 1978.

Acknowledgments

Whıle leadershıp is the driving force behind No Kill, saving lives is always a community affair. And it starts with a first-rate team. I want to thank my San Francisco SPCA team, particularly Michael Baus, Leslie Wilson, Emma Clifford, Dr. Jack Aldridge, L'Danyielle Yacobucci, and the rest of the CATs.

To my Tompkins County team, too numerous to name individually including staff, volunteers, foster parents, community members and institutions which supported not only the animals, but me as well. To Sandy Snyder, the best shelter manager I have ever worked with. And to Rick Matelsky, formerly of North Shore Animal League, for giving hope to kittens and puppies throughout the country.

To Ed Duvin, the first to articulate that the "salient issue is not suffering, but a deadly form of human ignorance that presumes 'killing them kindly' is preferable to what we all face: a life fraught with uncertainties." Until he lit the first match, the cause of animals in shelters had been shrouded in darkness for far too long—a darkness imposed by the very people who were supposed to be the animals' protectors.

To Erik Marcus for his invaluable advice and guidance about the entire publishing process, and for his encouragement throughout.

To Ellie Haith, Derek Holdt, Rob Monsour, and others who read drafts of the book and offered their comments. An added measure of thanks to my wife for her tireless support; to my animal loving kids, Riley and Willoughby, for keeping me on the path of righteousness; and to the first "cat lady" I ever knew, my mother, who instilled in me an abiding love for all things feline.

But most of all, I am deeply and personally indebted to Terry and Sharon Holdt, whose extreme generosity has allowed my wife and I to pursue our dreams.

NATHAN J. WINOGRAD
San Clemente, California

Index

About the Author

Nathan J. Winograd is a graduate of Stanford Law School, and is both a former criminal prosecutor and corporate attorney. An ethical vegan and lifelong animal rescuer, his passion has always been helping animals, and he left the law to dedicate himself to that task. He has helped write animal protection legislation at the state and national level, has spoken nationally and internationally on animal sheltering issues, has created successful No Kill programs in both urban and rural communities, and has consulted with a wide range of animal protection groups, including some of the largest and best known in the nation.

In 2001, he became the Executive Director of the Tompkins County SPCA. Under his leadership, Tompkins County became the first community in the nation to save all healthy dogs and cats, sick and injured treatable dogs and cats, and feral cats. By the time he left, Ithaca was the safest community in the nation to be a homeless dog or cat. In 2004, he started the No Kill Advocacy Center, dedicated to creation of a No Kill nation. He has helped agencies and municipalities all over the United States reduce rates of shelter killing.

He lives in Northern California with his wife, two children, and a menagerie of animal companions.

For more information, go to www.nathanwinograd.com.